REREADING FRYE:
THE PUBLISHED AND UNPUBLISHED WORKS

Edited by David Boyd and Imre Salusin

Following Northrop Frye's death in 1991, a large archive of his correspondence, unpublished criticism, and notebooks was deposited with
the Victoria University Library at the University of Toronto. This collection of essays, written by a distinguished group of Frye experts, begins
the process of reassessing Frye's thought and writings in light of the
extraordinary material contained in this archive.

The essays included here illuminate in new and significant ways both
Frye's critical theories and their philosophical underpinnings. They
show that Frye's was a many-sided and yet strikingly consistent process
of meditation that was not fully reflected in his published works, for all
their adventurous scope and brilliance.

This impressive collection highlights the continuing relevance of
Frye's ideas and gives a broader sense of his writing and his achievement.

(Frye Studies)

DAVID BOYD is Associate Professor, Department of English, University
of Newcastle, Australia.
IMRE SALUSINSZKY is Associate Professor, Department of English,
University of Newcastle, Australia.

A page from one of Frye's notebooks showing the series of symbols used throughout his diaries and notebooks (NFF, 1991, box 21, Notebook 21, p. 73; courtesy of Victoria University Library).

Rereading Frye
The Published and Unpublished Works

EDITED BY
DAVID BOYD AND
IMRE SALUSINSZKY

UNIVERSITY OF TORONTO PRESS
Toronto Buffalo London

© University of Toronto Press Incorporated 1999
Toronto Buffalo London
Printed in Canada

ISBN 0-8020-4252-x (cloth)
ISBN 0-8020-8094-4 (paper)

♾

Printed on acid-free paper

Frye Studies

Canadian Cataloguing in Publication Data

Main entry under title:

Rereading Frye : the published and unpublished works

Includes bibliographical references and index.
ISBN 0-8020-4252-x (bound)   ISBN 0-8020-8094-4 (pbk.)

1. Frye, Northrop, 1912–1991 – Criticism and interpretation.
I. Boyd, David (David V.).   II. Salusinszky, Imre, 1955– .

PN75.F7R47 1999   801'.95'092   C98-932505-9

University of Toronto Press acknowledges the financial assistance to its
publishing program of the Canada Council for the Arts and the Ontario Arts
Council.

For Jane and Deryck Widdicombe

Contents

Acknowledgments

Most of these essays developed out of a research seminar held at the University of Newcastle, Australia, in July 1994. For their generous help in funding the seminar, under the auspices of the Program for International Research Linkages, we would like to thank the International Council for Canadian Studies, Ottawa. Thanks, too, to Paulette Montaigne, of the Canadian High Commission in Canberra, and to the Association for Canadian Studies in Australia and New Zealand, for their help with our application.

We would also like gratefully to acknowledge the Research Management Committee, the Faculty of Arts and Social Science, and the Department of English at the University of Newcastle for their support of the seminar.

All quotations from the unpublished notebooks and diaries of Northrop Frye, including diagrams, are used with the permission of Victoria University Library (Toronto). Our thanks to Dr Robert Brandeis and his staff at the library for their friendly and professional assistance.

Finally, our thanks to Robert D. Denham for the hundreds of editorial inquiries he has fielded concerning Frye's unpublished notebooks and diaries.

D.V.B. and I.L.S.

Abbreviations

AC   *Anatomy of Criticism: Four Essays*. Princeton: Princeton University Press, 1957.

BG   *The Bush Garden: Essays on the Canadian Imagination*. Toronto: House of Anansi, 1971.

CDC *The Cultural Development of Canada*. Toronto: Massey College, 1990.

CP   *The Critical Path: An Essay on the Social Context of Literary Criticism*. Bloomington: Indiana University Press, 1971.

CR   *Creation and Recreation*. Toronto: University of Toronto Press, 1980.

DG   *Divisions on a Ground: Essays on Canadian Culture*. Edited by James Polk. Toronto: House of Anansi, 1982.

DV   *The Double Vision: Language and Meaning in Religion*. Toronto: University of Toronto Press, 1991.

EAC *The Eternal Act of Creation: Essays, 1979–1990*. Edited by Robert D. Denham. Bloomington: Indiana University Press, 1993.

EI   *The Educated Imagination*. Bloomington: Indiana University Press, 1963.

FI   *Fables of Identity: Studies in Poetic Mythology*. New York: Harcourt, Brace & World, 1963.

FS   *Fearful Symmetry: A Study of William Blake*. Princeton: Princeton University Press, 1947.

GC   *The Great Code: The Bible and Literature*. Toronto: Academic Press, 1982.

MM   *Myth and Metaphor: Selected Essays, 1974–1988*. Edited by Robert D. Denham. Charlottesville: University of Virginia Press, 1990.

NB   Unpublished notebook. The number following NB is the number of the notebook, and the number following the comma is the paragraph number, as these will eventually appear when the notebooks are published by University of Toronto Press as part of the Collected Edition of the Works of Northrop Frye.

NFC   *Northrop Frye in Conversation*. Interview with David Cayley. Concord, Ont.: House of Anansi, 1992.

NFCL   *Northrop Frye on Culture and Literature: A Collection of Review Essays*. Edited by Robert D. Denham. Chicago: University of Chicago Press, 1978.

NP   *A Natural Perspective: The Development of Shakespearean Comedy and Romance*. New York: Columbia University Press, 1965.

OE   *On Education*. Markham, Ont.: Fitzhenry & Whiteside, 1990.

RW   *Reading the World: Selected Writings, 1935–1976*. Edited by Robert D. Denham. New York: Peter Lang, 1990.

SeS   *The Secular Scripture: A Study of the Structure of Romance*. Cambridge: Harvard University Press, 1976.

SM   *Spiritus Mundi: Essays on Literature, Myth, and Society*. Bloomington: Indiana University Press, 1976.

SR   *A Study of English Romanticism*. Chicago: University of Chicago Press, 1968.

StS   *The Stubborn Structure: Essays on Criticism and Society*. Ithaca, N.Y.: Cornell University Press, 1970.

WGS   *A World in a Grain of Sand: Twenty-Two Interviews with Northrop Frye*. Edited by Robert D. Denham. New York: Peter Lang, 1991.

WP   *Words with Power: Being a Second Study of 'The Bible and Literature.'* New York: Harcourt Brace Jovanovich, 1990.

Contributors

Joseph Adamson is Professor of English and Comparative Literature at McMaster University. He is the author of books on Frye and Melville.

David Boyd is Associate Professor of English and Co-ordinator of Film Studies at the University of Newcastle, Australia.

Robert D. Denham is John P. Fishwick Professor of English at Roanoke College. For the past several years he has been editing Frye's unpublished papers, and was the editor of the first three volumes of the Collected Edition of the Works of Northrop Frye.

Michael Dolzani is Associate Professor of English at Baldwin-Wallace College in Berea, Ohio. He is co-editor, with Robert D. Denham, of Frye's notebooks for the Collected Edition of the Works of Northrop Frye, published by the University of Toronto Press.

A.C. Hamilton is Cappon Professor of English Emeritus at Queen's University. In addition to his work on Frye, he has published chiefly in the English literary Renaissance, and is now revising his 1977 edition of Spenser's *Faerie Queene*.

Jonathan Hart, Professor of English at the University of Alberta, was Visiting Fellow at Cambridge in 1993–4 and a Fulbright Faculty Fellow in Comparative Literature at Harvard in 1996–7. He has just completed *Representing the New World*.

Alvin A. Lee is Professor Emeritus, Department of English, McMaster

University. He is General Editor of the Collected Edition of the Works of Northrop Frye.

Péter Pásztor is a freelance teacher, editor, and translator, in Budapest. Among his translations are Mircea Eliade's *The Myth of Eternal Return*, Leszek Kołakowski's *Religion,* and Northrop Frye's *The Great Code* and *Words with Power.*

Imre Salusinszky is Associate Professor of English at the University of Newcastle, Australia. He is editing Frye's writings on the eighteenth and nineteenth centuries for the Collected Edition.

Preface

Much reading, thinking, imagining, and rereading – and careful scholarship – remains to be done before an overall, in-depth understanding of the life and works of Northrop Frye will be possible. This present book, edited by Boyd and Salusinszky, is timely. It shows how some of the most vital and expert parts of that intellectual enterprise now are taking shape. It also provides strong arguments that this particular cultural work is potentially one of the most important humanistic efforts taking place at this point in history.

During his lifetime (1912–91), Frye was exceptional among practitioners of the humanities in the extent to which he made known publicly the products of his fertile, constantly searching mind, as it played over and penetrated deeply into virtually the whole of Western culture and went well beyond into other cultures. In the course of a fifty-three year teaching career he gave thousands of lectures. He wrote thirty-three books and edited fifteen. His essays and chapters appeared in more than sixty books. His separately published monographs, journal articles, introductions, and reviews are many. Along the way there were as well miscellaneous writings and a host of utterances in interviews, dialogues, radio talks, television programs, and film documentaries. From among this rich and diverse published abundance certain important texts (*Anatomy of Criticism, The Great Code*) have been widely read and thought about throughout the world. They appear to be of such enduring substance that they will continue to attract major attention from serious students of literature and the workings of the human imagination.

Rereading Frye is an important early contribution to a new phase of Frye studies. The word 'rereading' in the title means two things. It tells us that the Frye texts which were published during or shortly after his life are still important in themselves, and that these are now being reconsidered in the cultural conditions of the late 1990s. If there are readers of this volume who hold the view that Frye's importance has receded into history, it is a safe prediction that at least some of them will revise that opinion as they work through the eight essays presented here. The second kind of rereading arises from the study of important new evidence. Beyond the large body of previously published Frye works, there are extensive writings which until recently have been unread and unknown by anyone except their author. These documents – described generically, quantitatively, and qualitatively by Robert D. Denham in the first essay of this volume – take up considerable shelf-space in the archives of Victoria University in Toronto. Beginning in 1996, the most important of these texts are becoming available as integral parts of the more than thirty volumes of the Collected Works of Northrop Frye (University of Toronto Press). In the light of this rich, newly available trove of additional reading material, earlier understandings of Frye – a great deal in fact of what we thought we knew and understood of this influential teacher, literary critic, cultural philosopher, and visionary thinker – now must undergo expansion and revision.

The immediate predecessor to Boyd and Salusinszky's path-breaking book is *The Legacy of Northrop Frye* (Lee and Denham, eds., 1994), the first volume in the Frye Studies series of the University of Toronto Press. That recent companion volume to this one represents a major retrospective/prospective effort by an international gathering of twenty-nine scholars to describe the depth, diversity, and significance of Frye's legacy. The present book involves several of the same Frye experts but greatly intensifies the critical focus. With one exception – Pásztor's account of the complexities involved in translating Frye into Hungarian, and into Hungary – the essays presented by Boyd and Salusinszky have been shaped, in varying degrees, by study of the newly available Frye papers, and by a heightened sense in several of the essayists of rapidly changing cultural conditions in the late twentieth-century world.

Rereading Frye readjusts perceptions of this major thinker in three important ways. It gives a better picture than ever before of the private workings of his mind. It brings into play for the first time two key concepts necessary for a better understanding of his work. It underlines how Frye, because he absorbed an astonishing number of the cultural products both of the past and of the twentieth century, without being enchained by either, was and is uniquely able to illuminate our present multicultural situation.

The first achievement of this collection is to provide a fascinating delineation of the actual intellectual processes that lay behind what was made public by Frye himself. In the notebooks in particular we can see what he was thinking day by day, and how through many starts, stops, circlings, repetitions, changes, frustrations, and, *mirabilu dictu*, breakthroughs in mental fight, he came upon utterances that are often stunning in their aphoristic brilliance and resonant with wisdom. This is a thinker who, year after year and decade after decade, pressed himself ferociously – and often playfully – to find the words of power and precision necessary for expression of the spacious, underlying vision that was driving him. All the essays in this new book cast light on these mental processes, but four have the workings of Frye's mind as their main subject.

Dolzani's highly informative account of the 'Great Doodle' and the ogdoad, which he and Denham have teased out from the notebooks, shows us what was in the back of Frye's mind throughout. This is an amazing story, whose implications will not quickly be digested. Denham describes lucidly the dialectical, synthesizing way in which Frye's highly energized mind worked. He helps us see how the involuntarily acquired aphorisms that Frye recognized as coming into his consciousness got arranged, once they had arrived there, into patterns of continuity and narrative sequence, and how some of these verbal arrangements became publications. Salusinszky convincingly shows that, unlike some critics, when Frye was talking about literature he really was talking about literature, and that his characteristic uses of diagrams, categorizational systems, and large architectonic theories were dictated not by preconceived notions about myth or archetypes but by the necessity of having mnemonic devices to deal with the encyclopaedic range of knowledge involved. Frye's visualizing patterns are a metaphorical map of a mind at work, says Salusinszky, a memory theatre in which knowing is made possible by spatializing its elements, and then retaining in visual mental form what has been learned, so that the knowledge gained will be available for recreative service in the work of what an early Frye bravely used to call civilization. Hart's essay, like those of Dolzani and Denham, works mainly from the notebooks. It tells the story of Frye's never-abandoned desire to write a novel, and his various attempts to do so. As one of the Press's readers of the manuscript version of this book says, Hart 'makes what Frye could not do seem nearly as significant, as a way of understanding his mental life, as the things he could do.'

The second achievement of *Rereading Frye* is conceptual. Much of the ground-breaking work in this realm has been undertaken by Nella Cotrupi in an important study soon to be published as part of this series by University of Toronto Press entitled *Northrop Frye: The Poetics of Process*. Cotrupi's work presents a new and insightful explanation of Frye's claims for a 'scientific' criticism. Cotrupi's explanation and rereading may well come to be seen as more illuminating than the usual social science (anthropology, psychology) partial explanation of Frye's science, suggested at times by Frye himself, though always, I think, uneasily and with qualifications. In her forthcoming volume Cotrupi discusses in detail the tradition that Frye consciously shared with Whitehead (*Science and the Modern World, Process and Reality*), Heraclitus, Plotinus, Longinus, Vico, and Blake. In his second essay in this volume, Denham, in his expert canvassing of some of these and other important links, including the crucial connection to eastern philosophies and certain Buddhist sutras, contributes to this fresh approach to Frye by focusing on the pivotal theme of 'interpenetration.' It seems that this crucial concept, explored in depth by Cotrupi and here illuminated by Denham, underlies everything Frye was trying to say, whether he was speaking of the Old Testament Deity as a process realizing itself or of a lyric taking its own centripetal shape, while simultaneously relating centrifugally to a whole multicultural world, both actual and potentially waiting to be imagined into being.

The third accomplishment of the Boyd/Salusinszky volume is to provide cogent arguments as to why Frye as a cultural philosopher should continue to be our contemporary, a much-needed articulator of a vision of human culture as 'the total body of imaginative hypothesis in a society.' Given the range and intensity of Frye's habits of thinking and imagining, and his ability to see an enormous number of relationships left undiscerned by more constricted minds, it is perhaps not surprising that Hamilton and Adamson, and also Pásztor from a quite different perspective, are able, in the editors' words, to present Frye as 'a social and cultural theorist who presciently addressed many of the concerns of current debates,' while doing so 'very much on his own terms.' Hamilton's essay is scholarly and vigorous in its argument that Frye was always a cultural critic and did not become one to follow the current fashion. But because he embodied a larger visionary culture, his work does not fall into the coercive determinisms of much of what is now known as the New Historicism, even though, like critics in that school, he too was always informed by an intense vision of social concern. For Hamilton, Frye as cultural critic is both a conservative and a radical, with his main allegiance in the latter role, where he is intent on pointing us to the real world of a transformed humanity in which primary human needs, in both their material and spiritual forms, are treated as paramount. This, obviously, is a world that we have yet to create.

Adamson's essay also is focused on Frye the cultural critic. This rewarding study takes us deep into an examination of why, in Adamson's view, Frye's conception of the autonomy of imaginative culture may be his 'single most important contribution to the history of thought.' It is the disinterested quality in art and science, Adamson says, agreeing with Frye, that can take us beyond the obsessive ideological commitments (treacheries) that are characteristic of much contemporary intellectual activity. In Adamson's words, 'The function of criticism ... is to look for a transforming energy in everything we read and to help set it free,' not to impose on the text or the cultural product being experienced and studied the particular agenda of whatever ideology is espoused by the critic. Hamilton and Adamson's essays demonstrate why Frye is one of the few Western thinkers whose writings, in increasingly numerous translations, now are being recognized and used on all continents, in linguistic and cultural contexts as ideologically complex and diverse as Pásztor's Hungary, Romania, France, Italy, India, Japan, Korea, China, and the Americas, to mention only some of the places in which Frye is now being read or reread. Pásztor's essay is a fascinating account of the actual usefulness of Frye's writings in one context among the many in the emerging new world order, whatever we practitioners of the humanities may yet help that turn out to be.

ALVIN A. LEE

Introduction

They might concur on little else, but most academic literary critics today would surely agree that the sort of 'literary chit-chat which makes the reputations of poets boom and crash in an imaginary stock exchange ... cannot be part of any systematic study.' If few critics would now admit to seeing the common pursuit of true judgment as their assigned role, however, dealing on the literary stock exchange has not actually been suspended in recent years so much as diversified, with the reputations of critics themselves now traded as briskly as those of poets ever were. And over the four decades since Northrop Frye originally made his famous pronouncement in the opening pages of the *Anatomy of Criticism*, no reputation has been more subject to the vagaries of a fickle market than his own, with the boom years of the 1950s and 1960s, when Frye was almost unchallengeably acknowledged as the most original and influential literary theorist of his day, inevitably followed by something of a downturn, if not quite a crash, in the 1970s and 1980s, when a new generation of theorists found it served their interests to displace the actual Frye with a travesty arch-formalist of their own creation.

Even the most casual observer of the workings of this market could scarcely fail to notice that a widespread renewal of interest in Frye's work is currently underway. The 1990s have seen major conferences devoted to Frye not only in Canada but in such less expected locales as China and Australia; there are now no less than three excellent full-length critical studies, by Robert D. Denham, A.C. Hamilton, and Jonathan Hart (all of them contributors to the present volume); and the monumental Collected Edition has started to appear from University of Toronto Press. But something more is emerging from all this activity than merely a renewed recognition of Frye's true stature as at least arguably the most important critic of the century. What we are beginning to see is not just a Frye who deserves reading, but one who demands rereading.

The single most important factor necessitating a rereading of Frye's work as a whole is simply the fact that a surprisingly large part of that work is only now becoming available for reading for the first time. Frye was not just a prolific writer, but a prolific jotter as well, and after his death in 1991 he left behind thousands of pages of notebooks, diaries, and letters. These papers were added to the other Frye materials in the Victoria University Library, and are now being transcribed and edited for publication in the Collected Edition. The general scope and contents of the unpublished papers are outlined by one of the editors, Robert D. Denham, in the opening article in the present volume, which is the first to make substantial use of this material.

The publication of these papers will not occasion a Canadian version of the de Man scandal – the papers are sensational, but not in that way. Frye talking to himself is still, happily, Northrop Frye, a man of tolerant left-liberal opinion, repelled from first to last by all forms of totalitarianism. But he is not quite the Frye that many confidently thought they knew, defined by the familiar strengths and weaknesses of a particular historical moment. What is beginning to emerge, instead, is a curiously Janus-faced thinker: on the one hand, a figure almost from another age, more alien to our own in his ambitions and habits of mind than we might ever have suspected, but on the other, a social and cultural theorist who presciently addressed many of the concerns of current debates – but did so very much on his own terms.

Although he showed very little interest in French structuralism – the working title for *Anatomy of Criticism* was 'Structural Poetics,' but no one in North American criticism had even heard of structuralism by the mid-1950s – we tend to think of Frye in the context of the wider tendency, in the 1950s and '60s, for system-building and architectonic metaphors within the humanities; the *Anatomy* certainly radiates a confidence about the new 'human sciences' that smacks of those years, and that has since passed so notably from the whole scene of the humanities. And so, like structuralism, Frye's work tended to accumulate in many readers' eyes that strangely mixed aura of clunky '60s modernity – like lava lights and polyester suits. The decline in his reputation in the 1970s and '80s was widely understood, accordingly, as the inevitable fate of a modernist in a post-modernist age.

But one of the most interesting things about the notebooks, and the most uncanny, is how essentially *pre*-modern they make Frye seem. This involves much more than simply a lingering fascination on Frye's part with certain long-outdated intellectual heroes of an earlier era, most notably Spengler. It is not the surface content of the notebooks that betrays this archaic element so much as their underlying structure, the way in which they reveal a drive less systematic than encyclopaedic: a desire to encompass all human knowledge within a single sprawling schema that seems to belong more in the sixteenth century than in the twentieth. Frye planned entire books on people and subjects we hardly knew he was interested in, and he thought of the thirty or so books he did publish as fragments of an extraordinary project dating back to his adolescence.

As Michael Dolzani, co-editor of the unpublished notebooks, describes in his 'skeleton key' to the notebooks, Frye conceived in his teens an elaborate symbolic system that was to be realized in eight gigantic intellectual documents. The nature of these documents shifted radically over the years. Originally they were to be concerti, later novels (Frye's unrealized ambitions as writer of fiction are examined here by Jonathan Hart), finally critical works, but the scheme itself was never abandoned. Frye's notes for this 'Great Doodle,' as he sometimes self-deprecatingly called it, are accompanied by a complicated apparatus of symbols and diagrams: what these most resemble are the constructions of the great medieval and Renaissance memory-artists discussed by Frances Yates, and it is perhaps there, as Imre Salusinszky argues, rather than in Lévi-Strauss or Jacobson, that the inspiration for the architectonic metaphors in the *Anatomy* and elsewhere is to be found.

If the notebooks often seem to present Frye in this unexpected role of Renaissance *magus*, however, inviting us to see the author of the *Anatomy of Criticism* alongside that of the *Anatomy of Melancholy*, the Frye emerging from the rereading currently in progress is by no means merely a historical curiosity. On the contrary, he is also a social, cultural, and religious thinker with something vital to contribute to current debates in the humanities, albeit in terms which challenge the current orthodoxy in those debates. His is a voice most vital, in fact, most needed at the present moment, precisely *because* of the challenge it offers that orthodoxy, particularly on the question directly addressed in the contributions to this volume of A.C. Hamilton and Joseph Adamson, the question of ideology.

The mistaken view of Frye as the leading Anglo-American representative of the high structuralism of the 1960s is misleading not only in the suggestion that he shares the spurious scientism of that school, but also in the implication that he shares its intellectual insularity. Joseph Adamson rightly emphasizes the centrality of Frye's 'highly sophisticated and complex defence of the *autonomy of literary and artistic culture*,' but it is precisely the sophistication and complexity of that defence which has too often been wilfully obscured. The real Frye, unlike the straw-man constructed by his critics in the 1970s and '80s, is anything but an arid formalist who wants to split literature off from the society it grows out of. In fact, he is a deeply historicist critic whose earliest endeavours were attempts to correct the dehistoricizing tendencies of the New Critics of the 1930s and '40s. He remains always conscious of literature's ideological involvements, but conscious too that literature is not identical with ideology. Rather, it occupies an intermediate space where ideology encounters something deeper, which he terms 'myth.' He saw in myth, and in a 'displaced' version in secular literature, a human vision that transcends both cultural change through time and cultural difference at a given time, a vision which necessarily lends his critical thought the theological dimension examined here by Robert Denham. It is this encounter between ideology and mythology, the local and the universal, in Frye's thinking that underlies A.C. Hamilton's closing prediction that 'the multiculturalism characteristic of his criticism will have its place in an increasingly multicultural world,' a claim for which Péter Pásztor's account of the introduction of Frye into the ideologically charged context of contemporary Hungary provides an intriguing case-study.

The very suggestion that there might be something, anything, which transcends ideology is of course anathema to the neo-historicists and cultural materialists who have been the dominant force in cultural criticism over the past couple of decades. Frye himself, as his notebooks show, was perfectly well aware of just how unfashionable his views were becoming, and supremely unconcerned by that fact:

I know that when I suggested the possibility of a human primary concern that overrides all conceivable ideologies I'm flying in the face of Roland Barthes and the rest of the Holy Family. It's high time that sacred cow was turned out to pasture. By the sacred cow I mean the omnipresence of ideology, & the impossibility of ever getting past it. (NB27, 276)

With benefit of hindsight, it is possible to view Frye's fall from favour on the literary stock exchange in the 1970s and '80s as a fortunate fall. In an academy more sensitive to the whims of that exchange than it likes to pretend, genuinely distinctive voices are rarer and more valuable than mere superstars and founders of schools. Frye's cheerful indifference to the demands of fashion, his willingness to embrace heterodoxy and slaughter a sacred cow or two, is one of the things that makes his voice so distinctive – and so indispensable.

DAVID BOYD AND IMRE SALUSINSZKY

REREADING FRYE

The Frye Papers

ROBERT D. DENHAM

The present volume is the first of its kind to draw substantially on the Northrop Frye papers at the Victoria University Library at the University of Toronto. This extensive collection of manuscripts, which occupies some twenty-three metres of shelf-space, was deposited in the library over the course of twenty-six years, beginning in 1967. By far the most important of the Northrop Frye fonds came to the library following Frye's death in 1991. They contain files of Frye's correspondence, books, articles, notebooks, diaries, notes, professional papers, offprints, and audio-visual materials, plus a large body of miscellaneous material. Included in the collection are the papers of Frye's wife Helen and a list of Frye materials, largely correspondence, in other repositories. A comprehensive catalogue of the collection, *Guide to the Northrop Frye Papers*, has been compiled by Dolores A. Signori. Over the next decade or so the most significant of Frye's unpublished work will appear as part of the Collected Edition of the Works of Northrop Frye, a project planned and directed by a committee under the general editorship of Alvin A. Lee.[1] The goal of the project is to produce an integrated critical edition of both Frye's published work and a generous selection of his unpublished writings. The first two volumes of the previously unpublished work, *The Correspondence of Northrop Frye and Helen Kemp, 1932–1939*, were published in 1996, and *Northrop Frye's Student Essays, 1932–1938* appeared in 1997. Frye's notebooks, diaries, professional correspondence, and miscellaneous papers will appear in due course. What follows is a brief overview of the most important units of material among the Frye papers.[2]

1. The Frye–Kemp Correspondence

These volumes contain 266 letters, cards, and telegrams that passed between Frye and Helen Kemp (later Frye) from the winter of 1931–2 until 17 June 1939. The letters, which come from the six occasions they were separated for extended periods during these years, provide a narrative of their early relationship, and what emerges, in Frye's case, is a portrait of a critic as a young man. But Kemp, about whom we have known less, is a compelling figure in her own right, and the letters bring her portrait as a young woman into much sharper focus. The story clearly has two centres of interest, and what we learn about both are the conventions of love stories: dreams and nightmares, desires and anxieties, triumphs and tragedies. But the story, as one might expect, is much more than a love story. The letters disclose, for one thing, the seeds of Frye's talent as a writer, illustrating that both the matter and the manner of his large body of work had begun to take shape when he was only nineteen. Frye was a prodigy, but Kemp had a very keen mind as well, along with a gift for expressing herself; and the correspondence would clearly have much less appeal were it not for the substantial amount of space they devote to exploring ideas – discussions of books, music, religion, politics, education, and a host of other topics.

The Frye–Kemp narrative has a very large supporting cast. Some play central roles, while others make only cameo appearances, but altogether more than thirteen hundred friends, acquaintances, teachers, confidantes, colleagues, relatives, artists, musicians, and writers figure in the story. The letters, therefore, always move out into other communities. There is the community of Victoria College, and within it members of the class of 1933, an extraordinarily tight-knit group in the 1930s, and it remains so, for those who are still alive. With only the evidence of these letters, one could write a fairly full account of Victoria and Emmanuel Colleges in the 1930s. There are the art and music communities of Toronto, in which both correspondents move quite freely. There is the community in and around Stone, a farming village in southwestern Saskatchewan, and Frye's reports from that desolate area contain as good a social history of the summer of 1934 as we are likely to get. There is the community of Frye's home town, Moncton, New Brunswick; the community of Kemp's neighbourhood on Fulton Avenue in Toronto; the summer community of Gordon Bay on Lake Joseph, Ontario; and the community of Frye's Merton College years at Oxford. The worlds of Helen Kemp and Northrop Frye continually expand, and after seven years we have travelled with them to Chicago and Ottawa, to Montreal and New York, to London and Oxford, to Paris and Brussels, to Rome and Florence. And we have seen through their eyes the early years of the Co-operative Commonwealth Federation, the struggles of the United Church of Canada, the activities of the Student Christian Movement, the appeal of Communism, the rise of fascism, and the beginnings of art education in the galleries of Canada.

2. Early Papers

The essays in this volume, containing twenty-two papers that come from Frye's student days, were written over the course of six years, from 1932 to 1938. Three of the papers – on primitivism, romanticism, and Browning – are from Frye's last year at Victoria College; seventeen date from his three years at Emmanuel College, the theology school of Victoria University, and the period immediately following that. The final two come from his years at Merton College: a paper on Eliot that Frye read at the Bodley Club in 1937, and a talk on Chaucer he presented at the Graduate English Club in Toronto in 1938, an expanded version of an essay he had written for his Merton tutor, Edmund Blunden, two years earlier. The Emmanuel College papers, written for Frye's courses in Old Testament, New Testament, theology, and church history, include essays on sacrifice, fertility cults, the Jewish background of the New Testament, the Epistle of James, St Paul and Orphism, the Church of England and nineteenth-century cultural movements, Augustine, the Reformation, Ramon Lull, the relation of religion to music and drama, and the doctrine of salvation. Two papers appear to have been written for the graduate English courses Frye took when he was enrolled at Emmanuel – one on Wyndham Lewis and the other on the forms of prose fiction. These papers provide a much more complete picture than we have had about the roots of Frye's later work. Frye often remarked that his writing kept circling back to the same issues, and these essays illustrate that his insights into a number of the questions that were to preoccupy him for more than sixty years came to him as a young man (the earliest paper was written when he was twenty).

As a second-year student at Victoria College Frye was already deeply immersed in Blake, but the presence of Blake in these early papers is minimal.[3] The most important presence rather is Spengler. In 1930 Frye had happened upon *The Decline of the West* in the library at Hart House, the student union at the University of Toronto, and he had reread it during the summer of 1931 while staying at the YMCA in Edmonton. In an interview Frye remarked that after reading *The Decline of the West* he was absolutely enraptured with it, and ever since I've been wondering why, because Spengler had one of those muzzy, right-wing, Teutonic, folkish minds. He was the most stupid bastard I ever picked up. But nevertheless, I found his book an inspired book, and finally I've more or less figured out, I think, what I got from Spengler. There's a remark in Malraux's *Voices of Silence* to the effect that he thought that Spengler's book started out as a meditation on the destiny of art forms and then expanded from there. And what it expanded into is the key idea that has always been on my mind, the idea of interpenetration, which I later found in Whitehead's *Science and the Modern World*, the notion that things don't get reconciled, but everything is everywhere at once. Wherever you are is the center of everything. And Spengler showed how that operated in history, so I threw out the muzzy Teuton and kept those two intuitions, which I felt were going to be very central. (*NFC*, 61–2)

One of Frye's first critical essays was a defence of Spengler against the attacks of Wyndham Lewis, and over the years he kept returning to Spengler.[4] Spengler makes his way explicitly into eight of Frye's early papers, and his influence is present in at least four more. In his paper on Augustine (no. 10), he refers to Spengler's *Decline* as 'perhaps the most important book yet produced by the twentieth century.' What attracted Frye to Spengler was not simply the meditation in the *Decline* on the destiny of art forms and the idea of interpenetration. It was also Spengler's view of the organic growth of cultures and his ability to assimilate a large body of material, to design a mythical structure from it, and to represent his vision of history schematically or creatively. As Frye was to say forty years later, 'If *The Decline of the West* were nothing else, it would still be one of the world's great Romantic poems' ('Spengler Revisited,' 187).

Spengler, then, as Frye reported in a notebook from the late 1940s, was one of two thinkers who 'focused the subject matter of practically all my theology essays' (NB42, 26). The other was Sir James Frazer. While other students at Emmanuel College were reading the German theologians, Frye immersed himself in *The Golden Bough*, especially volume 4, *The Dying God*, volumes 5 and 6, *Adonis, Attis, Osiris*, and volume 9, *The Scapegoat*. In his paper on 'The Jewish Background of the New Testament' Frye calls *The Golden Bough* 'perhaps the most important and influential book written by an Englishman since the *Origin of the Species*.' What attracted Frye to Frazer, whose imprint can be found in seven of the early essays, was the positive value the latter attached to myth and the implications of *The Golden Bough* for the study of symbolism: Frye came to see that the framework for religious studies need not be restricted simply to theology and history. In his essay entitled 'An Enquiry into the Art Forms of Prose Fiction' Frye refers to *The Golden Bough* as 'one of the greatest anatomies in the English language,' meaning that Frazer had a literary significance for Frye as well. Later he would call Frazer's massive anatomy 'a kind of grammar of the human imagination' ('Symbolism of the Unconscious,' 89).

Frye's long paper on 'Romanticism' is the first sustained instance we have of what were to become several of Frye's trademarks: his conceptual expansiveness, his ability to organize a large body of ideas, and his schematic way of thinking. Here Frye tackles practically the entire range of romanticism as a cultural force, not a fashionable topic in the 1930s when Eliot's classicism and the new humanism's antiromantic doctrines were still a forceful presence in criticism. After an introduction that draws on Spengler's notion of organic cultural growth and decline, Frye examines romantic philosophy from Rousseau to Bergson and Spengler himself, romantic music, and romantic literature, concluding with a glance at the political contexts of romanticism. In a note scribbled on the title-page Frye apologizes to Professor George Brett for the necessary but unmitigated evil of the length of his essay, this remark having been preceded by the wry confession that he has 'not had time to deal with the painting or with Continental literature.' The omission no doubt pleased Brett, who was faced with a ninety-four-page, marginless typescript of some 30,000 words.

The essay is an audacious undertaking, especially for a twenty-year-old, though it is a remarkable tour de force, and it contains the seeds of what were to become a number of Frye's basic principles. The fundamental dialectic of the essay is the space–time opposition. 'Obviously all cultural activity,' Frye announces, 'is comprehended through the two ultimate data of time and space.' They are the 'ultimate forms of perception.' Frye associates time and space with an extensive series of dialectical pairs: the blood and the reproductive faculty versus the sense and reasoning, being versus thought, feeling and intuition versus abstract systems, romanticism versus empiricism and positivism, history versus philosophy, dynamism versus stasis, narrative art versus pictorial art, the compulsion to action (morals) versus the compulsion to thought (logic), the religious period of culture versus the sceptical period, the creative versus the critical, architecture and music versus sculpture and drama, the lyric-essay versus fiction, philosophy of history versus scientific experiment, the world-as-will versus the world-as-idea, and so on.

A number of the oppositions appear on the vertical and horizontal axes of a diagram Frye provides, one of the earliest of the many visual representations of categories that appear throughout the unpublished papers, especially the notebooks. There are various permutations of the dialectic, and the categories here, like the categories that developed in Frye's later work, are fluid, even slippery. But they served Frye well over the years: time and space, the basic categories in the diagram just mentioned, are the principles that lie behind the separation of myth and metaphor, fictional and thematic, and a whole series of other bipolar divisions in *Anatomy of Criticism* and elsewhere. The space–time dialectic is everywhere in both Blake and Spengler, who speaks of time as 'a counterconception (*Gegenbegriff*) to space' (*Decline*, 1:126), but Frye was doubtless influenced as well by his readings in the history of philosophy, where time and space had been commonplace issues in philosophical discussion from the Greeks on.

The other deductive framework that Frye calls on repeatedly in these early papers is the truth–goodness–beauty triad that was to reappear twenty years later at the beginning of the Fourth Essay of *Anatomy of Criticism*. Even in his early twenties, then, Frye had already become a system-builder, having formulated a framework within which he could locate every philosophical, religious, social, and aesthetic issue. The early systems are less complex than those of his later work, but they clearly lie at the centre of the Victoria and Emmanuel College essays, determining and giving direction and shape to his speculations. The child is father of the man.

When Frye entered Emmanuel College in the fall of 1933, he was ambivalent about a career in the ministry. In a letter to Helen Kemp the previous summer he had said,

No, I don't want to be a professor. Theoretically. In practice I should like it well enough. But there is something about such an eminently cultured occupation that would make me feel as though I were shirking something. A professor is, as I think I have said before, an orchid, – highly cultivated, but no roots in the ground. He deals with a crowd of half-tamed little savages who get no good out of him except intellectual training and, in some cases, the radiation of his personality. He is not a vital and essential force in a community of live people. He is not a worker in the elemental sense of that word. Most professors, to gain a reputation, specialize so intensely in their work that they are cut off even from the undergraduate. These are the pedants. The rest are not so cut off from reality, but they are cut off from life. Oh, well, you get the idea. The ministry is my 'vocation,' etymologically. I have been 'called' to it just as much as any blaspheming fool of an evangelist that ever bragged about what a sinner he was before he was converted. But that doesn't mean that I am fitted for it, necessarily. It doesn't mean that I am not deadly afraid of it and would rather do a hundred other things ... I wonder what those writers who talk about relentless and inexorable Fate would say to a man who had two Fates, pulling in opposite directions. The trouble is that I can't quite figure out which one is God. (*Correspondence*, 1:52–3)

By the time he was halfway through his theological studies Frye *had* figured it out. In January 1935 he wrote to Kemp, 'The ministry, with its requirement of almost absolute versatility at an indefinitely high pitch, compelled me and yet finally frightened me away' (*Correspondence*, 1:397). But the decision not to become a United Church minister had little effect on Frye's program of study. As John Ayre says, 'Comparative theology and Bible studies all belonged to the same mythological universe as the literature of Blake' (94). But the Emmanuel papers illustrate that the circumference of Frye's vision continued to expand, encompassing by the end of his three years a large portion of what Vico called the *verum factum*, the world made by human beings – its literature, philosophy, theology, art, music, religious and political institutions. Still, the centre of this circumference, it can be argued, was ultimately religious, and these early essays served as a workshop for Frye to begin formulating his ideas about Christian symbolism, the katabatic and anabatic movements in the religious journey, the Incarnation (which would become for Frye the ultimate metaphor), and a philosophy of history, which, Frye assumes, must by definition have a religious base if it is to be universally applicable. The philosophy of history, he says in his essay on Augustine, 'is the ultimate theoretical activity of the human race, and can only be worked out by thinkers in the tradition of a true religion'; and in his essay on Calvin, he remarks that 'the most fundamental intellectual activity of the human race is a philosophy of history, an attempt to find a pattern in existence.' Searching for this pattern lay at the centre of Frye's lifelong quest.

3. Notebooks

Frye practised the notebook form of writing for more than fifty years. In one of his last notebooks he speaks of his longstanding preoccupation with recording the process of his mental life in this fashion: 'All my life,' he says, 'I've had the notebook obsession manifested by what I'm doing at this moment. Writing in notebooks seems to help clarify my mind about the books I write, which are actually notebook entries arranged in a continuous form. At least, I've always told myself they were that. For GC [*The Great Code*] I tried a different experiment: typing notes. They started off in the regular way, but before long I realized that I was just draining the "drunken monkey" babble of the so-called conscious mind off my skull. It didn't really work: I want to destroy those notes' (NB44, 326). Altogether there are 75 holograph notebooks among the Frye papers, all but two of which are in cloth or paper-covered books. (Two unbound notebooks were kept in loose-leaf binders.) They come in various shapes and sizes, the amount of material they contain varying from a few pages to 253 pages. The earliest notebook dates from the late 1930s, when Frye was at Oxford, and the final entries in the latest notebook were made in 1990, only a few weeks before Frye's death. Although portions of some notebooks are drafts of Frye's various writing projects, most of the material consists of neatly laid-out paragraphs separated by blank lines. The holograph notebooks contain approximately 750,000 words, excluding the drafts. Fortunately, Frye did not destroy the 'typed notebooks.' Some of these are practically identical to the holograph notebooks; others contain summaries of books Frye was reading with occasional commentary. The typed material constitutes another 350,000 words.

These notebooks are the most extraordinary material among the unpublished papers. In the notebook just quoted, Frye remarks, 'I keep notebooks because all my writing is a translation into a narrative sequence of things that come to me aphoristically. The aphorisms in turn are preceded by "inspirations" or potentially verbal *Gestalten*. So "inspiration" is essentially a snarled sequence' (NB44, 591).[5] While the notebook entries are ordinarily not as brief as an aphorism (they contain about 70 words on average), they do consist of discontinuous entries. But, as 'snarled sequence' suggests, the entries are by no means unrelated to each other, and Frye often refers to other sections of the notebook in which he is writing at the time and occasionally to other notebooks.

Michael Dolzani and I have completed the transcription of the notebooks and have arranged the material into seven volumes. Our intention is to have them published seriatim as we complete the annotations. The first volume will contain eight notebooks that relate to what we have called the 'late work' notebooks, written while Frye was at work on *Words with Power* and *The Double Vision*. The second volume, which we have called the 'third book' volume, will contain seven notebooks that come from the years after *Anatomy of Criticism*, when Frye was planning to write his next major work. (For an account of the 'third book,' see Michael Dolzani's 'The Book of the Dead' in the present volume.) Another volume in the series will bring together the notebooks from the *Anatomy* period. Still another will feature the notebooks from the years Frye was formulating his ideas on the Bible. The last three volumes will contain, respectively, early notebook material (including Frye's stories and the extant portions of his unfinished novel *The Locust Eaters*), his commentaries on romance (Dante, Spenser, Parzifal, Robert Chester, and notes for *The Secular Scripture*), and the 'typed notebooks.'

Here are 12 of the 821 paragraphs in 3 notebooks that Frye wrote during the last decade of his life:

I have some months, I think, to enjoy my Belacqua period, and wander in a palace of possibilities. For creation I shall have to read, or glance through, Karl Barth's tomes, I suppose. Perhaps the Marxist canon should be studied again: certainly Hegel, at least the Phenomenology would bulk largely in it. Law would mean a much firmer grasp of the conception of natural law, in Hooker & others, even though I think the notion is illusory; that is, illegitimately associated with moral law. Perhaps the Hegelian polysemous ladder should be attached to wisdom, and wind up the first section. (NB11c, 3)

Ancestor-worship is, I think, a projection of a much deeper impulse telling us that the dead have to be redeemed by the creative & charitable acts of the living. Christian doctrines are projections of the go-away-and-don't-bother-us feeling. The dead can do all sorts of things for us, I imagine, but they're not superior beings, or are in only one aspect. Another aspect lives on in time inside descendants (or others: the feeling that one *must* leave descendants is nonsense) and is beatified by them if they're lucky. Reincarnation may occasionally be a form of this. My conception of typology broadens. It's an element in the gospel stage (nunc dimittis). (NB11c, 13)

I apologize for adding another ingredient to the already over-spiced stew of metaphor and metonymy, and my debt to the essays of Roman Jakobsen is as obvious as my departure from them. There seem to me to be three possible contexts for 'metonymic': (a) as a figure of speech where one image is put for another, & which is hardly worth distinguishing from metaphor (b) as an analogical mode of writing & thinking where the word is put for something beyond it (more or less my use here) (c) as a form of writing where the word is put for the object (more or less Jacobsen's, & corresponding to my 'descriptive'). I think there are advantages in my arrangement, or I should not have proposed it, but it is of course not a right or wrong question. (NB11c, 17)

For years I have been collecting and reading pop-science & semi-occult books, merely because I find them interesting. I now wonder if I couldn't collect enough ideas from them for an essay on neo-natural theology. Some are very serious books I haven't the mathematics (or the science) to follow: some are kook-books with hair-raising insights or suggestions. (NB11h, 9)

A lot of modern writers want spirituality rather than religion. They are usually more attracted by Oriental cults (mainly kundalini and za-zen) but in of course a very cleaned-up version. This makes me impatient, and one of my motives in writing is to show that everything is in *this* tradition too. But of course the psychological *use* of religion is more Oriental. (NB11h, 11)

My Christian position is that of Blake reinforced by Emily Dickinson. At what point did Xy [Christianity] throw away Paul's spiritual–natural and pick up his dismal shit about a soul–body combination that separates at death, leaving us with a discarnate soul until God gives the order for the resurrection of the body? This evil notion was concocted to keep man under the priest-king hierarchy. I suspect the Filioque clause was added to subordinate the Spirit to the Son and reduce the former to continuing the priest-king authority in time. Not that the Eastern Churches did any better with it. Even if you do this, as Joachim of Floris realized, you turn history revolutionary and go through a 'reformation.' (NB11h, 13)

I must never forget that I'm a literary critic. Socrates' daimon, tutelary deities, angel guardians, may well be ourselves in a future stage of development. Henry James' Sense of the Past, one Ralph Pendrell imprisoned in the Regency & the other cruising freely in the future, yet still affected by his behavior. Or we could read 'higher' for 'future' above. Prospero recreating his enemies in a submarine purgatory. (NB11h, 21)

Yoga is the voluntary suppression of the involuntary actions of the mind. We're all born with a natural yoga: we're freed by objective energy and our consciousness freezes it into matter. Matter is mater, the mother. Materialism, dogmatism, the authority of elders and impotent kings, all assist the freezing process. A higher discipline that would freeze the mind could liberate the spirit. (NB11h, 24)

I'm naturally interested in the rapprochement of religion and science, but the Tao of Physics people seem to grab something denatured and out of its cultural context from Taoism or Zen or Vedanta. I think cultural specifics like exodus and gospel mean something, and I want to use them. (NB44, 23)

These people (David Bohm, Karl Pribram) also talk about dismantling the ego-centered thinker. What interests me here is the old chestnut about criticism as a parasitic activity. Perhaps criticism is the opposite of parasitism: it tries to be a transparent medium for the poets, many of whom are in the 'egotistical sublime' area. For some writers, at least, the ego may be a necessary spark plug to get the engine turning over. But the egocentric critic (Leavis) is apt to be a judging critic, perverting the whole operation. (NB44, 24)

I'm at the age to reread books I've forgotten: when an undergraduate F.H. Anderson told us to read Havelock Ellis' Dance of Life, & I read it with interest, but picking up a second-hand copy in a bookstore, I found I'd totally forgotten it, yet its spattery encyclopaedic style has certainly influenced my idiom, & it begins by saying that the fundamental arts are dancing & building (my freedom & shelter concerns). A footnote includes the sexual concern (mating dances of birds). (Unfortunately the stinker who sold the shop the book has razored out five pages, so I'll have to find another copy {I won't keep a mutilated book on my shelves}). (NB44, 81)

One very widespread myth (ancient Egypt, the Orient) is that the psyche consists of several elements, which break apart at death. Let's follow out the Oriental version for a bit. Everybody has, I've said, a lost soul, and should make sure it gets good & lost. When you bust up, the crucial question, as with multiple personality cases, is: which one is the real you? When Helen died, the real Helen became an angel in heaven. There was also a sulking and egocentric Helen, who would become a preta or unhappy ghost, and wander around Cairns for a few hours and then disintegrate. Lycidas was a Christian angel, a pagan genius, an absence, and a drowned corpse. Helen was a pile of ashes, an absence to me, and an angel: perhaps she's a genius to me (or anyone else who loved her and is still living or not living and still confused). (NB44, 747: the final notebook entry Frye wrote)

4. Diaries

Among the Frye papers are seven diaries which Frye kept, with greater and lesser degrees of zeal, during the 1940s and 1950s, the entries about the routine activities usually filling up an entire page. At the beginning of his 1949 diary, Frye says,

In the course of my life I have made several efforts to keep a diary, & in fact have produced some better than average ones, notably one that ran from July 12, 1942 until the opening of term. They have always proved to be sizeable writing jobs, but have been useful in recording the contemporary stage of my imaginative development. This year I want to tackle the diary scheme again on a bigger scale, as a means of systematizing my life. I'm not working hard enough, and I feel that a diary would be useful, as my job is mainly thinking & writing, & I need some machinery for recording everything of importance I think of. As a moral discipline, too, it's important for a natural introvert to keep his letters answered, his social engagements up to date, and his knowledge of people and events set out in greater detail. There is hardly any phase of my life that a diary would not be useful for. Reading the morning paper & mail leads to recording the social side of my life, marking essays affords material for a possible book on how to write English. Conversation, even at Victoria, occasionally produces ideas; lectures are very productive of ideas I often just let go to waste. The thing is not to be alarmed at the miscellaneous character of one's life & stylize the diary accordingly, as I've tended to do. It should be a continuous imaginative draft, not itself a work of literature. I also hope it will be of some moral benefit, in passing a kind of value judgment, implicit or explicit, on whether I've wasted the day or not, whether my schedule is in shape, whether my unanswered letters are piling up, etc. The feeling of meeting my own conscience at the end of the day may cut down my dithering time. I should be careful, however, not to ascribe exaggerated values to secondary duties merely because they are duties & I don't like them, but always to put writing, thinking & reading first. (pars. 1–3)

Frye followed the blueprint given here for five of the next seven years, setting down his reflections on the day's work, recording his conversations with Helen and with colleagues, reviewing his class lectures, planning his writing projects, analysing his dreams, noting social events, and registering other daily activities. He was not, however, able to maintain the 'moral discipline,' never completing the entries for an entire year. The most extensive diary runs from January 1 to September 7, 1950. Entries for the 1955 diary end in March; for the 1952 diary, in April; for the 1949 diary, in May. The 1942 diary begins in July and carries through November. The 1951 and 1953 diaries are quite brief, the former recording the activities of only a few days in March. Still, the diaries as a whole contain more than 250,000 words, and they provide a remarkable record of Frye's life during the years that he was writing *Anatomy of Criticism*, editing the *Canadian Forum*, publishing scores of articles, writing in his notebooks, and teaching a full schedule of courses at Victoria College.

5. Miscellaneous Papers

Among the Frye papers are a number of essays and manuscripts for addresses that were never published. These, as well as transcripts for a half-dozen or so of Frye's talks, will be collected into a miscellany volume, which will contain 'The Social Significance of Music,' a 1935 paper Frye presented to the Society of Incompatibles in Toronto; a paper on Chaucer he wrote for his Oxford tutor, Edmund Blunden (1936); 'The Present Condition of the World,' written during the spring of 1943 for an Emmanuel College book that was never published; 'The Literary Meaning of "Archetype,"' a paper read at the 1952 meeting of the Modern Language Association; talks on Shaw, Milton, Swift, Blake, and Orwell presented in the 'Writer as Prophet' series on CBC radio (1950); CBC radio reviews of books by Richard Ellmann, Reinhold Niebuhr, Herbert Butterfield, Lawrence Hyde, and Alessandro Manzoni; a talk on Joseph Pieper's *Leisure*; a report on television programs, prepared for the Canadian Radio-Television and Telecommunications Commission; 'The Social Content of Literary Criticism,' an address given at Cornell University (1968); 'The Social Uses of Literature' (1972); 'Literature and Language' (1974); 'Reconsidering Levels of Meaning,' a lecture given at Emory & Henry College (1979); an introduction to the papers of Harold Innis; a convocation address presented at the University of Bologna (1989); articles entitled 'Leisure and Boredom,' 'Articulate English,' and 'Shakespeare's Comedy of Humours'; and more than two dozen shorter pieces.

6. Correspondence

Frye's correspondence to and from friends, colleagues, and organizations is extensive: there are some 20,000 leaves in the general correspondence files. These letters are arranged in the Frye papers according to date of accession, and a large portion of the correspondence is filed alphabetically by the correspondent's name. Letters not filed alphabetically can be located in the comprehensive index of *Guide to the Northrop Frye Papers*. There are separate files containing correspondence with publishers and correspondence relating to translations, to speaking engagements, to administrative and curricular matters at Victoria College and the University of Toronto, and to media projects. The correspondence in these categories is, as one would expect, much less interesting than the general correspondence.

The correspondence holdings are not extensive before 1968, the year Jane Widdicombe became Frye's secretary and began keeping carbon typescripts of the letters. No one has yet made an exhaustive search for the letters Frye wrote before 1968, although some of this correspondence has begun to turn up in other repositories. The *Guide to the Northrop Frye Papers* lists information about Frye's correspondence in seventeen archives or special collections. A large number of letters written before 1968 are certainly in private hands, and the search for these letters has hardly begun.

The unpublished papers, once they make their way into print, will add substantially to our understanding of Frye's life and work and will result in considerable revisionary thinking about the scope, sources, content, and method of his criticism. The notebooks, to consider only that unit of material, significantly expand the Frye *oeuvre*. No twentieth-century literary critic wrote on as wide-ranging a subject-matter as Frye, but the notebooks reveal a mind of even broader scope than has previously been recognized: Frye writes on scores of topics he did not commit himself to in print.

Second, the notebooks are filled with dozens and dozens of diagrams and so reveal an even more schematic mind than emerges from Frye's books. They also reveal a highly deductive method of thinking. Frye always claimed that the first task of the literary critic was to make an inductive survey of the field. From his published works we know that he was extraordinarily well read, and the notebooks add to our knowledge of what he did read. Still, the notebooks make clear that Frye's general procedure was to begin deductively, to formulate first the large patterns or hypothetical schemes and to illustrate them with particular examples only after the containing categories had become clear to him. For a clear illustration of this, see, once again, Michael Dolzani's essay in this collection.

Third, the notebooks frequently reveal a much more engaged mind at work than appears in Frye's published work, which was typically disinterested. In the unpublished writing Frye's attitude toward his subjects is much less sublimated and displaced: he wears his attitudes on his sleeve. Frye was a deeply religious thinker, but his own commitments are often difficult to infer from his published writings because he almost always maintained a detached attitude about matters of belief. But this is not true of the notebooks, where we seem him struggling, often in a very personal way, to complete his religious quest. Or, to take another example, in his published writing Frye very seldom commented on his critics or engaged other critical modes. To be sure, in later writings one can sense his anxieties about deconstruction and sociocultural criticism, but these anxieties are quite muted. Not so in the notebooks, where he engages, say, Derrida directly and is very forward in his attitudes about the contemporary critical scene.

Finally, the notebooks reveal more clearly than previously known the scope of Frye's reading and reflection. There are entries in the notebooks, to give a highly selective list, on music and musicians, ancient Near Eastern astrological topics, the grammar of Renaissance imagery, Dante (to whom Frye devotes an entire notebook), the total-consciousness speculations of Erwin Schrödinger and David Bohm, Lacan and Derrida, Frances Yates and G.R. Levy, the French *symbolistes*, A.E. Waite, Michael Biagent's *The Holy Blood and the Holy Grail*, Brontë's *Shirley*, Joachim of Floris, Jung, the *I Ching*, Boehme, Eckhart, *The Tibetan Book of the Dead*, the *Rig-Veda*, Jnana Yoga, de Nerval, Patanjali, Gregory of Nyssa, Hindu philosophy, Julian Jaynes, the *Sepher Yetzirah*, the Lankavatara Sutra, Hegel's *Phenomenology of Spirit* (a key book for Frye), and Malekulan mythology.

The fifteen or so volumes of Frye's unpublished papers, once they make their way into print, will surely reinforce the estimate that he is one of the genuinely creative spirits of our age.

NOTES

1 John M. Robson was the general editor of the Frye project from 1992 to 1995. After his untimely death the general editorship was assumed by Professor Lee. The University of Toronto Press is in the process of publishing the Collected Works.

2 The first two parts of the overview borrow several paragraphs from the introductions to *The Correspondence of Northrop Frye and Helen Kemp, 1932–1939* and *Northrop Frye's Student Essays, 1932–1938*.

3 Frye's undergraduate paper on Blake's *Milton* and the papers he wrote for Herbert J. Davis's Blake seminar when he was a student at Emmanuel College have not survived.

4 See 'Wyndham Lewis: Anti-Spenglerian'; 'Oswald Spengler'; 'New Directions from Old'; and 'Spengler Revisited.' The last essay Frye describes as 'an effort to lay a ghost to rest,' but ten years later Spengler was still making occasional appearances in his essays.

5 Cf. NB38, 36: 'All my work consists in translating involuntarily acquired aphorisms into a pattern of continuity. The former has something to do with listening for a Word, the ear being the involuntary sense, the latter with the spread-out performance of the eye,' and NB27, 112: 'The main difficulty in my writing, as I've often said, is in translating discontinuous aphorisms into continuous argument. Continuity, in writing as in physics, is probabilistic, and every sequence is a choice among possibilities. Inevitable sequence is illusory, & especially so in logic, where, just as q is always followed by u, so "rigor" is always followed by "mortis."'

WORKS CITED

Ayre, John. *Northrop Frye: A Biography.* Toronto: Random House, 1989.
Cayley, David. *Northrop Frye in Conversation.* Concord, Ont.: Anansi, 1992.
Frye, Northrop. 'New Directions from Old.' In *Myth and Mythmaking,* edited by Henry A. Murray. New York: George Braziller, 1960. 115–31; rpt. in *FI,* 52–66.
– *Northrop Frye's Student Essays, 1932–1938.* Edited by Robert D. Denham. Toronto: University of Toronto Press, 1997.
– 'Oswald Spengler.' In *Architects of Modern Thought,* 1st ser. Toronto: Canadian Broadcasting Corp., 1955. 83–90; rpt. in *RW,* 315–25.
– 'Spengler Revisited.' In *SM,* 179–98. This essay appeared originally as '*The Decline of the West* by Oswald Spengler,' *Dædalus* 103 (Winter 1974): 1–13.
– 'Symbolism of the Unconscious.' In *NFCL,* 84–94. This essay appeared originally as 'Sir James Frazer' in *Architects of Modern Thought,* 3rd and 4th ser. Toronto: Canadian Broadcasting Corp., 1959. 22–32.
– 'Wyndham Lewis: Anti-Spenglerian.' *Canadian Forum* 16 (June 1936): 21–2; rpt. in *RW,* 277–82.
Frye, Northrop, and Helen Kemp. *The Correspondence of Northrop Frye and Helen Kemp, 1932–1939.* Edited by Robert D. Denham. 2 vols. Toronto: University of Toronto Press, 1996.
Signori, Dolores A. *Guide to the Northrop Frye Papers.* Toronto: Victoria University Library, 1993.
Spengler, Oswald. *The Decline of the West.* Translated by Charles Francis Atkinson. Rev. ed. 2 vols. New York: Knopf, 1928.

The Book of the Dead: A Skeleton Key to Northrop Frye's Notebooks

MICHAEL DOLZANI

– I'm suffering from schematosis.

Northrop Frye, Notebook 38, 10

I

'Everybody has a fixation,' says Northrop Frye at one point in the four thousand or so pages of notebook material he left behind him at his death in 1991. 'Mine has to do with meander-and-descent patterns. For years in my childhood I wanted to dig a cave & be the head of a society in it – this was before I read Tom Sawyer. All the things in literature that haunt me most have to do with katabasis [descent movement]. The movie that hit me hardest as a child was the Lon Chaney Phantom of the Opera. My main points of reference in literature are such things as The Tempest, P.R. [*Paradise Regained*], the Ancient Mariner, Alice in Wonderland, the Waste Land – every damn one a meander-&-katabasis work' (NB19, 356, ca. 1964–7). In related entries, Frye connects this downward-and-inward impulse with his introverted personality, and remarks, 'The point of introversion is perhaps always the world of the dead ...' (NB19, 342).

For several years, my own fixation has been exploring the labyrinthine caverns of the Northrop Frye notebooks. A certain portion of the astonishing volume of Frye's unpublished writing has been the sort of literary remains one would expect: notes on his reading, drafts, the bones and discarded flints on the floor of the cave. A smaller segment records his lifelong aspirations and failed attempts to write a novel or prose romance. But the heart of the Frye notebooks is something unique and fascinating, and something bound to be controversial, because it raises profound questions about the peculiar nature of Frye's creative processes.

For over fifty years, Frye filled notebook after notebook with a series of quasi-sequential paragraph-length notes; sometimes these represent earlier forms of material that later found its way into his published books, but, if that were all, the notebooks would be a more ordinary and less interesting phenomenon than they in fact are. Most of us need to write down the results of our reading, research, and thinking so as not to forget them, but Frye is usually not *recording*; his remarkable memory did not seem to need much jogging. Sometimes he is clearly trying to come up with the proper formulation of an insight; if he does, he will repeat it verbatim in various contexts over decades, like a kind of private oral tradition. But the really interesting passages are where he is in process; like many people, he thinks by writing.

It is what he is thinking about, however, that is unusual – in fact unique, at least in my experience. Frye worked by projecting huge writing projects, works of epic scope and ambition, often in multiple volumes. These projects were not based on content but upon form: what he typically does in his notebooks is attempt to formulate or fill out patterns, designs, schemata, charts, and diagrams. He rarely begins with a subject, say Shakespearean comedy, and then tries to find an organizing form for what he has to say; he needs to have the form in order to have something to say about Shakespearean comedy. The form *is* the content; the medium *is* the message.

Moreover, the organizing pattern of a single work was never conceived in isolation; it was part of a total pattern, an encyclopaedic vision, present to him from an early age, out of which all his books grew. As my co-editor Robert Denham and I worked our way deeper and deeper into the branching tunnels of about ninety unorganized, undated notebooks, transcribing Frye's difficult handwriting, we began to come upon references to eight one-word titles of what were clearly projected works, sometimes half-jokingly referred to by Frye as the ogdoad, as if they were a pantheon of eight gods – a suggestion that turned out to have several kinds of truth to it. We also encountered eight symbols or characters, clearly a kind of shorthand version of the titles, reminiscent of Joyce's code-symbols for his personae in *Finnegans Wake*. After two years of bafflement, we finally unearthed a typescript document called 'Work in Progress' from 1972; this, along with a few corroborating documents, provided some of the explanation that follows. It also provided welcome evidence that we could consider ourselves archaeologists rather than tomb-robbers, as there is no reason for Frye to have typed out merely for himself a lengthy exposition of a symbolic system whose language he had been thinking in for decades.

1. In their first form, the eight works were to be eight concerti, for Frye in his early teens had ambitions to be a composer. Considering that the ogdoad scheme is really a double fourfold, the first four works being the only ones whose conception was developed at all clearly, a more significant analogy might be to sonata form (Frye once planned to write a four-part novel in sonata form, though he never got further than the title page and a few-dozen-page draft of the first part). A composer might conceivably begin with themes that he or she decides to develop in sonata form; but it is equally likely that the decision to compose in a certain form comes first and guides, or at least catalyses, the creation or discovery of the themes.

2. In their second version, which also dates back to Frye's early teens, the works became eight novels with one-word titles, and, eventually, code-symbols (see frontispiece): *Liberal* (L), *Tragicomedy* (⅂), *Anticlimax* (Λ), *Rencontre* (Λ), *Mirage* (V), *Paradox* (⊦), *Ignoramus* (⊥), *Twilight* (Γ; occasionally ⌐ or ⊤). These had no specific characters or events: they were imagined entirely in terms of plot-type, in other words of significant design. *Liberal* was a witty comedy of manners; *Tragicomedy* was panoramic, with a complex plot; *Anticlimax* was 'austere and forbidding'; *Rencontre* was a war novel. According to Frye himself, they derived from his boyhood reading of Horatio Alger and Scott – in other words, of comedy and romance, genres in which form (or at least formula) predominates over realistic texture.

3. While living on Bathurst Street in Toronto in 1944, Frye had an epiphany while walking to his office, which he recorded in what I have begun calling the Pentateuch notebook (officially Notebook 42). Here, he conceived five interconnected critical works, on a 4 + 1 scheme, which almost immediately metamorphosed into his old ogdoad, with *Fearful Symmetry*, then in its later stages, as *Liberal*, or Genesis, or the Los book (in Blake's terms). *Tragicomedy*, or Exodus, the Orc book, would deal with Shakespearean comedy in terms of a cyclic form that Frye found as the basis of ritual and myth in Frazer, of history in Spengler, and of drama in Frances Cornford and in Colin Still's *Shakespeare's Mystery Play*. *Anticlimax*, the Leviticus and Urizen book, would draw together the theories of medieval polysemy, Renaissance allegory and

creative etymology, occult and alchemical symbolism, and a lot of other things into a general theory of levels of meaning in literature. *Rencontre*, or *Numbers*, the Tharmas book, branched in two related directions: one a study of Romanticism based on a study of the sophisticated, self-conscious, ironic prose romance strain that runs through Poe, Hawthorne, Melville, the ghost stories of Henry James, Flaubert, Joyce, and Proust; the other a study of modern crisis and the fragmentation of culture. And so on, through the second group of four, which were considered to be Blakean 'emanations' or counterparts of the first four (one thinks of the 'double mirror' structure of *The Great Code* and *Words with Power*: two inter-reflecting parts of four chapters apiece).

When the Blake book was finished, however, it was numbered 0 instead, and L became a study of epic. In Notebook 7 (ca. 1948–56), the attempt to write this with a focus on Spenser turned into *Anatomy of Criticism*, as a discussion of Renaissance allegory ballooned into a discussion of levels of meaning in literature and then into a synthesizing overview of literary theory. So the *Anatomy* had to be numbered 0 as well.

4. From the late 1950s, after the *Anatomy* was off his hands, until the early 1970s, Frye spun off a number of short books, most of them beginning as series of public lectures, but privately laboured over plans for what he called the Third Book, in other words the third major study after *Fearful Symmetry* and *Anatomy of Criticism*. At its heart was a diagram, meditated in numerous forms over two decades but never ultimately published, called the Great Doodle – though we can call it the cycle of *mythoi* for solemnity's sake. It developed out of the cycle of *mythoi* in the Third Essay of the *Anatomy*, but differs in two ways. First, it is what Frye would have called the thematic stasis of the Third Essay, taking its hero's-quest circular narrative and spatializing it into four quadrants which he calls *topoi*, by which he means to evoke 'particularly their literal sense as "places"' (NB19, 343). However, since 'his soil is man's intelligence,' in Stevens's phrase, each landscape, each 'place,' becomes the locus of an interconnected set of themes and thematic images, often lyric-centred. The recovery of lost time, for example, is one of an indefinite number of themes whose context is Eros, rising like the sun or the seven-storey mountain from the East to a zenith of Logos-wisdom in the north. Second, the Great Doodle is centrifugal rather than centripetal: that is, it is not intended to lay out the internal structure of literature as an 'order of words,' but to show how mythopoeic patterns inform and transform society, history, and individual life. In addition,

the Third Book was to explain how literature's order of words is the shadowy prefiguration (or 'Druid analogy,' to use the Blake term that Frye employed for it) of a totally revealed Word that is its antitype or realized form, a 'spiritual Other' that is beyond literature, even if it is only to be arrived at by going *through* literature. Here is one of Frye's own descriptions of it:

All my criticial career has been haunted by the possibility of working out a schematology, i.e., a grammar of poetic language. I don't mean here just the stuff in FS [*Fearful Symmetry*] & AC [*Anatomy of Criticism*] & elsewhere, but the kind of diagrammatic basis of poetry that haunts the occultists & others. Whenever I finish a big job I seem to return to this ... In other words, once again I have a hope of reviving or making precise & detailed suggestions about – let's say the diagrammatic basis of schematology. (NB12, 335, 1968–70)

As an analogy or type, however, the Great Doodle does appear in literature, and therefore implicitly in some of the shorter studies Frye wrote during the period. Without the notebooks, we would never have guessed that Frye thought of *A Study of English Romanticism* as a cycle, with Beddoes at the bottom or south (the underworld), Shelley east (the revolutionary dawn), Keats at the oracular north, and Wordsworth, who apparently got squeezed out of chapter one, as the representative of conservative Romanticism slowly declining in the west (NB19, 222). But the Third Book was still part of Frye's larger multi-volume ambition, which emerged again when he planned his sabbatical in 1964. At this point, *Liberal* was to be on epic, *Tragicomedy* on drama (especially Shakespearean comedy), *Anticlimax* a study of prose forms (especially satire).

5. By the time of the 'Work in Progress' memo of 1972, yet another metamorphosis had taken place. Frye now envisioned a four-volume work called *The Critical Comedy*, to be completed by the time of his death (he was then sixty). *Liberal* was now a book on the Bible; *Tragicomedy* embodied the Great Doodle, along with some of the lyric poems that he had been using to illustrate it in his graduate course on Literary Symbolism; *Anticlimax* became a study of prose forms, contracts and utopias, educational theory, and conceptual displacements of myth; *Rencontre* turned into, of all things, a history of English literature. The total work was to have one hundred sections, like Dante's *Divine Comedy*.

6. If we ask about the final form of this eightfold ghost that seems to

have haunted Frye for over sixty years, we get what at first seems to be a depressing answer, namely that Northrop Frye, like Coleridge, suffered from a strange compulsion neurosis that drove him to propose huge, abstract plans with no relation to practical reality, like Coleridge's always-about-to-be-written encyclopaedic treatise on the Logos. The ogdoad was never produced, though a lot of its materials were used elsewhere; the Third Book was abandoned; the books Frye did write never fit into the scheme. In the end, are we not forced to regard the whole business along the lines of Yeats's *Vision*, as an afterbirth that may once have helped nourish the author's real offspring but in itself has to be ejected as something of a bloody mess?

Even more seriously, by taking Frye's critical method to the point of self-parody, which it can sometimes seem to be, doesn't it end by discrediting his whole enterprise? Jung says in *Psychological Types* that the typical defence system of introverts is abstraction, a withdrawal from the fury and mire and ambiguity of experience into the controlled and meaningful order of the mind; out of a fear of death, such abstraction runs away from life – right into the land of death, Blake's Ulro, the spectral womb–tomb self-buried world of the solipsistic ego. In an amazing passage from Notebook 12, Frye looks the central accusation right in the eye:

I am intensely superstitious; but there are two kinds of superstition, related as self-destructive melancholy is to penseroso melancholy. There is the superstition based on fear of the future: this is based also on my character as a coward & weakling, & is of course to be avoided. There is another kind which consists of removing all censors & inhibitions on speculation: it's almost exactly what Coleridge calls fancy. It may eventually be superseded by imagination: but if there's not fancy to start with there won't be any imagination to finish with. Let's call it creative superstition. It works with analogies disregarding all differences & attending only to similarities. Here nothing is coincidence in the sense of unusable design; or, using the word more correctly, everything is potential coincidence – what Jung calls synchronistic.

Thus, noting that Blake's Zoa–emanation scheme & the I Ching trigrams are both an ogdoad or Noah's Ark family of eight, I seize on every resemblance there is, invent a great many that aren't, and disregard all differences, determined to find an analogy in the teeth of the facts – not that there are any facts, of course ... (329, 330)

Now, it's essential to catch the tone of this passage: Frye is playing devil's advocate in the spirit of Blake's Devils in *The Marriage of Heaven and Hell,* demonstrating once again, as he does so often, how he is a playful thinker in the *homo ludens* sense of Schiller, Huizinga, or Nietzsche:

My approach to faith turns it into *gaya scienza,* a joyful wisdom: most of the conventional approaches turn it into a burden of guilt feelings. Critics who distrust me because I don't seem too worried about inconsistencies (Murray Krieger, Bill Wimsatt) can't tune into this notion of faith as a dancing ballet of intuitions, affirmations, counter-affirmations, 'doubts' or retreats from dogma, & a pervading sense of 'anything may be. "true" or "false," but whatever it is, the whole pattern has a design and a movement.' (NB44, 649, 1986–90)

Thus, while the anatomy tradition, from *The Anatomy of Melancholy* to *Sartor Resartus* to *Finnegans Wake,* proceeds from the satiric deconstruction of encyclopaedic and schematic erudition, many passages in the notebooks make clear that the anatomy tradition is not subversive of myth or literature themselves but only of the attempt to accommodate them to logic, fact, or ideology. For the spirit of play is the very nature of myth, and therefore of literature: 'The old idea that all kinds of mysteries of knowledge can be extracted from myth is, in modern terms, the fact that discursive prose is verbal work, while myths, like literature, are verbal play, & consequently can be "deconstructed" endlessly ... This conception of play integrates the kookiest notion of criticism into the centre of contemporary theory' (NB44, 281).

In some moods, Frye is willing to defend his criticism's retreat from the experiential in terms of a refusal of mastery and aggressiveness: 'It's the same instinct that makes me a critic, withdrawing from experience until it becomes oracular. It goes back to my lack of physical confidence, or, more accurately, to my realization that that lack of confidence has a very sound basis. I am not one of those who attack & conquer events and surroundings. I turn away until they settle down' (NB11f, 199, 1969–70). Occasionally, this refusal of 'reality' seems to harbour a positive as well as negative virtue, the affirmation of inwardness against the demands of the group:

Now, I feel that extroversion is considerably more than three-fourths of life, as Arnold said of conduct: it's more like seven-eighths. But there does have to be some residual or saving remnant of introversion, some sense of communion identity with something that isn't society. Call it nature or God, or, as I say in the Keats paper, it's important that different people should call it different things.

It's built on the introversion of the child, the retreat into the world made for his benefit. (NB19, 337)

Still, it is possible to play devil's advocate so well that the devil wins his case, and I do not know which I dread the most after the notebooks are finally published: the critics of high seriousness (whether empirical or ideological) who will take phrases like 'disregarding all differences' as a final confession of irresponsible guilt, or the New Age and occultist types who will celebrate Frye's coming out as one of their own. The word 'essay' means trial or attempt, a tentative response; and the *Anatomy of Criticism*'s subtitle, *Four Essays*, bears thinking about, for it subverts – or, to use a more suggestive word, recreates – that sense of definitive and final order that the book's diagrammatic quality seems to entail. The remainder of the present essay makes a tentative response to the view of Frye's schematic imagination as totalizing.

II

Let us begin by noting that Northrop Frye did in fact succeed in writing four major works; and that those four might bear some relation to the first and most important half of the ogdoad scheme, at least if we 'deliteralize' that scheme by reading it according to its spirit rather than its letter (which was never fixed and stable anyway). Frye himself came to identify *Liberal* with *The Great Code*, and *Tragicomedy* with *Words with Power*, both the published books having been hewn from the abandoned Third Book in the way that Blake quarried *Milton* and *Jerusalem* out of the abandoned *Four Zoas*. It is speculative to identify the *Anatomy of Criticism* with *Anticlimax*; nevertheless, determined to find an analogy in the teeth of the facts, let me point out that, with its Aristotelian framework, it is his most Urizenic book, and it really did evolve out of a study of epic and Spenserian allegory, just as *Anticlimax* was supposed to in the Pentateuch plan. Once, briefly, its author did imagine a revised *Fearful Symmetry* as *Rencontre* (NB24, 205, 1971–3): it is, after all, a study of Romanticism reflecting the conditions of its writing during a period of cultural fragmentation, world war, and nihilistic crisis. If, with the appropriate playfulness, we do adopt this perspective, it would mean that Frye wrote his tetralogy, or whatever it is, in almost the reverse order that he planned to write it. There might be some point even to that: in some versions of the buried or hidden world of the dead, time is said to run backwards.

It may be possible to work our way to a deeper level of insight at this point, however. As he grew older, Frye had moments of recognition that the ogdoad might be, as he put it several times in the notebooks, books for him to read rather than to write (e.g., NB7, 255, 1950s; NB18, 38, 1956–62). In other words, each of them represents an abiding preoccupation or focus of vision, not a subject matter; put another way, they are mental configurations that informed his writing, but not, or not necessarily, the actual content of specific volumes. There are many terms for such flashes of recognition (disregarding, of course, all differences): Aristotelian *anagnorisis*, Biblical *metanoia*, Eastern *paravritti*. What they all imply is a reversal of perspective that turns our perception inside-out in a Blakean vortex. Suddenly, we realize that what we are talking about is not four works of literary criticism written by the bundle of accidents that sat down at a writing desk, but a mental vision of the Logos whose four 'wheels' or driving forces are Zoas, living forms. Thus:

Liberal is about the total Word. Hence it began as a study of an archetypal poet like Blake, opened into a study of epic and other encyclopaedic forms, and ended as a book on the Bible as the great code of art. This total Word is circumferential, all-encompassing, but it is not some abstract Unity or Monomyth. That is why the Blakean emanation of *Liberal* is *Twilight*, the last of the ogdoad, 'my *Tempest*,' as Frye calls it. *Twilight* was recurrently envisioned as a collection of aphorisms or century of meditations (e.g., NB44, 325–6); its theme is the decentralized, immanent, individualized Word, the world in the grain of sand. Perhaps it might have dwelt on long-time preoccupations of Frye's such as the Lankavatara Sutra, with its doctrine of interpenetration, as opposed to totalization or subordination to a unifying master-narrative.

Tragicomedy is the counterpart, or creative contrary, of *Liberal* in the sense of being about the secular scripture, the recreative efforts of a human Spirit to respond to the creative Word, or spiritual Otherness, in what *Words with Power* calls the dialectic of Word and Spirit. But that is on an ideal level, where literature, driving beyond even the anagogic (the most expanded level of purely literary meaning) begins to approach the borderline of what *Words with Power* calls the kerygmatic (see that work for a fuller discussion of these ideas). On a more profane and imperfect level, literature remains what Frye called the 'Druid analogy.' The phrase from Blake means that the total form of *fallen* human imagination is a cycle, a form of the Urizen-versus-Orc conflict between limitation and energy, law and desire, reaction and revolution, tragedy and comedy: 'tragicomedy' is a good name for the ironic mode of this vision.

But in both its ideal and ironic versions, the Great Doodle is still a cycle of *mythoi* derived from the quest-myth narrative. Therefore, the ultimate subject of *Tragicomedy* is *mythos*, the narrative aspect of the Word.

Anticlimax is about *dianoia*, and is thus in turn the Blakean contrary of *Tragicomedy*; in fact, Frye says in the Pentateuch notebook that the two (which as Orc and Urizen books comprise a total Orc cycle) amount to a history of Western culture up to about 1600. Polysemy, allegory, satire and anatomy, contracts and utopias, conceptual displacements of myth, literary and educational theory – all this is in the general area of *dianoia*, broadly conceived.

Rencontre is the counterpart or contrary to all of these in that while they are about myth and cosmos, it is essentially about *history*, and particularly about the great crisis that began with Romanticism and culminates in the crises of modernism, post-modernism, and whatever we are supposed to be convulsed in now. Adopting the contrasting terms in the title of Mircea Eliade's *Cosmos and History*, the other books, or at least the second and third, deal with *cosmos*, a vision of both nature and human society as organized according to an eternally renewing cycle that is all we know of the True, the Beautiful, and the Good, and all we need to know. But *Rencontre* is about the fall into the nightmare of history. History is a nightmare because it turns the sacred into the profane; it attempts to live without myth, but only succeeds in living by demonic parodies of myth – this last is the subject of many of the greatest works of the twentieth century: *Heart of Darkness*, *The Golden Bough*, Jung's *Psychology of the Unconscious*, *The Waste Land*, *Ulysses*, *Gravity's Rainbow*.

An ingenious recreation, perhaps: but does it really respond to the fundamental challenge? Why should everything be a part of a pattern, even one that allows for a lot of flexibility and diversity? Isn't pluralism a more suitably democratic view, especially in a period that is in full revolt against the demand of power structures, academic and otherwise, to 'fit in'?

Taking up these questions in a brief essay demands a lot of very compressed generalizations, but let us begin with the nature of the modern crisis that is the backdrop of *Rencontre*. In the first chapter, entitled 'The Case against Locke,' of his first book, Frye began his career with an explanation of how philosophy has continued to demonstrate the illusory nature of the subject–object dichotomy ever since Descartes set it up in the seventeenth century. Psychology has followed suit in showing that ordinary subjective awareness, the ego, is not necessarily a 'normal,' let alone superior, mode of consciousness: there is plenty of evidence that we screen out 'lower' (depth psychological) as well as 'higher' (Maslovian) levels of functioning. Various disciplines of the philosophy of language, deconstruction being only the most recent, have repeatedly insisted that the signified–signifier–referent notion of language – the word as a bridge between a concept in the subject's mind and an object in external reality – breaks down into a series of intractable paradoxes, precisely because it is founded upon the illusory subject–word–object view of experience. The social sciences join the chorus, inundating us with evidence that other, very different modes of symbolic figuration were ascendant in other times and places, some of them implying quite alien modes of perception and understanding that nevertheless possess an authority of their own. Finally, history, especially since Marx and Nietzsche, has exposed the degree to which Western culture (like any other) is an ideological rationalization of power and hierarchy, even if it is not *only* that. Whatever one thinks of Spengler, what Frye claimed years ago remains true: that we are all actually Spenglerians, because we all believe, for more than sufficient reasons, that we are at the end of a cultural era. A literal translation of Spengler's German title would be something like 'the going-under of the evening-lands' – the Western descent of the sun or solar-hero into the caverns of the grave, or what Blake called the dens of Urthona.

So long as one clings to ego-centred reality as the only one, this is a pessimistic view, indeed a nihilistic one. Because that is what most people do in fact believe, the modern world oscillates between a manic hysterical anxiety and a depressive alienated despair. Yet, though it thinks of itself as the reality-principle incarnate, the ego is in fact only a construct, a useful but limited instrument – limited insofar as it is founded upon the 'cloven fiction' of the subject–object perspective: 'Note that the subjective and objective worlds are the same, the individual ego being a historical product: it's just that they seem opposed because of a cloven fiction that really unites them' (NB44, 704). The ego is inevitably reductive by nature, remaining in existence by defining itself as 'I' against everything else that is 'not-I.' So its fundamental mode is alienation: from others, nature, God, even from its 'own' language or its 'own' self. Frye says: 'The Spirit is born, or reborn, from prophecy, and its enemy is Lacan's *moi*, the self-alienated ego or projected Narcissus. The *moi*, I suppose, must be the Spirit's twin brother, born at the same time and the hero of the dream world while the Spirit sleeps. The *moi* remembers everything except its spiritual heritage: if it remembered that it would vanish' (NB27, 103, 1985). In another place: 'Spirit, then, is the unity, expressible only by metaphor, of subject & object in which the essential reality of the two are one' (NB44, 382).

What the quotations call the Spirit is what St Paul called the 'spiritual man' (*soma pneumatikon*), the larger identity, 'I, yet not I,' into which we are born, or reborn, out of the 'natural man' (*soma psychikon*) who is our womb and tomb, the body of this death: 'There's an individual that isn't an ego, & there must be a dreaming individual that isn't just preoccupied with a wish to screw his mother. In waking life the storm clouds of the ego keep blinding us to reality, but every so often they clear & we see clearly & objectively. Something similar happens with dreams – everybody feels that some dreams are more oracular than others' (NB19, 7). It was Blake who identified our larger spiritual identity with the creative power buried in the caverns of our being, the imagination or 'Real Man.' (We should note in passing that the masculine pronouns need deconstructing; as Frye says of Scripture: 'In its historical & ideological context the Bible is male-centered, white-centered, Christian-centered, theist-centered. In its mythical & metaphorical contexts these limitations become metaphors for something that includes what they exclude ... One has to recreate ...') (NB44, 545). Apocalypse meant to Blake the resurrection of this power out of the depths in which humanity has tried to bury it throughout history, out of what Frye called 'a cave of myths, or encyclopaedic memory-theatre,' or 'a cave-theatre holding all the ghosts of imagination like the one in PU' (NB19, 344, 343). 'PU' could mean *Prometheus Unbound*, but it was also Frye's usual abbreviation for Jung's *Psychology of the Unconscious*: both identifications would work. The awakening of this Spirit or larger human identity is at the same time an *epopteia*, a manifestation of a God who is also man out of the depths as in the Eleusinian mysteries, the light suddenly ablaze in the despairing, uncomprehending darkness, and its kindling ignites a volcanic eruption, a harrowing of hell: 'The real God, from Blake on, is not the descendit de coelis God of imposing order & recreation, but the Promethean God tearing loose from death & hell with smoke & grime all over his face, the mad treading-the-wine-press Messiah of Isaiah' (NB11f, 166).

The ego cannot solve the problem of the One and the Many, either for itself or for society; it is stuck with a Hobson's choice between repressive unity and disintegrative difference. But the imagination perceives in configurations of patterns, in a unity-in-diversity of contraries that Frye usually calls interpenetration. The basis of the imagination is what Frye's late work calls ecstatic metaphor, in which we become what we behold (the Blakean formulations, admittedly frequent, seem inevitable). This is not some esoteric mystical state, nor is it a mere intellectual theory: everyday human life is held together by a series of identifications. Only a nihilist like Richard III says, 'I am myself alone'; healthy human identity evolves out of a lifetime of identifications with various forms of the 'Other' – friends, lovers, family, institutions, causes, vocations, nature, God, even with one's own self over time, i.e., the kind of time-binding by which we feel identified with (though not the same as) our own self at the age of seven. In a normal development, we are not submerged in or martyred to such identifications; on the contrary, our real autonomous individuality grows out of them.

Literature is, or can be, a process of meditation that intensifies the process of imaginative identification, to the point at which ordinary, unorganized, 'given' reality is recreated into a new, constructed reality that is neither objective nor subjective, a 'supreme fiction,' as Wallace Stevens calls it. And the first thing Stevens says of it in *Notes Toward a Supreme Fiction* is that 'It Must Be Abstract,' meaning stylized, patterned, designed. That is the basis on which, in his last years, Frye could record the following contention: 'The opening sentence of AC [*Anatomy of Criticism*] said I attached no particular importance to the construct *qua* construct. I think I've got past that now, and that it's only by means of such dizzyingly complex constructs that one can ever get anything substantial out of criticism. Those who appear not to have such a construct, like Johnson, are attached to an ideology; those who do often don't get it worked out, like Coleridge' (NB44, 99). It follows from this that the attempt to get 'beyond formalism' and into an examination of the social function and authority of literature and mythology does not, paradoxically, take us away from design or pattern: instead, it relates us to constructs more intensely, on an existential rather than simply hypothetical level.

Imaginative patterns are focused around the primary concerns; these have a physical basis but expand into a spiritual dimension where they become the more abundant forms of human life, as sex expands into love, eating and drinking into communion and community. The ultimate expansion of the supreme fiction is into an entire cosmology, a recreated human universe – or rather, that is its synchronic version. Yet Stevens's second requirement is: 'It Must Change.'

This brings us back to the Great Doodle, the cycle of *mythoi*: why did Frye abandon it after so many years? The Doodle, after all, does represent a cycle of change. On its compass-mandala, the East-to-North quadrant is the locus of the ascent of Eros, the comedy-romance climb to a higher level of reality. The North point is Logos, the vision of order at the top of the mountain. The North-to-West quadrant is Adonis, the tragic fall into a lower level of existence. The Western point is Nomos, the epiphany of law that sets the limits of the fallen world. West-to-South is the meander-and-descent quest into the caverns of the under-world, and the Southern point is Thanatos, the vision of Nothing, as Logos is the vision of All or plenitude. South-to-East is resurrection, or Prometheus unbound, but the Eastern point is 'the Nous point of iden-tity ... symbolized by the Platonic symposium & the Christian commun-ion supper ... the eucharist being defined by Blake as the formation of the appropriate society' (NB24, 15, ca. 1971–3). The vertical axis from Logos to Thanatos is the 'axis of concern.' As readers of *Words with Power* will have realized by this time, Frye did not actually abandon the circle: he verticalized it so that its four quadrants became four vertical levels of an *axis mundi* diagram. Why? Frye never really says, but certain lines of development in the late notebooks suggest an answer: because the Doodle, Great though it may be, remains just one more Monomyth, a closed cycle of return that is still caught in a synchronic repetition of 'the same dull round.' What it lacks is something that, in Frye's view, only the Biblical tradition can provide: a truly diachronic principle of recreation, a power that redeems history instead of merely escaping from it; only through time is time conquered.

The Bible as a closed and changeless canon is (like all canons) a demonic parody of the real thing. As far back in time as one can trace it, the Bible is actually in a constant process of recreating itself. Where the East and the Classical tradition give us a perennial philosophy ('We worship Zeus under one name, you under another, but all religions are really one'), the Biblical tradition's fanatical intolerance is the shadow-side of its greatest gift: a potentially revolutionary vision of revelation repeatedly and progressively refining itself in the fiery furnace of dialec-tical historical conflict. Out of the type–antitype relationship unique to the Biblical tradition developed the historical vision of Joachim of Floris, in which humanity evolves through three progressive ages of Father, Son, and Holy Spirit; Joachim was an influence in turn upon Romantic theories of history from Hegel to Blake to Marx. This is the progressively social side of the Biblical vision, and it remains a powerful force no mat-ter how many ideological perversions it has spawned.

But there is also an individualized version of the process of dialectical recreation, one that originates in Frye's remark (*WP*, 139) that the type–antitype relationship is closely parallel to the mythical–kerygmatic one.

What would the Great Doodle become if it were conceived kerygmatically instead of merely mythically or imaginatively – that is, if it became existentially realized, a 'myth to live by' instead of merely one to contemplate intellectually or aesthetically? Briefly, it would be transformed from a circle into a vortex, and it would represent what Blake called 'opening a centre,' the process by which ecstatic metaphor turns the ego inside out. What would this be like to experience?

To answer this, let us begin with another question: why is life always an *agon*, a struggle with some form of Other? Reluctant to admit it, one part of us nonetheless knows: because it is only through struggle that we develop and mature. Granted that not all struggle may be productive, it is the conflicts in our lives out of which our identity has been forged. Love, or creativity, or useful work: the real activities of human life demand a commitment from us, a discipline that becomes, again, a kind of refiner's fire. There are two aspects of this conflict of contraries: possession and sacrifice. Considered from one standpoint, we assimilate in this process something of the Other, make it a permanent possession, part of a new and expanded identity. This does not mean 'mastering' it, or annihilating its otherness. The lover with whom we become 'one flesh' is still a separate individual: '... love is interpenetration, but it has to extend beyond the sexual interpenetrating of intercourse. Every act of hostility is penetration with a threat, with a desire to dominate or acquire for oneself. Love means entering into and identifying with the other people and things without threats or domination, in fact without retaining an ego-self' (NB44, 501). Likewise, the text that we 'possess' still exists in itself and for others. True possession has nothing to do with sadistic domination or property rights, but is a manifestation of what Charles Williams (and Stephen Greenblatt after him) called the way of exchange, a Heraclitean circulatory system in which we die each other's lives and live each other's deaths. That is why, from another point of view, while we assimilate, eucharistically, what used to be alienated from us, our metamorphosis (or *metanoia*, to use the Biblical word) also demands a sacrifice, a death-and-rebirth initiation rite in which we die to the old ego-self: this is the antitype of which Christ's Passion is the type. Its demonic parody is either the sacrifice of the Other or the annihilation of ourselves as a scapegoat or *pharmakos*. Likewise, the true sense of deconstruction is the opening-out in a Blakean vortex of logocentric and egocentric language.

In whatever context, this death-and-resurrection rhythm transfigures death, and thus harrows hell. Death becomes purgatorial, not just the end of our being, much less an indefinite prolongation of the ego's fallen existence. It is an ordeal of suffering and endurance, yet not necessarily of meaningless and passive victimage. Something comes of it, as something comes out of the trials of Job, whose story, an epitome of the whole Bible, forms the conclusion of both *The Great Code* and *Words with Power*. In the midst of his suffering, Job's reality turns inside-out, and out of that whirlwind-vortex bursts a tremendous vision of reality as *God*, the terrible Other, sees it in all its awful sublimity, detached from the natural man's fear and desire; indeed, Frye suggests that Job's final restoration may be a *part* of that vision, and thus not just a wish-fulfilment happy ending in the fallen reality in which he began.

At any rate, this faith in a purgatorial creative process helps to explain Frye's hatred – the word is not too strong – of two great works of literature. In Notebook 6 we learn that 'The Iliad is a poem I loathe, and the Inferno was an act of treachery to the human race far lower than Judas, who could not possibly have acted from motives so debased as Dante's "practical" ones were' (59, 1968). The entry cannot be dismissed as the expression of a momentary irritation. In Notebook 12, speaking of the Thanatos point on the Great Doodle, he says, 'I've always hated this world, and the Iliad & Inferno are my bugbears' (10). So much for the misconception that Frye's rejection of value judgments in criticism means that works of literature cannot be criticized for the ideological damage they might do.

But why did he hate them so much? A later entry from Notebook 12 offers a first clue: 'The Prometheus element on the other hand is the one Dante left out: he turned his back on hell and didn't harrow it' (481). We may put this together with remarks elsewhere about the 'poco-curantism' of the *Iliad* and *Inferno* (NB6, 59), the apathy or indifference, citing especially the 'terrible myth' of Achilles in book 24, meaning presumably Achilles' famous speech about how an indifferent Zeus delivers good and bad fortune to humankind at random, so that there is nothing to do but resign oneself to what happens (NB12, 166). In other words, what Frye rejected in both works, even more than their sadistic violence, was the message 'All hope abandon.'

In contrast, three other works recur together throughout the notebooks like three interlinking rings: 'Thus I think now of my three favorites, *Tempest*, *P.R.* [*Paradise Regained*], & [Blake's] *Milton*, as all beginning essentially with Hermetic meander-&-descent patterns' (NB12, 402). The descent in these works is not literally into an underworld cavern or tomb; nevertheless, Frye says, 'Now The Tempest seems to me to belong with *Milton* and *Paradise Regained* in the purgatorial world, being in so curious a way on the other side of this one' (NB12, 285). This is the realm he often associates with the world called Bardo in *The Tibetan Book of the Dead*, the hidden side of this life in which the dead move from death to rebirth: 'The Buddhists keep saying, with tremendous and unending prolixity, that the subject–object duality is horseshit. Okay, it's horseshit: what's so infernally difficult about it? The fact that it's so difficult to overcome derives from the fact that the metaphorical kernel of subject & object is the contrast of life & death. The person for whom that's disappeared really is a sage' (NB44, 109). The image of 'the game of chess in the lower world' (e.g., NB24, 66) haunted him so much that he dreamed for years of writing a novel actually set in Bardo. (Charles Williams beat him to it in *All Hallows Eve*, he felt, although James Merrill's *The Changing Light at Sandover* is a far profounder treatment of the same theme.) The purgatorial descent, though, is a double gyre whose other movement is resurrection; this is clear in a remark from Notebook 12 that 'Critical treatment of *The Tempest* (top of Eros), *Paradise Regained*, (opening of Logos) & Blake's *Milton* (redemptive descent) [in Boddhisattva fashion] has to be extended ...' (13). This matches Dante's own descent in the *Inferno*, which is for him, unlike the damned, part of a process that is ultimately purgatorial or transformative, and rises by the end into a vision of the divine presence.

We have come by this point a long way from the picture of Northrop Frye as a refugee doodling abstractions on the walls of Plato's cave. In a deeply moving passage written after the death of Helen Frye in 1986, he says that he doesn't have faith, only hope; but he is hopeful that death is a purgatorial process, and that the woman he loved is not simply annihilated. He adds: 'Since Helen's death I've felt my love for her growing increasingly beyond the contingencies of the human situation. I begin to understand more clearly what Beatrice and Laura are all about. If the relation is reciprocal there is nothing to regret beyond the inevitable mechanisms of regret' (NB44, 203). When I first read Notebook 44, out of which *Words with Power* unfolded, I took this entry to be speaking about the *memory* of Helen, of its power to inspire a work that would be a *memorial* to someone dead and lost in the past. Yet such a work could only be a tombstone, and that is in fact the opposite of what Frye is really saying, as another paragraph clearly shows:

Meanwhile, let's think about the one idea all this grief has brought me so far. I said in GC [*The Great Code*] that the invisible world in the Bible was not a second order of existence, as in the Platonic tradition, but the means by which the visible world becomes visible, as the invisible air is the medium of visibility. The one really invisible world is the world across death: is that what makes us to see the seen? Is the visible world the world of faith (*pistis*), as in Plato, that is the *elenchos* [evidence] of the unseen? (NB44, 174)

In the invisible world, the world across death, Helen is far more than an inspiring memory: 'Helen was – that's the beginning of tears and mourning. Helen is. What she is, perhaps, is a central element in the unseen which will clarify my understanding, if such clarification is granted me' (NB44, 175). When he says that 'I find all my ideas regrouping around her in a way I can neither understand or explain' (NB44, 223), he means that he is actually undergoing the process which is to become the theme of the book: from literary metaphors, which are merely aesthetic and hypothetical, 'We move *through erotic* metaphors ... *to* existential metaphor, or experience of identity with light or spirit' (NB44, 340, my emphases; see also 243 and 353). And when consciousness achieves identity with spirit, it is no longer bound, like Prometheus, to the rock of space and time. The dead and the unborn – as they seem to the alienated ego – are then known to be always already present, though in another order of reality: 'Where religion and science can still get together is on the conception of the objective world as an "unfolding" of an "enfolded" or unborn order, which is beyond time and space as we experience them. David Bohm's book, *Wholeness and the Implicate Order*, has something on this' (NB44, 19). In truth, it is *we* who are the dead (as in Joyce's famous short story), and to experience identity with spirit is to become born: 'The soul–body complex is to spirit as embryo is to baby, as type is to antitype, as illusion is to reality (after what we call reality has vanished into illusion)' (NB44, 336).

Such an order of reality is counter-logical: 'Spirit, then, is the unity, expressible only by metaphor, of subject & object in which the essential reality of the two are one' (NB44, 382). This is enough for most people to dismiss it, though Frye protests, 'I've been called a (Platonic) dualist, but I'm not one, and neither was Plato. There is only one form of dualism, the Cartesian cloven fiction of subject & object, a formidable barrier to thought because our language is Cartesian' (NB44, 347). What's more, it is counter-historical: 'We enter a world where Jesus is still alive, a world opposite to anything "the quest for the historical Jesus" could ever reach. This direct inner deconstructing search is the "mystic" Boehme-Blake approach – at least that's a very direct kind' (NB44, 341). Again, the crowds thin and disperse, though Frye splutters, 'Why do people call *me* anti-historical? I talk about myth, and it's *myth* that's anti-historical' (NB44, 285). He that hath ears, etc. But by the time of the late notebooks, Frye's thinking was driven by more urgent motives than his status in contemporary critical fashion. *Words with Power* no longer had a hundred sections, but it was what remained to complete of a critical comedy whose first dim outlines he had begun to discern when he first met his Beatrice-figure almost fifty years before. As he says in Notebook 27, 'My whole conscious life has been purgatorial, a constant circling around the same thing, like a vine going up an elm' (486). Or like the process that alchemy calls the *circumambulatio*, the progressively clarifying meditation that spirals asymptotically towards a mysterious centre of revelation.

For interpretation does not merely build up a centripetal order of words; it invites us to ask the question that Jung said compelled his whole career: 'What myth are you living?' The purgatorial vision, which is the thematic stasis, or antitype, or fully clarified form, of the ogdoad, would have been Frye's answer; for it was not merely his anatomy but his confession or 'mental history,' the true form of his life. The last two of his notebooks are probably both his profoundest and his most personal. In one of them (Notebook 53, written during the composition of *The Double Vision*), he renders the vertical *axis mundi* image from the second half of *Words with Power* in terms that become directly autobiographical:

The 'body' is preoccupied with primary concerns on the physical level, and is also the part of the psyche that we should now call the unconscious. It 'knows' nothing except that the soul or mind or consciousness that keeps bullying it is all wrong about everything. Above the soul is the spirit, and when the 'body' makes contact with that, man possesses for an instant a spiritual body, in which he moves into a world of life and light and understanding that seemed miraculous to him before, as well as totally unreal. This world is usually called 'timeless,' which is a beggary of language: there ought to be some such word as 'timeful' to express a present moment that includes immense vistas of past and future. I myself have spent the greater part of seventy-eight years in writing out the implications of insights that occupied at most only a few seconds of all that time. (267)

From the other 'last' notebook (NB44) comes a passage, informed by the imagery of Yeats's *Byzantium*, that dispels any misconception that this 'writing out' can ever be the reverie of a detached intellectual sitting in his study, picking out the *mots justes* to articulate his vision of a pure and ideal mandala of Forms: 'All human creativity drifts upward through the ivory gates from libido to ego, bringing a mixture of vision and violence, love and cruelty. A sense of articulate order comes down through the gate of horn. Creativity is a purgatory fuelled by the "blood-begotten spirits," refined into love & wisdom through words. Without words, it's only the Babel of power with its confusion of tongues' (603). Once again, the Spirit ascends to meet the descending Word in the air: this is the dialectic of Word and Spirit.

In the same notebook, Frye quotes a remark by Hans Kung: 'Purgatory is God himself' (219). God in this view is less an external being than a process, a *power* or transformative energy, in which we live and *move*. Blake says that energy is 'eternal delight'; the third and last thing Stevens says of the supreme fiction is, 'It Must Give Pleasure.' This is the substance of things hoped for, the phoenix power that rises from the cave.

Frye and the Art of Memory

IMRE SALUSINSZKY

I think that Frye is certainly the finest prose writer among modern critics. He has the expository force and some of the wit of Shaw ... I once said of his book *Fools of Time* that, if necessary, he will depart from the major systematic arrangements of the *Anatomy* and make up new ones. I suggested that really they are a kind of memory theatre, just mnemonic aids. He wrote me a rather snappy letter saying 'Well of course they are: what did you think?'

Frank Kermode, 1987[1]

The long tradition of phenomenological literary scholarship has made us accustomed to looking at an author's works in order to try to discover, through those works, a sense of the way in which the author experienced his or her world – to find, if you like, a map of the author's mind. Would it be possible, by analogy, to look in criticism for a guide or map to the critic's mind? Obviously, just as this works best with writers like Dickens or Joyce who seem to contain an entire world, so it would only work with major critics who have unfolded an entire, and original, vision, or *summa*, or theory of literature. Just as the great writers seem to make us feel what someone else has seen and felt as they have experienced reality, so the great critics who have shifted the paradigms of literary criticism often seem to make us aware of what someone has seen and felt as they have experienced literature. This sense of an authentic consciousness, or living presence, behind the text may be an illusion, a logocentric fiction, but the point is that this illusion may inhere in criticism as well as in the art it deals with.

In terms of setting out a *summa*, a complete vision of literature, Frye is outstanding in modern criticism – we have to go back centuries to find parallels. So how did Frye's mind work? Or to put it another way: how did it look? Do his works provide us with a metaphorical map? I think that this is now one of the more interesting questions that Frye studies can set itself, but I don't think that the evidence for it is buried deep in the Frye Papers at the Victoria University Library; it's not something that we'll find the key to one day, hidden in a blue-grey cardboard box (though what *is* in those boxes can certainly help, as I will show). No, the central evidence for how Frye experienced literature is in his published works, especially *Anatomy of Criticism*. And this may seem odd when we consider that Frye's style in these works, though witty and conversational, is also famously objective: there is none of the sense of a modern aesthetic critic like Harold Bloom, say, recounting his soul's adventures among masterpieces. When Bloom talks about literature he is really, as he freely admits, talking about himself; when Frye talks about literature, he is really talking about literature. Frye is a skilled rhetorician in the classical and humanist tradition that he describes in *The Critical Path*:

The typical humanist strives to be sane, balanced, judicious; he is not a prophet nor an angry man ... He avoids both technical and colloquial language, and has a deep respect for conventions, both social and literary. As a professional rhetorician, his instinct is to save the face of the situations he encounters by finding the appropriate words for them. (90)

Yet Frye does reveal a great deal to us about his own mind as he talks about literature – perhaps even more than Bloom. One of Frye's mottoes, from John Stuart Mill, is that the poet is not heard but overheard: the same may be true of the critic; but it is hard to overhear someone when he is shouting at you.

Of course, among the anecdotes about Frye, there are many concerning his prodigious memory. Jane Widdicombe, his secretary for more than twenty years, will confirm his ability to provide his books' allusions, even long quotations, without having to consult originals. The first time I spoke to Frye, in 1982, he told me that, when he came to Toronto from the Canadian Maritimes as an undergraduate in the late 1920s, he had to telegram his mother to send on some of his books: because he *saw* certain passages as appearing on certain pages, he was having trouble checking the quotations for his student essays in library editions. Frye certainly recognized that his unusual powers of recall were intimately connected with his work as a critic, and with his notoriously introverted personality as well. He wrote in a notebook in the early 1970s: 'My "recluse" existence is not wholly laziness & inertia. My work depends on a good memory, & the way to keep a good memory is not to make too many waves of experience in between. The hours I spent in Mob Quad reading about Old English literature are as vivid to me still as the hours I spent last week at a CRTC hearing ...' (NB24, 230). At other times, though, Frye can be much more ambivalent, and even conceives his own extraordinary memory as a kind of burden:

In my speeches I often speak of earlier moments of intensity. They were usually not moments of intensity, but only look so when I remember them. In a sense, therefore, I'm simply lying. But perhaps this is what the memory is for, to bring to life past moments. If so, the memory, like the sensory apparatus, is selective & exclusive. Screen memory is the only memory. Nietzsche says that when the memory says 'I did that' & pride says 'I didn't,' the memory gives way. I wish to hell mine would, & that I didn't remember so many silly & humiliating things. Maybe it's a disease that it doesn't, & it should. Perhaps that's the meaning of Lethe, losing the memory of sin, in Dante. Of course an old man in complacent dotage, with a battery of stories showing him in a good light, isn't exactly the noblest work of God. But memory is the key to identity. And perhaps (as Coleridge once suggested) the key to resurrection too. My own memory, employed in this way, brings an almost intolerable weight of nostalgia with it: I want to go back to an earlier & simpler time when all those people were alive. (NB11f, 158)

It is interesting that Harold Bloom, Frye's most distinguished successor in so many ways, has a prodigious memory too; but the two appear to react to their powers of recall in opposite ways: the poets in Bloom's head become claustrophobic, and begin their bitter struggles for *lebensraum*; Frye just builds bigger and bigger rooms for his tenants, so that even Eliot and Pound, whom he dislikes, get to share a granny-flat.

There is a way of talking about memory and memorization in Frye that is less anecdotal than his ability to remember passages from books, though his ability to remember passages from books is not divorced from it. The reason I suggest that Frye's critical vision may provide us with a unique insight into his interior landscape is that I now regard that vision as a contribution to the art of memory. This type of inquiry is less concerned with Frye's psychology, or even with a conventionally phenomenological approach to his criticism, than it is with placing him in a tradition that he has not been placed in before: the tradition of pictorializing and spatializing knowledge in order to render it memorable. Frye's notebooks reveal that he was much more interested than we have previously suspected in mnemotechnics – the system of training what was once called 'artificial memory' – and in the history of the art of memory, as set out in particular by Frances Yates. (There are numerous references to Yates in the notebooks, as well as to the people she writes about, especially Giordano Bruno, and Ramon Lull, on whom Frye wrote an undergraduate essay.) Whether or not Frye consciously practised formal mnemotechnics, he was deeply interested in it. That Frye's *criticism* may be both enabled by, and a contribution to, mnemotechnics has not previously been considered. It was, however, suggested to me in passing, over a decade ago, by Frank Kermode, in the epigraph to this essay; I have been thinking about Kermode's hint ever since. One other place that a kind of mnemonic imagery has been used in connection with Frye is in an analogy that Angus Fletcher drew, and Frye appreciated, between the structure of the *Anatomy* and Haussmann's design for Paris, with its broad, unbroken avenues linking the different districts (31). The beauty of this analogy is that it recognizes that Frye's categories are really kinds of places: Frye says in Notebook 19 that by calling the quadrants of the Third Essay *topoi* he meant 'particularly their literal sense as "places"' (343). This suggests that the *Anatomy* and its schemas may actually be reread as an anatomy of Frye's own memory of literature, and, as Kermode hinted, as descriptions of the memory-rooms in its author's mind.

The art of memory was one of the central branches of classical, medieval, and Renaissance thought. The anonymous *Ad Herennium*, ca. 82 B.C., lists *memoria* among the five parts of rhetoric, but calls memory 'the custodian of all the parts of rhetoric' (see Yates, 5). Trained memory, which was called an 'art,' or what today we would probably call a method or expertise, is distinguished in classical rhetorical theory from 'natural' memory, the things we recall without memorization. (This sense that artificially trained memory, usually analogized as a kind of mental inscription, exists in tension with a more 'natural' memory inhabits mnemotechnics from the beginning, and never leaves it – it is still apparent in Kermode's description of memory-theatres as 'just mnemonic aids.') The most important feature of the art of memory is also the feature most relevant to Frye: it is architectonic and pictorial, operating through the placement of mental images in imaginary buildings.[2]

The method, in all its variations, works through two sets of rules: rules for places, or *loci*, and rules for images, or *imagines*. The most suitable images were considered to be those that had some grotesque quality or, even better, involved movement (the latter were called *imagines agentes*). What the practitioner of the ancient art does is to construct buildings in the mind, which are called palaces or theatres, and then place the information to be memorized in the memory rooms as mental images. When the material needs to be recalled, the memory artist walks through the rooms until he finds the image, which is connected to the information through some kind of association. Some classical memory artists had palaces containing over 100,000 rooms. And as Mary Carruthers points out, the art of memory was always considered a very different thing to rote learning – a difference that has steadily been eroded through the centuries:

The 'art of memory' is actually the 'art of recollection,' for this is the task which these schemes are designed to accomplish. They answer to principles that define and describe how reminiscence occurs, what it is, and what it is supposed to do. And among those tasks, iteration *per se* was clearly not considered vital. The crucial task of recollection is *investigatio*, 'tracking-down,' a word related to *vestigia*, 'tracks' or 'footprints.' All mnemonic organizational schemes are heuristic in nature. They are retrieval schemes, for the purpose of *inventio* or 'finding.' (20)

In other words, mnemotechnics in classical, medieval, and Renaissance scholarship merges with epistemology itself; the shape in which knowledge is committed to memory *is* knowledge. The Middle Ages took the classical discourse of artificial memory and turned it to ethical and religious ends: a properly trained memory became an attribute of Prudence. An epic poem like the *Divine Comedy* was seen as part of the art of memory. Dante takes Paradise and Hell, which were already in a sense recognized as memory places, and populates them with grotesque images that will remind us how to live prudently. Yates notes that for Thomas Aquinas, the central figure in medieval memory, memory-theatres are used to hold a vast *summa* of knowledge in memory.

In the Renaissance, Yates's argument continues, in the work of rhetoricians like Bruno and Lull and Camillo, artificial memory blends with occult and hermetic information-systems like the zodiac and the kabbala. These writers think that they can penetrate the secrets of the universe simply by unfolding in its vast entirety the picture-book of memory, since the universe stands to the mind as macrocosm to microcosm. The famous memory theatre of Giulio Camillo – an actual travelling exhibit that you could walk into – was based on classical mnemotechnics but, says Yates, 'is to represent the order of eternal truth; in it the universe will be remembered through organic association of all its parts with their underlying eternal order' (138). She also points out that Renaissance memory-artists saw their memory-images much as what we today would call archetypes or mandalas. Bruno tried to arrange all human knowledge, not into memory-rooms, but in the related form of enormous diagrams, featuring images and wheels that could be combined and adapted in memory, and that revolved inside each other in the mind.

As well as being occultists, these writers are of course anatomists. Although Frye works hard in *Fearful Symmetry* to rescue Blake from being swallowed whole into this occult tradition, the notebooks show him as much less certain of his *own* wish to be rescued from it, precisely because of its diagrammatic basis: 'All my critical career has been haunted by the possibility of working out a schematology, i.e., a grammar of poetic language ... the kind of diagrammatic basis of poetry that haunts the occultists & others ... once again I have a hope of reviving or making precise & detailed suggestions about – let's say the diagrammatic basis of schematology' (NB12, 335).

The collapse of the great art into modern memory-training, a gimmick for making friends and influencing people, is one of the scandals of post-Romantic culture – although now, with the rise of artificial intelligence, artificial memory is also making a comeback. The memory 'cells' in our PCs are a revitalization of a traditional mnemotechnic image; and when we ask each other, 'How much memory do you have?' we could almost be Renaissance memory-artists. And in the oddly related development of deconstruction (people forget that the *Grammatology* begins with a discussion of cybernetics), pictures of mind that rely on inscriptive metaphors have likewise made up ground on those that rely on natural or organic ones. This may help improve the fortunes of even so logocentric a subject as mnemotechnics.

Romanticism, especially Blakean Romanticism, is of course partly to blame for the decay of artificial memory, which it figures as mechanical and reiterative, and opposes to vital, creative imagination. Blake associates the memory with Selfhood: 'Imagination,' he says, 'has nothing to do with Memory' (783). Now this is an opposition that Frye himself did a good deal to reinforce in the 1950s and 1960s. Carrying the militant banner of Blakean imagination and the Age of Sensibility into battle against later Romantic backsliders, Frye writes in 1956 that 'With the 1800 edition of *Lyrical Ballads*, secondary imagination and recollection in tranquillity took over English poetry and dominated it until the end of the nineteenth century' (*FI*, 137). Interestingly, however, the notebooks reveal him as much more ambivalent about Blake's assault on memory – to put it mildly: 'Blake was very sloppy about memory: straight reversion to the spectres of the past is one thing, but the practice memory he himself insists on is quite another. Granted that memory has to be transformed by the imagination, still the developing of a pattern out of the chaos of memory is essential ...' (NB7, 84).

When Frye refers to 'practice memory' here, he means something synonymous with what Samuel Butler called 'habit,' the subject of Frye's 1988 essay, 'Some Reflections on Life and Habit.' Here Frye opposes habit, or practice memory, or 'unconscious memory,' to conscious memory, in which I simply recall an event from the past. When I play a piece 'from memory' on the piano, I am not conscious of remembering every note, just as I am not conscious of remembering how to perform every act in a craft or an art at which I am skilled. Repetition or habit has referred these acts to unconscious memory, but that is only possible because of an inbuilt human potential that was already there: Frye calls practice memory 'a continuing of the evolutionary process we hooked into at the beginning of our lives,' and argues that it is the foundation of the education process (*MM*, 151). In Notebook 3 Frye says that 'Art is based on the creative repetition of practice, which is memory coming into being, or Being' (27). In his view this kind of memory, far from being in some kind of contradictory relationship with imagination, is the very ground from which imagination proceeds:

Blake's 'imagination has nothing to do with memory' is about the least helpful comment he ever made. I wish he had said, 'imagination begins in reversing the current of memory.' Memory progressively dematerializes images and rearranges them into a Narcissus-mirror of ourselves: imagination (as Blake meant it) goes in the opposite or presenting direction of *ut pictura poesis*. In memory the metaphorical context is formed by association; in imagination it is formed by an assigned context. If not narcist, memory simply follows the conventions of tradition: this is what bothered Blake. Yeats in *A Vision* was pursuing images back into the Great Memory. (NB27, 357)

The art of memory suggests an answer to what is a fundamental puzzle in Frye: the apparent split in someone who proselytizes for militant Blakean-Romantic imagination, but whose own work is informed by the very sense of order that we identify with classicism. If the classical vision in Frye is not a sense of order that he's imposing on literature so much as an exploration of his own memory-rooms, then the whole procedure becomes a variety of internal quest-romance, and at that point folds back into Romanticism.

It would be surprising if, after all, 'mechanical' memory, rather than 'creative' imagination, were to hold the key to understanding Frye, but then nothing is more pronounced in his work than a relentless imaging and spatializing of knowledge. This is, in fact, precisely what he suggests in the 1950s that criticism needs to turn its attention to: 'We begin to wonder,' he says in the Polemical Introduction, 'if we cannot see literature, not only as complicating itself in time, but as spread out in conceptual space from some kind of center that criticism could locate' (*AC*, 17). Frye is *the* architectonic thinker in modern criticism, and many of the earlier thinkers who matter most to him – Spengler, Jung, Vico – tend to be architectonic too.

To choose a prominent example from Frye's work, take the Third Essay in the *Anatomy*, the Theory of Myths. Here Frye classifies archetypal imagery into four categories; each category contains seven levels or 'worlds' of imagery (vegetable, animal, mineral, and so on); and each level of imagery has its own cycle or movement. Famously, Frye then goes on to explain archetypal narrative by thinking of all the stories ever told as parts of an enormous revolving mythic wheel. The wheel's upward movement is comic, its downward movement tragic, and it contains quadrants corresponding to spring (comedy), summer (romance), autumn (tragedy), and winter (satire). In what even Frye concedes is a 'formidable' piece of additional symmetry, each quadrant further contains six phases, the first three of which correspond to the last three in the previous quadrant. Compare Yates's recreation of just one of Bruno's revolving concentric memory-wheels: 'The three hundred and sixty degrees of the zodiacal circle are divided amongst the twelve signs of the zodiac, each of which is subdivided into three "faces" of ten degrees each. These latter are the "decans" each of which has an image associated with it' (213).

In Frye's work, these pictorial configurations are not contained in literature itself, but in Frye's memory of literature: they *are* his memory of literature, as Kermode hinted to me. To use the *Anatomy*'s own language, they come from the deductive, not the inductive, effort of criticism. If we read Frye's notebooks, we are constantly struck by his sense that he is discovering something; but it is often difficult to decide whether it is something about literature, or his own mind, or the mind of all humankind – partly, I think, because from quite early on these things all interpenetrate for Frye. From Notebook 8: 'Well, I'm sorry, but I've just discovered that, apart from the big circle, there are four little circles, each for each genre, as each genre can cover the whole range of drama from its own point of view' (249).

Perhaps if Frye had included diagrams in the *Anatomy*, the fact that the book is his own memory-palace, in addition to whatever else it is, would have been clearer. It certainly became clearer when Denham's *Northrop Frye and Critical Method* was published, with diagrams that bear an astonishing similarity to those of Renaissance memory-artists. My guess is that Frye did not include his own diagrams in the *Anatomy* because, with New Critical organic metaphors for poetry still in force, it would have further increased the likelihood of the claim, to which he was sensitive, that his method reduced criticism to mere 'pigeon-holing' (another mnemotechnic metaphor, by the way). On the question of diagrams, in the 1975 essay 'Expanding Eyes' Frye says:

The view of literature set out in *Anatomy of Criticism* has many points in common with a mandala vision, so much so that many people have drawn up mandalas based on the book and have sent them to me, asking if this was what I really had in mind. I generally reply, with complete truth as far as I am concerned, that they have shown much more ingenuity in constructing their models than I could achieve myself. (*SM*, 117)

This is slightly disingenuous, as is Frye's comment to a graduate student in 1963 that he had specific diagrams 'in mind' while writing the *Anatomy* (Tucker, 42). The notebooks reveal that Frye drew hundreds of *real* diagrams, much more 'ingenious' than those suggested by anyone, even Denham.

These diagrams (for an example, see page 48) are among the strongest direct evidence of a link between Frye's project and the art of memory. Sometimes he labels areas in the diagrams 'zones' – there cannot really be a 'zone' in literature, but mnemotechnics recognizes that there are 'zones' in memory. The word makes Frye's diagrams sound like what Bruno's diagrams are: two-dimensional keys to an imagined three-dimensional space. Like Frye in the *Anatomy*, Bruno uses categories like vegetable and animal; and like Bruno, Frye in his notebooks uses symbols from the zodiac, musical keys, and the points of the compass among many other devices for arranging literary themes and images across the eight great intellectual projects he called his 'ogdoad' or

Frye's diagram illustrating symbols associated with death and rebirth (NFF, 1991, box 36, file 11; courtesy of Victoria University Library). A typed version of the diagram is shown opposite.

'Great Doodle' (see Michael Dolzani's essay in this volume). For Frye, as for Aristotle, knowing seems inevitably to be a kind of seeing.

In one of his later notebooks, Frye reassesses the architectonic and schematic elements of the *Anatomy*. He is much less apologetic about it all now: the New Critics are long gone, and, as well as Frye, structuralism has helped to reinvigorate diagrammatic thinking in the humanities.[3] Frye now writes:

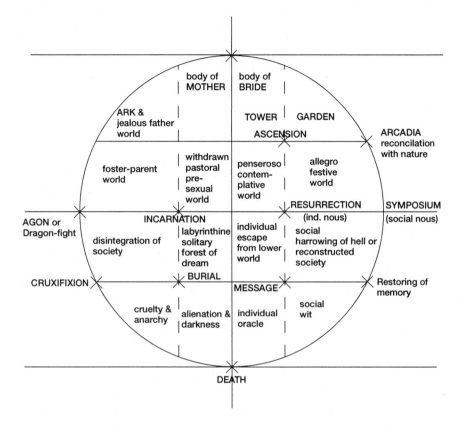

I'm beginning to feel that the schematic structure of the Anatomy is a key to a much larger principle. People don't have to remain doorkeepers in it forever, as in Psalm 23: they can go out to build palaces of their own. I suspect also that the key to philosophy is the exact opposite of what philosophers do now. It's the study of the great historical systems, each of them a palace and a museum, that's genuine philosophy. At a certain point they interpenetrate into a house of many mansions, a new Jerusalem of verbal possibilities, but that's a tremendous state of enlightenment. (NB44, 110)

He also remarks in this notebook that 'If there's no real difference between creation & criticism, I have as much right to build palaces of criticism as Milton had to write epic poems' (108). The use of the images of palaces and museums in these quotations is strictly mnemotechnical, as is the connection between these and epic. And Frye also says that he's reassessed the view he expressed at the beginning of the *Anatomy* that he attached no particular importance to the 'construct *qua* construct': 'I think I've got past that now, and that it's only by means of such dizzily complex constructs that one can ever get anything substantial out of criticism' (99).

What specific internal characteristics of Frye's theory are illuminated from the perspective of mnemotechnics? I noted before that the art of memory combined rules for places, *loci*, with rules for images, *imagines*. In Frye, it seems to me that the *loci* correspond to the four categories of imagery – divine, romantic, realistic, and demonic – that were mentioned earlier: these are the rooms in which Frye places his images. Importantly, Frye believed that these categories are not exclusive to literature; they are the way that the imagination creates a human world within nature. That is why he saw all epistemic shifts, notably Romanticism, as changes in 'the spatial projection of reality' (*StS*, 203).

As for the *imagines* of classical mnemotechnics, these correspond to the actual archetype in Frye's system, which he defines as 'A symbol, usually an image, which recurs often enough in literature to be recognizable as an element of one's literary experience as a whole' (*AC*, 365), and which he further classifies into seven different levels or 'worlds.' And what of the *imagines agentes*, those ideal memory images that inscribe themselves upon artificial memory through movement? These are the Frygian *mythoi*, the four archetypal narratives – comedy, tragedy, romance, and irony – seen as quadrantal movements of the giant mythic wheel.

But there is a deeper level of analogy between Frye's theory and mnemotechnics. The most important revision that Frye worked upon the New Criticism was his introduction of what, borrowing from Aristotle, he called a poem's *dianoia*: the meaning of the poem visualized as an image. We experience narrative in time, but when we have finished listening to a poem or novel or play, says Frye, we *see* what it means, in a simultaneous experience that is outside time. (This is yet another example of Frye's pictorializing habit, as indeed are all the versions in which *vision* is stressed throughout his work.) And in order to see what a poem means, in order metaphorically to view its archetypal organization, Frye says, *contra* New Criticism, that we need to 'stand back' from it, the way we stand back from a painting in a gallery. Here is a memorable example from the *Anatomy*: 'If we "stand back" from the beginning of the fifth act of *Hamlet*, we see a grave opening on the stage, the hero, his enemy, and the heroine descending into it, followed by a fatal struggle in the upper world' (*AC*, 140). This seems to me a perfect instance of an active memorial image. It is at once a statement about *Hamlet* from the perspective of archetypal criticism, *and* a description of how *Hamlet* is represented in the timeless rooms of Frye's critical memory – a congruence that *dianoia*, one of the *Anatomy*'s cardinal concepts, embodies.

Frye also talks about literature as a whole as expressing 'man's revelation to man' (*EI*, 105), a dream of lost and recovered identity that is most completely set out in epic, and in the Bible. This, it seems, is the sense in which, for Frye, literature is a path towards *humanity's* vast unconscious memory-palace. And it is also the sense in which that memory resembles medieval *Prudentia*: it reminds us that we want community and love, not alienation and war, even though we behave as if we don't. Frye's controversial insistence that this level of myth is something deeper than an ideology – something like the buried memory of all mankind – and hence transcends different social formations is where I think his theory of myth, his own method, his theory of unconscious or practice memory, and even his views on critical theory, all coincide with mnemotechnics.

This is hinted at at several points in the notebooks, as when he is thinking about Shelley in the 1960s:

The dead is the unalterable; whatever reshapes the past performs an act of resurrection ... Maybe I should have put this into the Shelley essay, where I more or less passed over the conception of a cave of myths, or encyclopaedic memory theatre. The point is ... that the world of the dead is also the world of the unborn. It's the cave-womb we emerge from, & knowledge in this world is an anamnesis of the cave of myths or the memory theatre. Note too that there is no *time* in the memory theatre: it's a spatialization of knowledge. (NB19, 344)

And much later: 'The memory selects, rejects, rearranges, condenses and displaces. In short, it *mythicizes* our history' (NB27, 211). Giordano Bruno also saw the study of myth in mnemonic terms, as well as having precisely Frye's sense that the meaning of a myth is not some hidden truth hinted at by the story, but is the story itself. As Yates notes:

Bruno introduces memory into his theory of mythology. He reverses the usual statement, that the ancients concealed arcana in the myths, when he says that, on the contrary, they declared and explained truths through the myths in order to make them more easily remembered. (291)

And if we look at Yates's recreation of Camillo's theatre, we see that it is really a gigantic arrangement of Greek and Roman mythologies.

The 'evolutionary' or inherited quality that Frye attaches to practice memory is also a quality of humanity recognized by Blake – 'Innate Ideas are in Every Man, Born with him' (459) – and, just as important, by Jung, in his idea of the collective unconscious, which he attaches directly to myth. Jung says that the collective unconscious 'is not to be thought of as a self-subsistent entity; it is no more than a potentiality handed down to us from primordial times in the specific form of mnemonic images or inherited in the anatomical structure of the brain.' He goes on to say that the archetypal images contained in the collective unconscious 'give form to countless typical experiences of our ancestors. They are, so to speak, the psychic residua of innumerable experiences of the same type' (80–1). Although Frye always resisted the Jungian reduction – he calls the collective unconscious 'an unnecessary hypothesis in literary criticism' (*AC*, 112) – it is impossible not to see a connection between these 'innumerable experiences of the same type' and what Frye calls 'concern': the fundamental needs and desires that all human beings share, that lie deeper than any social ideology, and that have no language in which to express themselves except the language of myth and literature, of imagination. If unconscious memory is also the collective unconscious, and hence the site of the empty forms that the artist fills to create new narratives, then Northrop Frye's memory theatre, like Camillo's, is a pathway to the Great Memory.

I have argued elsewhere that Frye saw criticism as the *dianoia* of literature as a whole – the only way of *seeing* what all of literature, as a single gigantic poem, is trying to show us ('Frye and Romanticism,' 71). The art of critical memory is what I now think he was teaching. Certainly some of the language Frye uses to describe the function of criticism – which became very much, in his hands, a 'spatialization of knowledge' – has a mnemotechnic quality. Sometimes this quality registers as a positive, sometimes as a negative. Frye wrote in many places that the highest form of criticism is the 'possession' of literature. This sounds like a metaphysics of presence, yet one thing Frye could mean is that one 'possesses' a book by placing an image associated with it in a memory-room – just as Mary Carruthers says medieval memory-artists believed that 'A work is not truly read until one has made it a part of oneself' (10). But Frye also talks, in a less optimistic register, about criticism as 'a monument to a failure of experience' (*CP*, 27). A monument is a memorial, and what Frye seems to be getting at in these strange passages is that a full imaginative communion between critic and artist, even perhaps when the identification is as close as his own with Blake, can never be recaptured in critical terminology. This is the price you pay once you accept that criticism is intimately tied up with memory, or perhaps even with the memory of memory, as Frye acknowledges in a diary entry on 23 January 1949: 'The vast organization of memory known as scholarship seems to me to be what the dreams we can remember are: wandering in the limbo of the past, just outside the gate we have as yet no golden bough to enter.'

In conclusion, I am far from saying that Frye's work is the only place in modern criticism where we can find mnemotechnical images and metaphors. Eliot's image of tradition as an 'ideal order,' which influenced Frye, is another obvious example, and all the varieties of modern formalism are bound to contain traces of it. However, Frye's work presents the most *complete* memory-theatre that modern literary scholarship has produced. And at a time when ideological developments, particularly in the late nineteenth century, loom so large in the accounts being given of the rise of English studies, the memory of Frye invites us to remember that something much older may still be lodged deep within our discipline – that mysterious, totalizing dream called the art of memory.

NOTES

1 See Salusinszky, *Criticism*, 104. I would like to thank Robert D. Denham and Michael Dolzani for allowing me to use their transcripts of Frye's notebooks and diaries. I would also like to thank the Northrop Frye Centre, Victoria University, in particular its former director Eva Kushner, for a fellowship that enabled me to research this essay.
2 The following discussion is indebted to Yates and Carruthers.
3 The most obvious structuralist analogue to Frye is Bachelard's *Poetics of Space*, published a year after *Anatomy* in 1958, but not well known among English-speaking critics for at least another decade. Bachelard writes: 'Topoanalysis ... would be the systematic psychological study of the sites of our intimate lives. In the theater of the past that is constituted by memory, the stage setting maintains the characters in their dominant roles. At times we think we know ourselves in time, when all we know is a sequence of fixations in the spaces of the being's stability – a being who does not want to melt away, and who, even in the past, when he sets out in search of things past, wants time to "suspend" its flight. In its countless alveoli space contains compressed time. That is what space is for' (8).

WORKS CITED

Bachelard, Gaston. *The Poetics of Space*. Translated by Maria Jolas. Boston: Beacon Press, 1969.

Blake, William. *Complete Writings*. Edited by Geoffrey Keynes. London: Oxford University Press, 1966.

Denham, Robert D. *Northrop Frye and Critical Method*. University Park: Pennsylvania State University Press, 1978.

Carruthers, Mary. *The Book of Memory*. Cambridge: Cambridge University Press, 1990.

Fletcher, Angus. 'Utopian History and the *Anatomy of Criticism*.' In *Northrop Frye in Modern Criticism*, edited by Murray Krieger. New York: Columbia University Press, 1966. 31–73.

Jung, C.G. *The Spirit in Man, Art, and Literature*. Translated by R.F.C. Hull. London: Routledge & Kegan Paul, 1966.

Salusinszky, Imre. *Criticism in Society*. London: Routledge, 1987.

– 'Frye and Romanticism.' In *Visionary Poetics: Essays on Northrop Frye's Criticism*. Edited by Robert D. Denham and Thomas Willard. New York: Peter Lang, 1991. 57–74.

Tucker, Mary Curtis. 'Towards a Theory of Shakespearean Comedy: A Study of the Contributions of Northrop Frye.' Ph.D. diss., Emory University, 1963.

Yates, Frances A. *The Art of Memory*. London: Routledge, 1966.

The Quest for the Creative Word: Writing in the Frye Notebooks

JONATHAN HART

The longer I've lived the more I realize that I belong in a certain context. The more completely I am that, I think the more I am acceptable to others. It's the law in literature, which I've often expressed, of Faulkner's devoting himself to a county with an unpronounceable name in Mississippi and getting the Nobel Prize in Sweden.

Northrop Frye in Conversation, 215–16

In an interpenetrating world every community would be the center of the world.

Ibid., 65

Northrop Frye, despite his gift for language and structure, could not find a place as a novelist. In his notebooks, however, Frye is given to the invention of possible worlds of putative novels. Occasionally, he writes a paragraph, a sketch, or a fragment of a novel, but we do not have a novel by Frye in a finished and published form. Even though he published some poetry and short fiction, and over twenty books of cultural, biblical, and literary criticism, Frye could not, or would not, complete a novel for a reading public. But his desire to be a novelist haunts some of his notebooks.

My essay is concerned with how Frye approaches a fiction without ever attaining it; what might be called the asymptote of fiction, or asymptotic creativity. The talk about a novel becomes more than 'notes towards': it is metonymic and represents an interpretative or ideological substitute for *mythos* or mythology itself. The only hope Frye has of overcoming this slide into the entire necessity of ideology, which he recognizes, is to mitigate it by rendering the ideological partial through re-creating the word, through the 'theoretical imagination.'[1] In this fictional space alone can fiction be redeemed as something that is theoretically in and of itself, even when it is part of a practical continuum of discourse and signs, where boundaries blur? If Frye's desire for the novel is a description without a place, an ideological argument in search of a mythology unmoved by time, then it calls into question the possibility of the 'in-and-of-itselfness' of fiction or literature and the autonomy of literary criticism or theory, the central idea in *Anatomy of Criticism* and, perhaps, in Frye's career.

Throughout the notebooks, Frye pursues the poet's vision of human life, without which all that is left is the ideological and instrumental (*AC*, 319). Frye is involved in a quest myth, like the myth of romance that he describes in *Anatomy*, as he looks for a proper form in which to create an order of words. In this perilous journey, like the hero of romance, Frye meets uncertainty and illusion, hoping to survive this internalized crucial struggle in the traces of fame, to be exalted after death. Without straining this metaphor of the journey through the notebooks in search of poetry or fiction, I am suggesting that for Frye, as for the romance poets he describes, the search for recognition, in oneself and in the world, involves the classical quest of *agon, pathos,* and *anagnorisis* (*AC*, 187). While Frye's notebooks refract this visionary pattern, they are not so linear, so that I offer the quest as one of the ways into Frye's poetics: that is, the no-man's land between poetry and theory, the various imaginations on the literary landscape. One of the anxieties for Frye was to succeed in declaring the independence of the theoretical imagination so well that he might not achieve recognition in the more ready and traditional forms of literary representation. To imagine the word successfully in literature and criticism seemed to be something that could consume this writer-as-hero in agony. What follows is a brief anatomy of that quest as recorded in the notebooks, personal papers, or diaries that combine theoretical frameworks and fictional longings. Whatever their relative merits the imaginings of both theory and fiction play off each other in fascinating ways. It is possible that Frye's notebooks, which are about becoming, become a hybrid genre, a charged and suggestive cross between literary theory and practice in 'autobiographical' terms. Here, then, is Frye's fable of identity.

The desire for recognition resides in the double vision of the local being universal, what might be called the Faulkner principle. Frye hoped that his own Canadianness would, paradoxically, appeal to the world, and he extends this hope to his craft of fiction. In *Locust Eaters*, the Kennedy–Megill novel that I have discussed elsewhere, Frye uses a contrast between Western Canada and English Canada, of alienation and the *civis* of the university, as a means of expressing his own experience and world (see Hart, *Northrop Frye*, 287–93; and 'The Road,' 231–2).[2] Frye, however, unlike Faulkner, or Margaret Laurence, was not able to create a full fictional world of the place in which he grew up: he does not hide his Canadianness in his criticism, diaries, or fiction, but except for *Locust Eaters* his fictional worlds do not develop a Canadian setting. It is Frye's expression of the desire to create fiction while abandoning it that is the central paradox of his spectral career as a novelist. As someone with a theoretical imagination, Frye struggled with the novelist's craft. More generally, Frye's talk about novels seems to become a substitute for the novels themselves. Frye cannot sustain a fictional equivalent of *Fearful Symmetry* or *Anatomy of Criticism*, but his fiction and notes suggest that this unfinished business reveals much about his imagination, and his road not taken. Fiction is Frye's blue guitar.

Locust Eaters, which I once thought might be identical to another novel Frye talked about in the mid-1930s, *Quiet Consummation*, and which I called the Kennedy–Megill fragment, is scattered Osiris-like through Notebooks 1 and 2 (see *Northrop Frye*, 287–93). In the first notebook there are notes for *Locust Eaters*, comments on characters, possible additions, reflections on the art of the novel, plans for another novel and for giving up *Locust Eaters*. The second notebook begins with sixteen pages of *Locust Eaters*, which Frye had begun during the 1940s, and ends with two pages of notes from 1962 towards a Bardo novel (discussed below). This partial draft of *Locust Eaters*, which is related to another fifteen-page typescript comprising the 'work,' is probably a later version of a first draft that has not survived. The method of composition and the state of the scattered fragments suggest that Frye's creation is incomplete, his attention to novels being partial, or, perhaps, his mode being more Menippean than he himself might have realized.

In the fifteen-page fragment of *Locust Eaters*, Frye centres on the Reverend Lyman Kennedy and Sarah Megill. The story is divided into four parts. The first part includes a good deal of satire in its physical descriptions, and in the introduction of Kennedy's family and the parishioners' response to his sermon; the second part represents Kennedy, a native of Western Canada, returning home from Eastern Canada to Bad Land and seeing the landscape of his youth with new clarity; the third part, like the first, shows life in Pilkey, a town in Eastern Canada; the fourth part moves back east to Champlain, where Kennedy trained and where Sarah Megill wanted John Goremont, her 'alleged grandson,' to study. This fragment ends after a discussion of conventional society and returns to Sarah Megill, the character who holds the four parts together thematically and structurally.

Whereas this fragment is coherent, the notes in Notebook 1 are much more discontinuous. The only comments I am interested in here are those on Canada, because Frye claimed, as in my first epigraph, that the more dedicated he was to his context, the more universal he would be. In his notes on Kennedy's daughter Vanya, he writes: 'The usual United Church minister's daughter who turns C.C.F. worker. I wonder if I have to mention the United Church & the C.C.F. There's really no reason why I shouldn't' (NB1, 16). (Frye often claimed that these two institutions kept him in Canada.) Some of Frye's notes for dialogue include speeches reflecting the politics of the period:

The security police in Canada have complete files on everyone in the country for whom freedom of speech is important, & could wipe out all freedom of speech quite easily in ten days. The only reason they don't is that a government supporting a laissez faire economy has no philosophy of government, & wouldn't know what to do with such an access of power if they had it. On the other hand, it wouldn't dare dissolve the security police because you never can tell. So our alleged liberties depend solely on the fact that a political party with a dogmatic philosophy of government hasn't yet come to power. But sooner or later one is bound to, & democracy is merely the interval of waiting for it. (NB1, 32)

Frye, as I have argued elsewhere, devoted many of his energies in fiction and criticism in the 1930s and early 1940s to unmasking fascism (see *Northrop Frye*, 3–4, 14–15, 276–9, and 'The Road,' 223–4). *Locust Eaters*, then, in its fragmentary notes and slight four-part draft, attempts to create a Canadian setting for a novel of ideas with international appeal.

The novel, for Frye, becomes the unofficial geography of his imagination, the private musings and representations in his notebooks, a counter-terrain to his public acts in lectures, interviews, and books. In this private fiction, as in his published short stories and poems, Frye seeks a voice and a place, looking for the physical and spiritual markers of his life in Canada, or his years as a student in England: indeed, he wrestles with the green and pleasant land of his mentor, William Blake, and its difference to the hostile environment of the Canadian prairies he experienced one summer as a student preacher (see Ayre, 100). *Locust*

Eaters contrasts the university town of Eastern Canada, an analogue for where Frye felt at home, with the alien landscape of the endless land under the big sky, where outsiders feel naked and watched.

Frye, who, like T.S. Eliot and Wallace Stevens, sought to escape personality, could not do so in his fiction. It is sometimes raw and bare and autobiographical, despite the wit, irony, and dialogue of ideas. Frye's attempts at fiction presented problems at the level of the local and personal, as well as of the practical and theoretical roles of fictionality itself; his struggle for and with the novel produces interesting fiction with significant problems, but not a novel. In some ways this lack of an actualized *telos* is more attractive, leading us to an anatomy of the desire of desire.

If literature is like the dark side of the moon that we know from inference, or a black hole we recognize indirectly through the detection of a gravitational pull, then the asymptotic nature of Frye's work as a novelist – much of which was unpublished, unseen, private, incomplete – does not mean that at one level Frye is not a novelist. His notebooks might be considered one large serial modernist novel, a prose song of the self, a cross between the mythical fragments of Blake's marginalia and unfinished epic, Eliot's *Waste Land* and its notes, and the metafiction of Borges. The notebooks perform other tasks, but they are a parallel and unofficial *mythos* to the public tale of Frye's criticism and theory.

Frye's notebooks are full of comments on stories he is writing and publishing, and on novels he never sees into print, or never writes at all. During the middle and late 1930s, while he is at Merton College, Oxford, and then upon his return to Canada, Frye wavers between confidence and doubt. In his letters to Helen Kemp he displays this contradiction and ambivalence: 'I shall never write a novel until I reach maturity, which will be whenever the summation of my past experiences takes on a significant unity' (*Correspondence*, 1:443), and 'I want to get a novel written and published. I've got the stuff of an unusually good writer in me' (*Correspondence*, 2:899). This double attitude can also be seen in Frye's realistic assessment of his art on the verge of his twenty-third birthday, and the Menippean tradition he traces for his sonnet-form novel, which seems to be *Quiet Consummation*.[3] The first claim about his novel Frye makes to Helen on 28 June 1935:

I rather think it will be either so bad I shan't do anything with it, such as showing it to my friends or re-reading it, or good enough to be accepted. Somehow I don't think I'll write an unreadable novel. I've got a fair idea of prose rhythm, a fairly decent literary education (for a novelist), a fairly good eye for caricature, and a fairly good idea of what comedy is about. Anyway, we'll see. Just another experiment. (*Correspondence*, 1:463–4)

The second claim, probably written a couple of years later at Oxford, sounds like the systematic genre-critic turning his analytical gaze back on his creative work:

The sonata-form novel will be my great anatomy, perhaps containing the whole Summa and Cassandra schemes. Its ancestry goes through Ulysses, Sartor Resartus, Tristram Shandy, Gulliver's Travels and A Tale of a Tub, The Anatomy of Melancholy, to Rabelais. Recalls from ancient history, fantastic romance & realist sketching, generalized character study, extracts from an unpublished book, will all be tucks, and the Protestant scheme recalls the anti-Catholic outlook of all the great anatomies, just as the sonata form recalls Sartor Resartus & the triple organization of Burton & Joyce, and the complete scheme of four parts of Gulliver's Travels and the musical schemes of Sterne. (NB4, 3)

Frye's doubting confidence contains enough truth to shed light on his fiction. His talk about writing, not so quiet a consummation, may have been a substitute for the novel itself, something that scholars will have to test as they search the Frye papers for a complete version of the sonata-novel. However, it is likely that *Anatomy of Criticism* will always remain Frye's great contribution to the genre of the anatomy.

Frye's inventory of invention for fictional worlds shows a young writer searching for stories. He is ironic with himself, aware of his predicament: 'A historical novel on the English 14th c. might be a possibility, when I find something out about the 14th c.' (NB4, 14). Many of the themes in his fiction are taken up in the notebooks as well. At Oxford, he writes a note about a ghost story that parodies fascist art: 'Ghost story – when supernatural event strikes Lew his first feeling is enormous sense of relief & exhilaration – he can now throw away his belief in tiresome scientific exactness. Say, this has possibilities. Devil tempts him, & he rides off on a broomstick [cackling?] joyously: this combines End of World & Fascist novel parodies. Second study in the end of the world. Better in Chap. V' (NB4, 15). Frye's published fiction certainly includes ghostly themes and parodies on fascism. In 1936, *Acta Victoriana* published Frye's story 'The Ghost,' which is a story about the moments after death, and in 1940 *Canadian Forum* brought out 'The Resurgent,' a satiric parable about fascist art. In paragraph 79 of Notebook 4, Frye associates abstention with fascism: 'Wine will be the ruin of France, is an actual temperancer's statement. The trouble is the Petain crowd agree.' In 'Affable Angel,' a story published in *Acta Victoriana* in 1940, Harry remarks, 'Not bad chaps, Nazis ... But could I get them to drink? Not them' (4). In the notebooks, Frye associated the Middle Ages with a life-affirming drinking of beer (NB4, 95). The imminent apocalypse of war in the late 1930s appears to have informed Frye's notebooks and fiction alike.

In 'Reflections in a Mirror,' a draft of which appears in Notebook 20, Frye sets out a fiction that involves parallels between the visible and invisible worlds:

I have been struggling for some time to think of a new fiction formula, and all my ideas tend to revolve around Rilke's idea of the poet's perceiving simultaneously the visible & the invisible world. In practice that means a new type of ghost or supernatural story, possibly approached by way of some science-fiction development. The idea is a vision of another life or another world so powerfully plausible as to make conventionally religious & anti-religious people shake in their shoes. (NB20, 1)

This visionary fiction parallels the visionary poetics of Frye's criticism, in which Frye was much taken with the visions of Blake, Yeats, and other writers.[4] Another instance of the parallelism and supplementarity is the relation between a note at Oxford and a story published a few years later. The note provides a sketch: 'Two men walk along the Thames embankment in a fog, talking of unpredictable feelings from the dismal: Dickens & Eliot: surrealism. Work up to expecting supernatural: radiant angel appears: won't do as too cheerful & normal' (NB4, 22). Over the centre of this paragraph is the word 'done.' The closest story to this description is 'Affable Angel.' Megill and Mrs Kennedy, from *Locust Eaters*, are scattered throughout Notebook 4, which is full of best-laid plans: the young Frye is teeming with ideas for novels. Whereas Frye's notations about fiction usually seem to have acted as substitutes for the fiction itself, they sometimes adumbrated or supplemented his published stories.

One of the most interesting interplays in Frye's writing is between the talk about writing a novel, and the actual fragments of novels in his diary. Near the beginning of his diary for 1949, he reveals the tension between life and art, miscellany and narrative: 'The thing is not to be alarmed at the miscellaneous character of one's life & stylize the diary accordingly, as I've tended to do. It should be a continuous imaginative draft, not itself a work of literature' ('Frye's Diary,' 1). Frye's diary, written over many years, is a substitute for other writing, including novels, and an example of the art of writing; it is like an autobiographical novel. The entry for 20 August 1942 gets to the nub of the tension in Frye's diary, and perhaps in all diaries, between the shaping of *mythos* and the flow of everyday life. Unable to see his own reflection in Pepys, Frye hypothesizes that the gulf of individualism and Romanticism separates them:

I've been reading in Pepys, to avoid work. I can't understand him at all. I mean, the notion that he tells us more about himself & gives us a more intimate glimpse of the age than anyone else doesn't strike me. I find him more elusive and baffling than anyone. He has a curious combination of apparent frankness and real reticence that masks him more than anything else could do. One could call it a 'typically English' trait, but there were no typical Englishmen then and Montaigne performs a miracle of disguise in a far subtler & bigger way. Pepys is not exactly conventional: he is socially disciplined. He tells us nothing about himself except what is generic. His gaze is directed out: he tells us where he has been & what he has done, but there is no reflexion, far less self-analysis. The most important problem of the Diary & of related works is whether this absence of reflexion is an accident, an individual design, or simply impossible to anyone before the beginning of Rousseauist modes of interior thought. ('Frye's Diary,' 16)

Language cannot escape its rhetorical surfaces even in the service of sincere self-revelation. For Frye, Pepys becomes a visionary who enables the reader to visualize clothes and cultural surfaces, a man who conceals as he confesses. Pepys tells of his life without being autobiographical:

Pepys knew perfectly well what he was doing: he wrote a book which he well knew to be an art-form. His motive in doing so is not obvious, because his genre, the diary, is not a branch of autobiography, as [John] Evelyn's is. He was a supreme observer, making himself a visionary, se faire voyant, as much as Blake or Rimbaud. And he knew perfectly how effective & oracular the random is: his camera keeps on clicking after he gets in bed with his wife because he knows better than to shut it off. A real artistic passion for observation in itself with no attempt at a creative follow-through is rare, but it exists. (NB16, 69)

Frye too deflected the world from his personality. In his diary of 1949, he says of the diary: 'I also hope it will be of some moral benefit, in passing a kind of value judgment, implicit or explicit, on whether I've wasted the day or not, whether my schedule is in shape, whether my unanswered letters are piling up, etc.' ('Frye's Diary,' 1). Is Frye, the diarist and critic, as abstract as he accuses Pepys of being? Frye continues his entry on the great diarist:

And there's a riddling, gnomic quality in the photograph absent from painting. When I try to visualize Pepys I visualize clothes & a cultured life-force. I have a much clearer vision of the man who annoyed Hotspur or Juliet's Nurse's husband. I feel that Pepys makes the dead eerie and transplanetary, not our kind of species at all. He does not observe character either: I can't visualize his wife or my Lord. Even music he talks about as though it were simply a part of retiring for physic. ('Frye's Diary,' 16–17)

This comment on Pepys's abstract chronicle of his times raises a similar question about Frye, whose diaries provide a commentary on books and criticism, together with sketches and observations towards his own writing of fiction. The paradox persists: the writer reveals the self to hide it.

In the diaries, Frye is both ironic and hopeful in expressing his various motivations for wanting to write and publish fiction. In jest and earnest he gives money, distraction, fame, talent, and genius as motives, and suggests schemes for detective, historical, domestic, religious, philosophical, historical, speculative, and satirical novels, and many other modes of fiction. On 21 July 1942, his diary discusses his book on Blake, and ironically offers fiction as a compensation should that critical work fall on deaf ears: 'If the public doesn't like it I shall write a novel which shall earn me a million tax-free dollars, exclusive of movie rights, & lose me my job. The Verlaine-Rimbaud story would make a swell novel, as I dare say two or three thousand people have thought before. It could be combined with the de Nerval one' ('Frye's Diary,' 8). Here Frye is following up on his earlier entry of 18 July, where he describes Marcus Adeney, a cellist who played in the Toronto symphony and edited a magazine. Frye says that Adeney's intellectual development was arrested in his teens, and such a conclusion leads him to the idea of writing a novel about such a person in a village: 'I'd like to do a novel on a small-town genius *in vacuo*, by the way, ending up with a de Nerval finish: subjective apocalypse, objective collapse. That's really the kind of thing I've been trying to dope out all along' (Frye's Diary, ' 7). Between these entries on this possible novel, Frye analyses detective and ghost stories, and obliquely suggests what kind of detective story he himself might write: 'I should think a story in symposium form, with a Marlow-narrator supplying clues and his auditors all guessing shrewdly & wrong, would have its points' (Frye's Diary, ' 10).

Not surprisingly Frye also planned an academic novel. It seems to have been separate from the 'Megill–Kennedy crowd' of *Locust Eaters*. As early as 1939, Frye had considered an academic element in one of his planned novels described in a notebook he calls a diary: 'Novel on two brothers: one a direct-action revolutionary, other a studious weakling who admires him & wastes his own time & talents in a futile effort to compete' (NB4, 31). In Notebook 20, after considering a novel set in 'Bardo' (the state between death and rebirth in Tibetan Buddhism), which is one of many novels in his inventory lists, Frye says: 'Well, anyway, that's one idea. Another, and a much more immediate one, is my university novel. The theme of that is simple enough: I have the theme, but I need a matching (or rather a containing) plot' (NB20, 6). From the plan for a speculative fiction on the relation between dream and waking, the spiritual and material, Frye shifts the action to a liberal arts college, where the centre of the novel is a dispute over curriculum reform and, therefore, more immediate to Frye's professional life. He says he will have to read Mary McCarthy, James Reid Parker, and others who have produced academic novels. For Frye, the situation at the college is malignant: university presidents in Canada are not totalitarian, but are put in 'dictatorial situations.' The dramatic tension is to come from the struggle between the president and a professor of English: 'I think of the focus of the book as a vigorous agon between two highly articulate people. The relation between them is one of enmity but not one of hatred' (NB20, 9). Of the two antagonists he would create, Frye observes that 'they fight with complete detachment' (NB20, 9), just as Frye himself keeps some ironic distance from the fictional dreams of his fictions. In his detached mood he is willing to speculate on the relation between his two sides: fiction and criticism. The academic novel reminds him of his general views on that relation as well as bringing back the idea of the Bardo novel:

Every once in a while I get a fit of euphoria, probably induced by gas in the stomach, in which I feel that I'm capable of writing good fiction. The old superstition that fiction is creative & criticism second-rate & second-hand talking about creation dies hard, although I've lived to see most criticism, including mine, become more creative than most fiction. Finishing the A of C left me willing to speculate about Bardo again. (NB20, 10)

At various times over his career, Frye tries to describe the Bardo novel he wants to write (see Hart, *Northrop Frye*, 269–74). This is a type of ghost story, which Frye thinks of as a form related to the afterlife, a literary convention for religions. This observation leads Frye to wonder whether there are parallel ways of conceiving of reality; a new shape, which represents unconscious meaning, might be found in the romance and anatomy traditions. As in his criticism, Frye is interested in the relation between religion and literary convention and between the subjective and objective. Frye, like Blake, explores the visionary, where poetry engages the supernatural (see *FS*, 127). It is not an accident that Frye, for the lectures that became the basis for his posthumous book, *The Double Vision*, returned to a poem in Blake's letter to Thomas Butts on 22 November 1802:

> For double the vision my Eyes do see,
> And a double vision is always with me.
> With my inward Eye 'tis an old Man grey;
> With my outward, a Thistle across my way. (817)

The Bardo story in particular, and the ghost story in general, appeal to this 'two-eyedness' or parallelism between the physical and spiritual worlds.

This double vision is a humanizing of the world, a recognition that the senses are not sufficient, that a subject recognizes itself as part of what it perceives. Poet and critic recreate the word in different ways, the one with possible worlds including the supernatural, the other in giving human understanding to the superhuman. This represents the doubleness and tension in the spiritual Frye. He recognizes the otherworldly as something he wants to suppose in his fiction, but the critic in him reminds himself that such suppositions are not actual knowledge of the afterlife or superhuman, but literary conventions. Blake holds out the challenge of seeing at once the thistle and the old man: Frye's dilemma is how to represent the inward and outward vision, not just within his fiction, but between his critical and fictional worlds. Perhaps Frye's longing for fiction in his notebooks and diaries is a feeling that criticism is not enough. Although he declared the creativity and independence of criticism from literature, Frye seems to have felt that writing fiction would give him something that criticism, as important as it was, could not. The resurrection of the soul, the poetic spirit, and the critical understanding, are distinct but related. The identity with God and nature through writing becomes one of Frye's primary goals. Recognition or epiphany through reading the signs, and purifying them through writing, is another way of stating the embodiment of this aim. This is why I have called Frye a paradoxical visionary, whose first and last books, *Fearful Symmetry* (1947) and *The Double Vision* (1991), are on vision (see Hart, *Northrop Frye*, 264). The wholeness and atonement of imagination in the separate but related realms of religion and literature are Frye's concern.[5] Frye had declared the independence of criticism from literature, but then wanted it to be creative in the same way as stories, poems, and plays – through metaphor. *Anatomy* does have a metaphorical and fictional structure, and its examples are often examples or metaphorical shards from other stories; but at another level it is a theoretical structure. The theoretical imagination is imaginative, and sometimes in similar ways to the poetic imagination, but they are not identical.

The critic and the writer coexist sometimes uneasily in Frye's notebooks. In planning fiction Frye is often theoretical; in his theory he often uses story and metaphor. His thematics overlap and oppose each other. In Notebook 20, Frye speculates that the formal principles of art are found within us, so that a heightening of the senses through light and darkness, or a mental disturbance through mescalin, might allow a person to 'see the real formal principles: the apocalyptic world of metaphor, with its jewelled trees & the like, & its demonic opposite' (NB20, 15). In speaking about a possible story involving 'the luminously realistic,' Frye turns the possibility into a negation of his dreams of writing fiction: 'I've already said that I've never written fiction because [Aldous] Huxley's novels are there to remind me how bad it would be' (NB20, 18). After saying that he will not write fiction, Frye returns to a desire to write. And one type of writing that fascinates Frye is ghostly or occult fiction, something that treats the inside and outside: 'The outward or extroverted energy is for dealing with the world as given or created – anyway, as it is. An inward-turned energy explores the powers that create it: that's always the first principle of all occultism' (NB20, 20). Huxley's luminous realism has made Frye think about a detective story, but Huxley's example also suggests Tolkein and Le Fanu. Like Robertson Davies, Frye is fascinated with the occult and the whole atmosphere of 'spirit' fiction:

I've been reading Tolkien, who has certainly come very close to the kind of thing I'd like to do. The magic ring, the talisman on which the story turns, is an evil thing: when you put it on you become invisible to the ordinary world (which in this book includes dwarfs and elves), but visible to evil spirits. Hence you gain great power over the ordinary world at the price of being enslaved by evil. In Le Fanu's Green Tea story green tea (cf. Huxley's mescalin) breaks down the barrier between ordinary & dark worlds & a hideous monkey appears as a hallucination to a respectable bachelor clergyman. The story is derived from Swedenborg, who says that evil spirits live in a man but can't see him because he can't see them. If he could, he'd be in for it, because they'd try to destroy him. (NB20, 21)

Frye's notebooks reveal the tension between his longing to write fiction, and the critical self-restraint that delays or arrests such a project. In 1962, Frye was still pursuing the idea of a Bardo novel, but something prevented him from making fiction a part of his published record, or an equal half of his metier: 'I don't want supernatural materialism either. The book's ideology would be a Bardo projection of my own: perhaps the deadee would not regret having developed my kind of outlook and would go back to get it. It wouldn't be quite as bald as that in presentation, but it would be in essential theory. God damn it. This kind of mooning isn't fiction-writing' (NB2, 16). In a similar vein, but reversing the structure from self-praise then self-criticism to detraction then compliment, he refers to his own 'fictional reveries' as prophetic, and as sometimes showing up in the works of professional writers. Frye then calls his Bardo novel a koan to think about and exercise the mind, and in an ambiguous justification says that he should let someone else write such a novel, someone who needs bread to eat more than he does (NB2, 17–18). The Bardo novel, then, represents a complex of ideas for Frye, and is another example of ambivalence and contradiction. This kind of fiction has a crisis that most often represents 'a threshold scene, a plunge into another order of being' and includes a recognition that is a return (NB2, 19). The boundary between life and death, from ghosts through apocalypse to resurrection and redemption, fascinated Frye so that much of his fiction, as well as his criticism on the Bible and on romance and comedy, focused on this theme. Human and divine comedy, especially in the structural sense, from the U-shaped narrative of the Scripture to Prospero's magical resolution and restoration, can be found both in the fictions and in the metafictions of the notebooks.

Even though these notes over the years contain various webs of fictions, of the road not taken, Frye is sometimes hard on himself as a novelist or aspiring writer. Sometimes he criticizes his style: 'The idiom of what I have written seems to be wrong: I don't seem to be fundamentally interested in writing the way novelists write, collecting the sort of data they collect, or throwing myself into the novelist's attitude with any conviction. What I write, with all its wit, is still pedantic' (NB1, 60). Frye thinks that he avoids the themes of novelists, the externals of the world like business and war, and 'that the novel is decidedly not my main interest, & so is hard to integrate to the rest of my activities' (NB1, 60). Here is a young scholar who will become one of the greatest critics writing in English, someone who has written some interesting fiction, dreaming of writing great novels and stories but also being brutally honest with himself. Recognizing his penchant for satire, Frye wonders whether he should write 'intellectual slapstick' rather than novels (NB1, 60). Of one of his largest novel-fragments, Frye declares: 'I feel that the Locust Eaters, though clever, is mediocre, fits a too-well-established pattern, & would embarrass my friends. It's crotch-bound: it hasn't the Frye swing & confident brilliance, & represents the sort of careful synthetic wit I should have been producing at twenty & couldn't. As a novelist I suffer from abnormally arrested development' (NB1, 60). He sees in his many plans for a novel the usurpation in fiction of what was planned for non-fiction: 'I think that, as I'm not essentially a novelist, I should disabuse myself of the dream of huge complex masterpieces, especially as my dream of eight has gone back to an original essay ambition which growing familiarity with the novel usurped' (NB1, 63). This critique leads Frye to say that he will keep *Locust Eaters* short, but does not make him abandon it. About twenty years later, Frye is still expressing his dream of being a novelist. Meanwhile, during the 1940s and 1950s, Frye spins out inventories of ideas for novels. Here is a metafictional description whose style and ideas might find themselves turned into a novel of ideas, like Thomas Mann's *Magic Mountain*:

When I think of myself as a fiction-writer, I feel that I could produce dialogue, characterization, & wit enough to pass muster in a good detective story, if I could write a good detective story, which I couldn't. That's why I feel the need of a containing formula, not a tight one; something that has run through Lucian & Rabelais, to give me something an amateur could work on in odd moments. One idea I had a long time ago was a variant of the Jesus novel. Archeologists dig up a fifth gospel, which sheds a quite different light on the rise of Xy (more Gnostic, I should think): authenticity unquestionable. The churches can't absorb it, so their struggles are interesting experiences in doubletalk. If I could invent a Gospel that sounded authentic it'd be terrific – a Grand Inquisitor theme.

I think also of a time machine that reconstructs the past but doesn't allow the viewers to be seen or take part in past ages. Such things are used like TV sets (except that they have to occupy the same Newtonian space as what they represent). They supersede history & do a lot of things – no good for the future.

Reconstructing texts by inspecting authors, etc. (NB20, 25)

Ideas, scholarship, and criticism were something Canadians excelled in during the first half of this century, but to be an artist was a more difficult thing. A novel of ideas might be possible for Frye, but he had an international scholarly audience for his criticism, through universities, academic publishing, and conferences of learned societies. In Canada, painters, especially the Group of Seven, were making claims to an international art based on new views of the Canadian landscape. In Frye's generation it appears to have been difficult for Canadian writers to achieve an international audience, and it was not until the 1960s and 1970s that some writers could use the Canadianness of their landscape, and their experience, to attract large international audiences. Morley Callaghan's shifting settings between Canada and the United States in his fiction were, for the most part, a thing of the past. Frye obviously struggled to find various forms in which to express his desires and understandings, and his fiction is a little-known but important part of his *oeuvre*. His notebooks represent his *agon* for expression: the attempt to hammer out an identity for 'Northrop Frye.' In this venture into confession and into observation of the self and the world – where desires, plans, and records mingle, and where Montaigne, Pepys, Rousseau ventured before – Frye leaves us with a question, the same one he asks of Pepys: whether he conceals as much as he reveals. Despite the irony and the wit, does he deflect with analysis, plans, and schemes that seldom dig deep into the labyrinths of the self, or is that the Frye there is – a verbal prism that blinds us with its sound?

The desire to write fiction persists in a Frye who is contradictory and ambivalent. He dreams, he calls himself on his dreams. The drama in the notebooks, both in the fiction and in the comments on fiction, is about whether Frye will attain his goal and whether the writing about fiction will take on the dramatic power of fiction itself, and join Frye's published criticism as a displacement or metonymy for the fiction itself. In such a supposition the supposed failure to produce a novel would become the success of the notebook-diary as a Menippean form of fiction-autobiography. The reinvention of a mode would be an appropriate form of success for the great critic of genre. He would cross some

borders as he had wanted to and would, like Coleridge, be a spirit or
'genius' (to assume one of Frye's favourite words) of the fragmentary,
unfinished, but brilliant talk overheard.

NOTES

1 This is a phrase I use in my book on Frye, and as its subtitle. In chapter 7 I discuss the relation between ideology and mythology. For other discussions of
ideology in Frye, see *NFC*, and Salusinszky in Lee and Denham, eds.
2 I wish to thank Robert Denham for his kind help over the years, especially in
providing me with copies of his transcriptions of Frye's unpublished fiction
and his comments on fiction in the diaries and notebooks. In a letter to me
(23 February 1996), Denham clarifies that the novel in Frye's notebooks that
we had been calling the Kennedy–Megill fragment or novel is *Locust Eaters*.
3 I will avoid a discussion of this novel, the problems of which I have discussed
elsewhere. See *Northrop Frye*, 267, 294, and 'The Road,' 231.
4 On Frye's visionary criticism, see Hart, *Northrop Frye*, chapter 8.
5 As I have said elsewhere, including in my writing on Frye, religion in literary
and cultural studies is often occluded and suppressed but represents a return
of the repressed. For recent discussions on Frye, religion, and culture, see the
essays by A.C. Hamilton, Thomas Willard, Hayden White, Craig Stewart
Walker, Margaret Burgess, Imre Salusinszky, Deanne Bogdan, and Michael
Dolzani in Lee and Denham, eds.

WORKS CITED

Ayre, John. *Northrop Frye: A Biography*. Toronto: Random House, 1989.
Blake, William. *Complete Writings*. Edited by Geoffrey Keynes. London: Oxford
University Press, 1966.
Frye, Northrop. 'Affable Angel.' *Acta Victoriana* 64 (January 1940): 2–4.
– 'The Ghost.' *Acta Victoriana* 60 (April 1936): 14–16.
– 'Northrop Frye's 1942 Diary.' *Northrop Frye Newsletter* 7 (Fall 1996): 1–34.
– 'The Resurgent.' *Canadian Forum* 19 (February 1940): 357–9.
Frye, Northrop, and Helen Kemp. *The Correspondence of Northrop Frye and Helen
Kemp, 1932–1939*. Edited by Robert D. Denham. 2 vols. Toronto: University of
Toronto Press, 1996.
Hart, Jonathan. *Northrop Frye: The Theoretical Imagination*. London: Routledge,
1994.

– 'The Road Not Taken: The Fictions of Northrop Frye.' *British Journal of Canadian Studies* 9 (1994): 216–37.
Lee, Alvin, and Robert D. Denham, eds. *The Legacy of Northrop Frye*. Toronto: University of Toronto Press, 1994.

The Treason of the Clerks:
Frye, Ideology, and the Authority
of Imaginative Culture

JOSEPH ADAMSON

But man lives in two worlds, the world of nature and the world of art that he is trying to build out of nature. The world of art, of human culture and civilization, is a creative process informed by a vision. The focus of this vision is indicated by the polarizing in romance between the world we want and the world we don't want. The process goes on in the actual world, but the vision which informs it is clear of that world, and must be kept unspotted from it. If it is not, ritual is degraded into compulsive magic and the creative energy of the poet into the anxieties of the kind of social concern that has been called, very accurately, the treason of the clerks.

Northrop Frye, *The Secular Scripture*, 58–9

Frye speaks at the beginning of *The Great Code* of his creative repetitions, of the way he keeps coming back to an old insight and renewing it in a more fully developed context. The epigraph to this essay, taken from *The Secular Scripture*, is in fact a reworking of a statement Frye made in *Anatomy of Criticism* twenty years before:

Just as no argument in favor of a religious or political doctrine is of any value unless it is an intellectually honest argument, and so guarantees the autonomy of logic, so no religious or political myth is either valuable or valid unless it assumes

I am grateful to Robert Denham, Jeffery Donaldson, Michael Happy, Alvin Lee, Imre Salusinszky, and Jean Wilson for taking the time to read and comment on this essay. Their help and encouragement have been invaluable. I would like to thank the anonymous readers who reported to the press for their very helpful comments and observations.

the autonomy of culture, which may be provisionally defined as the total body of imaginative hypothesis in a society and its tradition. To defend the autonomy of culture in this sense seems to me the social task of the 'intellectual' in the modern world: if so, to defend its subordination to a total synthesis of any kind, religious or political, would be the authentic form of the *trahison des clercs*. (*AC*, 127)

The reference in both passages is to Julien Benda's *La Trahison des clercs*, a book published in 1928 in the midst of the intensely political and nationalistic furor of intellectual life between the wars in Europe. Benda denounced what he saw as the betrayal of 'disinterested intellectual activity' by the turning of thinkers and writers to the 'perfecting of political passions': 'Every one knows that innumerable critics to-day consider that a book is only good insofar as it serves the party which is dear to them, or as it manifests "the genius of the nation," or as it illustrates a political doctrine in harmony with their own political system, or for other reasons of the like purity' (75). Thus a 'realist attitude' (58) is imposed on aesthetic judgments, along with the 'preaching of particularism,' the insistence on considering 'everything only as it exists in time, that is as it constitutes a succession of particular states, a "becoming," a "history," and never as it presents a state of permanence beyond time under this succession of distinct cases' (101). Any reaching after the trans-historical, according to such a view, is 'a form of the child's taste for ghosts, and should be merely smiled at' (101). What makes a work valuable is 'whether it expresses "the present" aspirations of "the contemporary soul"' (102).

Frye's allusion to Benda's polemical work – not just in the two passages quoted above but also elsewhere – points to what is perhaps the Canadian critic's single most important contribution to the history of thought: his highly sophisticated and complex defence of the *autonomy of literary and artistic culture*, his insistence on the priority of a fully developed imaginative response to literary works and on the central role of the verbal imagination in human culture in general. This is a particularly valuable point of view today when so many of our critical approaches to literature are driven, as they were in Benda's time, by ideological and political beliefs and agendas. From deconstruction, through New Historicism, to cultural and race and gender studies, the last two decades have been dominated by a criticism that assumes an overtly *interested* use of language.

There are good reasons for regarding this recent shift of focus as the consequence of a dramatic failure of nerve on the part of literary studies, an anxious and largely unconscious response to a threat levelled from another quarter. The policies of universities are increasingly commanded by a normative scientific and technological ideology that disregards and undervalues the role of imaginative culture in society. The serious study of the cultural realm is implicitly disparaged and condemned as anti-objective and anti-realistic; at best it is seen as a waste of time and money, at worst as one more obstacle to the unfettered hegemony of purposeful knowledge.[1] In a rather perverse way, this tendency to deny the significance of art and culture has now come to invade literary studies. Deconstruction, New Historicism, and cultural criticism have made rigorous scrutiny, critique, and de-mythologization – intellectual values associated with a more scientific attitude to the world – the order of the day, while critics and scholars primarily interested in issues of gender, race, and class tend to treat literature and culture largely in terms of immediate social goals. In the very field of study, then, in which one might expect a defence and affirmation of the imaginative dimension of human experience, reigns instead an attitude of profound *skepsis* with regard to the inherent value of culture as an area of creativity free of direct ideological and political investments. This attitude regards so-called 'naive' – that is, non-ideologically oriented – approaches to the understanding of literature as outmoded and obsolete. The words 'imagination' and 'creativity' are now stigmatized terms, and references to them are viewed as hopelessly naive and retrograde – 'a child's taste for ghosts,' as Benda says.

Given the pervasiveness of such an attitude, it is little wonder that Frye's work has been simply bypassed, hardly contested even – for the most part simply stepped around and left behind on the way to something else. Once an object of great interest and controversy, his work has receded into a perceived irrelevance. Its incongruity with the dominant critical concerns of today is best captured in the tone of authority that he characteristically adopts. It is one that suggests a clarity and objectivity dramatically at odds with the tortuous self-questioning of the contemporary critical field, and thus it seems presumptuous and out of place. Many simply find it difficult to accept such objectivity and authority as something that can belong any longer to the field of criticism. They are equally reluctant to accept the human imagination either as a mental activity that can approach the authority of the world of science, or as an area of interest that can command the kind of attention owed to imperative questions of social justice.

This is where Frye's work may be of the utmost significance. Indeed, his most important tenet, without which the rest loses its force, is that the imaginative dimension of a culture has a decisive *authority* that separates it from its ideological and historical background. The substance of a culture is made up of a body of hypothetical statements about the world, and this corpus is the centre of a society's *tertium quid*, 'some cultural element in the middle,' as he puts it in a fascinating essay on Harold Innis, subtitled 'The Strategy of Culture,' that manages to escape 'from the competing pressure groups by having something of its own to communicate that neutralizes the conflicts of interest' (*EAC*, 160). In *Words with Power*, Frye makes a closely related distinction between primary and secondary concerns, a distinction which involves the differing uses of a culture's mythology. Fiction and poetry, in Frye's view, address human anxieties and desires, but they do so in the mode of *as if*, and in a language and imagery of *primary concerns*, of universal areas of essential human interest and urgency. 'Universal' here refers quite simply to the fact that no human society is conceivable that could exist without such fundamental desires and fears. These concerns – food and shelter, love, property, freedom of movement – are the raw material of myth and literature. Freedom of movement, however, as Frye emphasizes, 'is not simply the freedom to take a plane to Vancouver; it must include freedom of thought and criticism. Similarly, property should extend to scientific discovery and the production of poetry and music; sex should be a matter of love and companionship and not a frenetic rutting in rubber; food and drink should become a focus of the sharing of goods within a community' (*DV*, 8). It is the close relationship of the imagination to these concerns that makes literature more than a game and endows it with its great seriousness and substance.

Ideology, on the other hand, has to do with *secondary concerns* or identifiable matters of belief that a society or a group tries to enforce. In *The Critical Path* Frye speaks of a society's myth of concern, a protected and restricted area of belief. An imaginative myth, in other words, becomes an ideology when it takes the form of a social mythology whose universality is asserted and imposed. In this, ideological critics are right to be sceptical of claims of universality, for here 'universality' is the ruse of a structure of authority with a vested interest in maintaining the status quo. Ideology, Frye says, 'conveys something of this kind: "Your social order is not always the way you would have it, but it is the best you can hope for at present, as well as the one the gods have decreed for you. Obey and work"' (*WP*, 24). Frye would concur whole-heartedly with Roland Barthes that the preferred alibi of ideology is nature. Its strategy is to treat a purely human creation – for instance, a particular socio-economic system – as something natural and therefore unchangeable. The ideology of a social establishment thus acts like the remote sky-god Urizen in Blake's vision of history: Urizen, as Frye conceives of this figure, is 'the human belief in the objectivity of nature' and in his cruelty he 'stands for the barring of nature against the desires and hopes of man' (FS, 210, 209). This appeal to a natural order is no less the case when, as in the current neo-conservative resurgence of capitalist ideology, a special premium is placed on the idea of economically driven change and technological innovation. The appeal is just as clearly to the necessity of an unalterable and inevitable order of things. Today's ideology of 'change' perfectly illustrates the divorce of secondary concerns from primary ones.

There is, of course, no such thing as a pure myth, unadulterated by ideology, and in 'an age dominated by clashing ideologies, there is a good deal of suspicion of myth as the inspiration of bad ideology' (WP, 25). Frye reverses this customary conception of the subordination of mythology to ideology. Ideology, he claims, is inspired by myth, and, as he writes in his notebooks, '[t]he function of literature is to recreate the myth behind the ideology' (NB44, 4). The exception to the rule are what he calls '[s]econdary myths ... spawned from an anxious ideology that wants to eliminate the other half of itself. When Frank Kermode gives anti-Semitism as an example of a myth, he is (a) expressing a very common prejudice against all myth (b) defining the kind of myth that's spawned by a hysterically one-sided ideology' (NB44, 128). In another notebook entry he ruminates:

After thirty years, I'm back to page one of the Anatomy. My opposition to socio-logical criticism is based on the principle that mythology is prior to ideology, the set of assumptions being always derived from a prior story. The story says nothing, and you say nothing: you listen to the story. Criticism often assumes that the ideology goes all the way: that there's no point at which the literary work stops saying things & keeping open the possibility of answer. If it's obviously moving from statement to myth, well, that's because of certain social pressures the writer had to conceal as well as reveal his meaning, had to be oblique instead of direct. Nonsense: obliquity is fundamental: it's the core (psychologically, anyway) of revelation. (NB27, 394)

Ideology relies on myth – on story – and 'the mythology, good or bad, creates the ideology, good or bad' (WP, 25). 'An ideology,' in other words, 'starts by providing its own version of whatever in its traditional mythology it considers relevant, and uses this version to form and enforce a social contract. An ideology is thus an applied mythology, and its adaptations of myths are the ones that, when we are inside an ideological structure, we must believe, or say we believe' (23).

The passages just quoted are from *Words with Power* and from two notebooks (27 and 44) that served as a drawing-board for the latter. They are an indication that in the closing decade of his life Frye felt a particular need to respond to the prevalent ideological view of culture with his own view of its role in society. In his introduction to *Myth and Metaphor*, a collection of essays from the latter part of Frye's career, Robert Denham observes that 'ideology is very much on his mind, the word itself appearing in all but one of the theoretical essays of the first two sections' (xvi). In *Words with Power* the emphasis is even more marked. 'The very structure' of the book, as Eleanor Cook points out, 'is meant to speak to contemporary theory' (16). One of the specific goals in the book seems to have been to defend the imaginative world of words against many of the assumptions of current critical practice, assumptions about cultural identity, for one thing, which are often disturbingly narrow in scope. Thus he remarks in a notebook entry: 'I know that when I suggested the possibility of a human primary concern that overrides all conceivable ideologies I'm flying in the face of Roland Barthes and the rest of the Holy Family. It's high time that sacred cow was turned out to pasture. By the sacred cow I mean the omnipresence of ideology, & the impossibility of ever getting past it' (NB27, 276). Frye ends *Words with Power* by evoking the Book of Job and the figure of Elihu, 'bumptious, confident, proud of his close relations to the contemporary, sure of his ability to defend God and condemn Job' (313). Such a figure brings to mind today's ideologue, caught up in the noisiness of the current period of criticism – Frye compares it to the 'stage of Eliot's "word in the desert"' – in which we 'hear all the rhetoric of ideologues, expurgating, revising, setting straight, rationalizing, proclaiming the time of renovation' (313). He then concludes by envisioning that moment when – he is alluding to the book of Job and the voice of God in the whirlwind – 'the terrifying and welcome voice may begin, annihilating everything we thought we knew, and restoring everything we have never lost' (313).[2]

Frye's interest in ideology may be more pronounced at the end of his career, reflecting the state of criticism in the 1980s, but already in *Anatomy* Frye insisted upon separating the concerns of literary criticism from ideological ones, though the concept of ideology often went by other names. It is false to assume that there has been some momentous change in the world of literary studies, a decisive opening of our eyes that has expelled us all from the garden of innocent readings forever. For anyone who bothers to read the Polemical Introduction to the *Anatomy* would be struck, I think – to take the kind of long view that was characteristic of Frye – by how little things have changed, by how naive we still are. 'The use of criticism,' he observes in a notebook entry in the mid-1980s, 'to denigrate criticism, and eventually literature itself: the feeling that if we root criticism deeply enough in phenomenology or what not we can turn literature into a document of something else. I said that 30 years ago, & it's only increased since' (NB27, 423). As Imre Salusinszky has observed, *Anatomy* emerged 'out of Frye's sense that such ideological approaches, such surrenderings of criticism to secondary concern, such "definite positions" as he calls them, had reached a dead end' (81). Cultural criticism, however, as Salusinszky goes on to point out, 'takes ideological criticism to a point that Frye could not have imagined: it folds not only literature and other forms of representation, but all previous attempts to study these representations, back into secondary concern' (81). Frye's cogent argument in 1957 against the 'treatment of criticism as the application of a social attitude' (*AC*, 22) – that is, as an essentially ideological mode of criticism – has only gained in relevance. The same is true of his statement that 'Every deliberately constructed hierarchy of values in literature ... is based on a concealed social, moral, or intellectual analogy' (23). These days, indeed, we are encouraged to confess our analogies, and to dispute those of others, openly and as often as possible. Never has the *positioning* of criticism – a metaphor, as Salusinszky notes, 'that Frye so heartily disliked' – been so in vogue.

One need not look hard today to illustrate amply Frye's observation that '[r]hetorical value-judgments are closely related to social values' (21), or his statement that 'there are critics who enjoy making religious, anti-religious, or political campaigns with toy soldiers labelled "Milton" or "Shelley" more than they enjoy studying poetry' (24). Forty years ago, Frye saw comparative value judgments as falling into two main camps – biographical criticism and tropical criticism – both of which he defined as 'essentially rhetorical forms of criticism, as one deals with the rhetoric of persuasive speech and the other with the rhetoric of verbal ornament, but each distrusts the other's kind of rhetoric' (21). These forms of criticism are still with us in the form of New Historicism, cultural studies, and deconstruction. Frye envisioned in their place a genuine dialectic in relation to which biographical and tropical criticism are a 'pseudo-dialectics, or false rhetoric' (25). As he saw it, the biographical critic, in order to form a genuine field of knowledge, must become the historical critic, whose attitude to his field is that there is nothing in it that 'he is not prepared to read with interest' (24). This sounds very much like one of the essential principles behind New Historicism. By the same token, tropical criticism – New Criticism then, deconstruction and post-structuralism now – must become ethical criticism, which, unlike the ideological approaches of today, '[interprets] ethics not as a rhetorical comparison of social facts to predetermined values, but as the consciousness of the presence of society' (24). Ethical criticism involves 'the sense of the real presence of culture in the community' (24), in which art is understood as 'a communication from the past to the present.' It 'is based on the conception of the total and simultaneous possession of past culture' (24).

This conception corresponds strikingly to some of the things that the psychoanalyst Donald Winnicott has to say about the 'location' of cultural experience. It is worth quoting the following passage, which contains, it appears, an allusion to Eliot's argument that the originality of new works of art depends on a larger cultural development that 'abandons nothing en route, which does not superannuate either Shakespeare, or Homer, or the rock drawing of the Magdalenian draughtsman' (39) – a view of the relation between tradition and the individual talent that Frye's entire life-work, devoted to a comprehensive elaboration of the 'order of words,' more fully clarifies and develops. Winnicott writes:

In using the word culture I am thinking of the inherited tradition. I am thinking of something that is in the common pool of humanity, into which individuals and groups of people may contribute, and from which we may all draw *if we have somewhere to put what we find* ... No doubt a very great deal was lost of the early civilizations, but in the myths that were a product of oral tradition there could be said to be a cultural pool giving the history of human culture spanning six thousand years ... It interests me ... that in any cultural field *it is not possible to be original except on a basis of tradition.* (117)

Winnicott speaks of the unique attitude we take towards what he calls 'transitional phenomena and objects,' among which he includes cultural experience. Faced with such phenomena we tacitly agree never to ask the question: 'did you create this object, or did you find it conveniently lying around?' (113). This is the attitude appropriate to a genuine criticism, as Frye sees it. In contrast, the understanding of culture that predominates among literary scholars today is reluctant to accept the trans-historical values of imaginative culture and is primarily concerned with the rhetorical, political, and ideological levels of a text. In the context of a minute exploration of all-pervasive power relations, the positive social value granted to cultural phenomena is restricted to that of a *resistance to power*: there is no conception of a cultural content that is not primarily ideological and political. The question nevertheless remains: what is the source of this resistance to relations of power?

The relative absence of Frye's name from contemporary discussions, given their ideological tenor, should not be surprising. Still, it would not be an exaggeration to say that his work was prophetic of the present emphasis on culture and on the interactions between the artistic and the sociopolitical spheres. The current belief that the study of literature must be rooted in an understanding of a period's entire cultural frame-work can, in fact, be traced back to the beginning of his career. From *Fearful Symmetry* on, Frye assumes the relevance of such a framework and insistently speaks of a culture as a human, and therefore entirely historical, creation that is separate from nature, a sort of artificial 'enve-lope' through which we experience the world around us. Unlike the dominant approaches today, however, Frye's understanding of this framework presupposes that culture is something more than a social and political battleground.

We should note that there are different meanings of the word 'culture' that need to be taken into account. In an essay entitled 'Levels of Cul-tural Identity,' Frye divides a nation's cultural life into three levels: an elementary level, 'the sense of custom or life-style: the distinctive way that people eat, dress, talk, marry, play games, produce goods, and the like' (*EAC*, 168); a middle level 'of cultural identity, which is the product of tradition and history, and consists of the distinctive political, eco-nomic, religious, and other institutions that shape a nation's life and give direction to the main currents of its ideology' (168); and finally 'an upper level of culture as the product of a nation's specialized creative powers' (169). In other words, we have: culture as custom, as ideology embodied in institutions – what Louis Althusser calls the Ideological State Apparatus – and as the arts and sciences. Frye is interested more often in the third sense of the word.

One of the weaknesses of current criticism is its inability or unwilling-ness to make such distinctions. The ideological and the political are assumed to have an absolute value and veto over all other concerns. Everything is ideology; *all* levels of culture are collapsed into the ideological level. Frye calls the practitioners of such criticism 'pan-ideologues' – 'They can't conceive of any myth that doesn't come in an ideological form' (*NFC*, 90) – and he speaks in the notebooks of an irony that equally applies to the aggressiveness of today's political criticism: the fact 'that Marxism, which tried to define ideology as the rationalizing of non-Marxists, should have turned into the one movement of our day that absolutizes ideology' (NB44, 28).

Frye sees verbal culture – the privileged mode of cultural experience in general – as characterized by an interpenetration of a number of distinctive modes of language, ideology being one mode in particular, and all of them interconnected in an encompassing mythological framework. His final assessment of these verbal modes in *Words with Power* is already outlined in *Anatomy* and elsewhere. The *Anatomy* (244–6), for example, already contains an encapsulated version of the discussion of rhetoric that later turns up in *Words with Power*. But Frye's most elegant (in the mathematical sense) formulation is his last. In *Words with Power*, he places the ideological between the conceptual and the literary (or imaginative). In asserting itself, each mode excludes a hidden initiative of language that runs counter to it, and this initiative, secretly operative but marginalized or repressed, forms the core of the superseding mode. The excluded initiative in the conceptual is what he calls 'a subjective desire or energy' (*WP*, 12), the personality which is 'speaking through the mask of argument' (13). Nietzsche is the philosopher most famous for uncovering the significance of personality and of the controlling will to power behind philosophical thought. Along with Kierkegaard, Nietzsche is often thought of as one of the first existential thinkers, and existentialism, as Frye points out, is a philosophical movement in which this subjective factor, with its appeal 'to commitment rather than reason' (13), comes most dramatically to the fore.

To describe this third mode, Frye speaks of the ideological and the rhetorical. The rhetorical refers to the verbal tactics of 'a speaking personality addressing a listening audience' (15). Ideology is a system of belief that is promulgated through the use of such tactics to persuade or compel an audience – a social group, an entire society – to subscribe to certain ideas and to carry out certain actions. Dialectic wishes, by the undeniable force of logic, to force its audience to accept the truth of its argument; ideology uses rhetorical techniques, often covert linguistic devices, to achieve the same end. As Frye puts it, 'the aim is to persuade and create a response of conviction. In oratory, an identification of speaker, speech and audience is what is aimed at' (17).

One of the theories of ideology that has influenced current criticism is that of Louis Althusser, and Frye's terms here recall Althusser's conception of the way ideology interpellates or 'hails' its subjects, an operation which is essentially rhetorical in kind, involving a similar type of identification: the subject responds to such interpellation the way an individual responds to his name, in an act of acknowledgment and self-recognition: Yes, here I am, what is it? Perhaps the most obvious place to look for such tactics is in the persuasive techniques of the highly commercialized media in Western capitalist societies – advertising, television, and film – and indeed much of the criticism informed by semiotics and post-structuralism has tended to focus on these areas of so-called popular culture (an area of exploration, it is worth noting, for which Frye's liberal conception of artistic culture in *Anatomy* helped to clear a path). The dramatic influence of the work of Jacques Lacan, for example, in the analysis of how instrumental social and cultural identities are constructed at an unconscious level clearly reflects this focus on the rhetorical means of 'subliminal' or unconscious compulsion.

A good deal of contemporary criticism has been committed to uncovering this *figurative* or *tropological* dimension of literature. In *The Critical Path*, Frye describes New Criticism, as he did in *Anatomy*, as 'a rhetorical form of criticism,' one which deals, not with persuasive oratory, but with 'the figuration of language' (20). This approach to literary texts found new life in deconstruction, however much the latter ventured in a radically sceptical direction. 'A great deal of the deconstructionists' brilliant analysis of rhetoric,' as Alvin Lee points out, 'is devoted to laying bare [this subordination of dialectic to rhetoric], what Frye calls the tactics of ideology' (40). Frye briefly analyses the relationship between the conceptual and the rhetorical or figurative modes in his essay on genre in *Anatomy*. There, he makes the point that

verbal association is still a factor of importance even in rational thought. One of the most effective methods of conveying meaning in translation, for instance, is to leave a key word untranslated, so that the reader has to pick up its contextual associations in the original language from his own. Again, in trying to understand the thought of a philosopher, one often starts by considering a single word, say nature in Aristotle, substance in Spinoza, or time in Bergson, in the total range of its connotations. One often feels that a full understanding of such a word would be a key to the understanding of the whole system. If so, it would be a metaphorical key, as it would be a set of identifications made by the thinker with the word. (335)

Derrida's seminal essay 'La mythologie blanche' has become the model for a radical critique of a philosophically pure language. But from the beginning it was basic to Frye's way of thinking that at the heart of any great conceptual system is a figurative core that cannot be outgrown. This, however, already carries us into the imaginative world of metaphor and myth. As Frye complains in a notebook entry: 'I still can't make any sense out of Derrida's assertion that metaphysics excludes writing. But of course his *écriture* includes everything that's visualizable. I have studied the metaphorical diagrams underlying some metaphysical systems, and however shallow such study may be, it convinced me that *that* is the *écriture* basis of conceptual thought' (NB27, 280).

This tension between the dialectical and the rhetorical is implicitly addressed by Althusser. An ideological approach to culture implies, of course, a conflict of ideologies: one ideology – to state a commonplace of contemporary critical theory – can be critiqued only in favour of another. While Althusser takes great pains to portray Marxism as a science, he recognizes that as an ideology it has an important, indeed a crucial role to play, since it is ideology that shapes our lived experience of the world. Marxist ideology, however, he is careful to remind us, must remain subordinated to dialectic, in an ancillary role which reflects, in fact, the traditional philosophical view of the proper relationship between these two verbal modes. It is clear, none the less, that scientific knowledge is inadequate on its own, and that reason must be supplemented both by persuasive tactics and by an existentialist *engagement*. A deeply interested element enters the scene in this mode. When we move from the conceptual to the ideological mode we are moving, as Frye sees it, from *reason* to *commitment*, and this is certainly a good way of understanding the shift from deconstruction to critical approaches such as feminism, New Historicism, and cultural criticism – from an approach devoted to the rigours of an essentially apolitical and impersonal dialectic to approaches that are intensely ideological and interested.[3]

The development of Roland Barthes's career is exemplary in this regard. He began his career by focusing on what he called *mythologies*, a word he uses, of course, in a very different sense from Frye's. A myth, for Barthes, is essentially a lie perpetrated by the rhetorical tactics used in mass culture to disguise ideological messages by investing them with an aura of the 'natural.' He ends his career by focusing on the transformative role of the reader as a sort of Nietzschean bestower of value and meaning, as the primary creator of meaning. This shift reflects a general foregrounding of the reader over the last decades. More recently, this focus on a subjective energy has become intensely politicized, and is most obvious in the confessional aspects of a good deal of contemporary criticism. Suspicious of any discourse that presents itself as objective and non-ideological, the critic of today is thus careful not to pretend that he or she is free of ideological motivation. The self-conscious act of drawing attention to one's own subject position, for example, is now so routine a gesture as to have become a convention of academic style. However, this critical self-awareness can quickly become an obstacle to the free and open exchange of ideas. Salusinszky has exposed the circularity of this device of making one's own position 'part of the problem under investigation ... And so there commences an endless positioning and repositioning, until finally I find myself firmly positioned at last: in a corner, with wet paint on every side' (82).

The underlying assumption, treated now almost as a dogmatic truth, is that art and culture are primarily a platform for social and political struggle. For all its purported sophistication, such an assumption is still bound to what Frye calls, in *The Secular Scripture*, 'the prestige of a displaced and realistic tradition,' the tendency 'to concentrate on what the book talks about rather than on what it actually presents' (43), as well as to an essentially 'Platonic-Christian framework,' in which '[t]he serious literary artists who tell stories in prose ... also tell us something about the life of their times, and about human nature as it appears in that context' (41). As he observes in the same study: 'The critical method suggested by realism begins by detaching the literary work being studied from its context in literature. After that, the work may be discussed in relation to its historical, social, biographical, and other nonliterary affinities. Such a method, inadequate as it is, is often rationalized as a proper emphasis on the "uniqueness" of the work' (59). Contemporary theory has declared itself quite inimical to the realistic tradition that Frye depicts here, criticizing realism on the grounds that it conceals the constructed and ideological nature of what it presents as objective reality. The assumption remains, none the less, that the serious artist is the one who is faithful to a nonliterary world of objective reality, however that may be defined at any given period. The realistic bias has never really been eclipsed. It flourishes with renewed strength in today's mainstream of criticism, in which what one 'talks about' is clearly more important than what one 'actually presents.'

Applicable here is what Frye says, in the same study, of the two thrusts of literary criticism prescribed by the Stalinist bureaucracy, where the revolutionary and the realistic are combined: 'The essential idea of this version of "social realism" was protest before revolution, panegyric afterward' (*SeS*, 164–5). Protest (against the dominant culture and its ideology) and praise (of minority voices and cultures) are essential aspects of the current critical focus on issues of gender, race, and class. In such a context, literature is understood as a form of 'realism with an allegorical basis' (NB44, 282). The problem of such criticism, in which 'an ideology [tries] to make all literature into an allegory of its own obsessions' (*WP*, 149), is already clearly articulated in the tentative conclusion to *Anatomy*:

Culture may be employed by a social or intellectual class to increase its prestige; and in general, moral censors, selectors of great traditions, apologists of religious or political causes, aesthetes, radicals, codifiers of great books, and the like, are expressions of such class tensions. We soon realize, in studying their pronouncements, that the only really consistent moral criticism of this type would be the kind which is harnessed to an all-round revolutionary philosophy of society, such as we find not only in Marxism, but in Nietzsche and in some of the rationalizations of oligarchic values in nineteenth-century Britain and twentieth-century America. In all these culture is treated as a human productive power which in the past has been, like other productive powers, exploited by other ruling classes and is now to be revalued in terms of a better society. But as this ideal society exists only in the future, the present valuation of culture is in terms of its interim revolutionary effectiveness. (346)

The protest and panegyric dominating current criticism are clearly in danger of repeating the type of codification and pedagogical selectivity described here. New Historicism, cultural criticism, and the highly politicized studies of race and gender are all subject to Frye's warning that 'just as historical criticism relates culture only to the past, ethical criticism uncorrected relates culture only to the future, to the ideal society which may eventually come if we take sufficient pains to guard the educating of our youth' (*AC*, 346).

It is this version of ethical criticism that Bernard-Henri Lévy, in *L'Éloge des Intellectuels*, claims has led to the banalizing of culture. Writing in the tradition of Benda, Lévy points to Sartre's book on Baudelaire as an exemplar of the dangers of this latest *trahison des clercs*:

Bref, ce qu'il [Sartre] lui reproche, c'est d'avoir été lui-même, Charles Baudelaire, auteur d'un livre genial mais noir, qui s'appelait *Les Fleurs du Mal* – et non un bien-pensant, gentiment socialo-quarante-huitard qui se serait contenté de mêler sa voix a la grand-messe du moment. On parle souvent de l'acharnement avec lequel l'auteur du Flaubert reproche a son héro de ne s'être pas 'engagé.' Il faut lire, relire ce Baudelaire comme model de ce que peut donner de pire, quand elle va au bout de sa folie, la reduction politique des écrivains. (57–8)

[In short, what he reproaches him for is having been himself, Charles Baudelaire, the author of a dark but genial book called *The Flowers of Evil* – and not a right-thinking, pleasantly socialistic forty-eighter who would have contented himself with adding his voice to the high mass of the moment. The relentlessness with which the author of the Flaubert reproaches his hero for not having 'committed' himself is often commented on. One should read and reread this Baudelaire as a model of the worst that can result from the political reduction of writers when it is pushed to its crazy extreme.]

Lévy is defending here the need for a critical *opposition* in a society that is not simply a counter-ideology. What he is really talking about is the objective and disinterested authority of art and culture. The call for moderation or balance that he advocates against the potential madness of political rectitude recalls Frye's insistence, in *The Critical Path*, on the need for an ongoing and never resolved tension in society between freedom and concern. However, much of Lévy's argument is itself one-sided, and recalls the strident tone of Harold Bloom's (and Alan Bloom's) attack on the so-called school of *ressentiment*. The problem is that such attacks on groups allegedly driven by *ressentiment*, like that of Nietzsche on the entire Judaeo-Christian tradition, are often secretly driven themselves by the very emotions they denounce in others.

They are, at any rate, *arguments*, and their highly subjective and polemical nature can be heard in the rhetorical style and in the antagonistic tone of voice. In his interview with David Cayley, Frye explained his reluctance to enter into discussion with contemporary ideological critics: 'I detest arguments. You're going to lose any argument with an ideologue, because you can only argue on the basis of a counter-ideology, and I'm not doing that' (*NFC*, 91). Such argument is a level of understanding that, for Frye, is ultimately transcended and subsumed by the modes of the imaginative and the kerygmatic, as he describes them in *Words with Power*. Frye carefully avoided the generally confrontational mode of academic debate, and obviously felt more comfortable, in person and in his books, with the style of teacherly exposition and demonstration that he practised in the classroom. Ultimately, he regarded polemic and argument as the opposite of the dialectical, for they tend to freeze and polarize opponents in their positions, to fix them at an ideological or legalistic level of understanding, rather than to free them to a more expansive level of insight.

This is because such disagreement is about winning or losing, in which it is the strongest argument or, as with Harold Bloom, the most powerful (mis)reading which prevails. In *Words with Power*, Frye opens his discussion of ideology with a reference to the opening debate over justice between Socrates and Thrasymachus in *The Republic*. Sophists such as Thrasymachus, as Frye points out, 'were concerned with rhetoric, not dialectic' (13), in that they were basically concerned with training people to win arguments. Socrates' opponent is a relativist and a legalist, an anti-foundationalist, a sort of early day Stanley Fish, the latter being a critic whose theory of interpretive communities is as rhetorical and sophistic an argument as one can get. When Thrasymachus argues about the definition of justice, he is, Frye writes, 'speaking for the wordless world of power. He is a forerunner of Machiavelli and Hobbes and Marx and the late Nietzsche, who tell us about a world where material or other forces of power are effective and words are not, and where the use of such a word as justice means chiefly that someone who holds power is rationalizing the fact that he is going to go on holding it' (14). The debate between Socrates and Thrasymachus is about the relationship between knowledge and power, and the general thesis today that knowledge – especially what one's opponents call knowledge – is always a manifestation of a will to power has been most systematically explored in the work of Michel Foucault. His influence has been enormous in shaping current critical views. But Foucault's critique of structures of power, like Marx's, clearly involves an assumption that subordinates power to something else. The impassioned desire for justice and truth that motivates such a project in the first place depends, in fact, on the language of primary concerns – the values, for example, of freedom, community, and discovery – that Frye describes, and that, for him, are the very core of a culture and its mythological framework. It is at this point, Frye would argue, that the creative imagination comes into play.

According to Althusser's famous definition, 'ideology represents the imaginary relationship of individuals to their real conditions of existence' (162). In a rather orthodox way, Althusser groups literature and art under the cultural Ideological State Apparatus. Apparently aware, however, of the need to distinguish between the imaginative and the imaginary, he elsewhere differentiates art and literature from ideology:

Balzac and Solzhenitsyn give us a 'view' of the ideology to which their work alludes and with which it is constantly fed, a view which presupposes a *retreat*, an *internal distantiation* from the very ideology from which their novels emerged. They make us 'perceive' (but not know) in some sense *from the inside*, by an *internal distance*, the very ideology in which they are held. (223)

Althusser subscribes, almost dutifully at times, to a normative scientific ideology, and art, of course, cannot be a form of *scientific* knowledge: 'Neither Balzac nor Solzhenitsyn gives us any knowledge of the world they describe, they only make us "see," "perceive" or "feel" the reality of the ideology of that world' (223). This qualification made, art is conceded the ability to detach itself from and even expose the nature of ideological discourses. This capacity stems from a perceptual and affective element, a counter-rational and counter-logical power that reveals the reality of ideology, even when the latter 'is identical with the "lived" experience of human existence itself' (223) and purportedly reaches so deep that it constructs our very subjectivity.

The authority peculiar to both science and art is, as Althusser suggests, the disinterested quality of both. One place where Frye works out the relationship between literature and ideology is in his famous conclusion to the *Literary History of Canada*. There he speaks of the 'garrison mentality' in early Canadian literature, the sense of solitude, the experience of the isolated individual or parochial community of being surrounded by a menacing environment. He links this attitude to the tradition in Canada of the 'arguing intellect' (*BG*, 227), of partisan, rhetorical, and ideological argument, and contrasts it with the 'disinterested structure of words' (228) that characterizes a highly developed literary culture. Disinterestedness, in the context of literature, is something very different from a lack of concern. It refers to literature's essential detachment, the fact that it does not make assertions. 'Literature,' he writes in *The Critical Path*, 'is the embodiment of a language, not of belief or thought; it will say anything, and therefore in a sense it says nothing. It provides the technical resource for formulating the myths of concern, but does not itself formulate' (101).

If ideology, then, reveals itself to be anxious and interested, literature shows itself to be, paradoxically, both *detached* and *concerned*. The concept of concern is central, in the latter part of Frye's career, not just to his examination of the social context of literature, but to his understanding of the role of religion in a culture. Literature's concern refers to the *relevance* of imaginative culture in the deepest sense, that is, to its relation to essential human needs and desires: 'Nobody would accept,' Frye says in *The Critical Path*, 'a conception of literature as a mere dictionary or grammar of symbols and images which tells us nothing in itself. Everyone deeply devoted to literature knows that it says something, and says something as a whole, not only in its individual works' (*CP*, 103). As deconstructive criticism would seem to dispute such a statement, ideological and politicized criticism – as the antithesis answers the thesis – would seem to confirm it, or at least an aspect of it. But both are polarized ways of thinking, and Frye never dissolves the paradox. As he goes on to say: 'Precisely because its variety is infinite, literature suggests an encyclopaedic range of concern greater than any formulation of concern in religious or political myth can express' (103). The range of concern that literature allows for is, in other words, an expression of the detachment of the imagination, and the tension between these two – concern and detachment – is one of the things that separates imaginative culture from ideology.

We have mentioned the postulation of a *tertium quid*, 'some cultural element in the middle' that neutralizes ideological conflict. This disinterested element, part of 'the fight for human freedom,' as Frye calls it, is identified with three things: with law, with 'the objectivity of scholarly and scientific knowledge' (*EAC*, 161), and with 'the creative and imaginative culture a society produces in the middle of all its power struggles' (160). As noted, Winnicott locates culture in precisely the same place, a 'third area,' the place of transitional objects and phenomena, which is a potential space of play between the subject and object worlds, between the self and its environment: 'The place where cultural experience is located is in the potential space between the individual and the environment (originally the object). The same can be said of playing. Cultural experience begins with creative living first manifested in play' (119). Sounding very much like Frye, Winnicott insists that in positing such a space one is not devaluing the other two areas of subjective experience and of objective world: 'Nevertheless, playing and cultural experience are things that we do value in a special way; these link the past, the present, and the future; they take up time and space. They demand and get our concentrated deliberate attention, deliberate but without too much of the deliberateness of trying' (128).

Winnicott's observations here coincide with the views of Jan Huizinga, as presented in fascinating detail in *Homo Ludens*, that 'culture arises in the form of play, that it is played from the very beginning' and that '[i]t is through this playing that society expresses its interpretation of life and the world' (46). Play and culture are 'distinct from "ordinary" life' and their purposes are 'external to immediate material interests or the individual satisfaction of biological needs' (9). What distinguishes play from work is not the energy expended, but precisely the quality we have been emphasizing: its disinterestedness. In societies where a significant amount of human energy and attention can be freed from instrumental concerns, such as the relentless effort to provide the necessaries of life, play-forms flourish and develop into the complex forms of culture associated with law, scientific knowledge, and art. Inherent in these cultural forms and institutions is an objective element that grows out of the self-contained quality of play, and a deep-rooted respect for the autonomy of such forms would seem to be an organic part of a free and open society. This may be more obvious in the worlds of science and law, where tampering with the 'rules' clearly has a deleterious effect on the validity of results or the sense of justice. But an analogous need to protect the conditions of objectivity can be recognized in art and literature as well, where the 'playful' quality of the structures is all the more apparent. In his discussion of the classical epic in *Anatomy*, Frye offers a very specific example of what he means by the objective nature of the authority of imaginative culture, of literature and art's concern-*cum*-detachment:

It is hardly possible to overestimate the importance for Western literature of the *Iliad*'s demonstration that the fall of an enemy, no less than of a friend or leader, is tragic and not comic. With the *Iliad*, once for all, an objective and disinterested element enters into the poet's vision of human life. Without this element, poetry is merely instrumental to various social aims, to propaganda, to amusement, to devotion, to instruction: with it, it acquires the authority that since the *Iliad* it has never lost, an authority based, like the authority of science, on the vision of nature as an impersonal order. (319)

Without this objective and disinterested element – the point is not that literature does not in any way accommodate the instrumentalities that Frye enumerates (propagandistic, hedonistic, religious, aesthetic, pedagogic). The point is that it *also* possesses an imaginative breadth of meaning that supersedes immediate goals and interests. Out of the sense of disinterested as a hypothetical, non-assertive, non-descriptive, 'playful' use of words ('the poet never affirmeth') emerges this other sense of disinterested as literature's objective authority.

In the latter part of his career Frye came to focus on verbal culture in its broadest scope and the nature of its relationship to what he refers to, in his initial formulations, as a myth of concern. In *Words with Power*, Frye offers his final formulation of the importance of this myth in human societies. It is here that he elaborates the already discussed distinction between primary and secondary concerns. Secondary concerns, to reiterate, are essentially ideological ones and have to do with political power and social authority and control, the particular application of a myth in a society in the interests of enforcing certain beliefs and actions and discouraging others. Primary concerns, on the other hand, involve those matters that are essential to human life in all societies. These are the concerns addressed in myth. In the *Anatomy* Frye speaks of 'universal symbols' which are the imaginative material of the anagogic phase of meaning in literature: 'I mean that some symbols are images of things common to all men, and therefore have a communicable power which is potentially unlimited. Such symbols include those of food and drink, of the quest or journey, of light and darkness, and of sexual fulfilment' (118). A group, that is, 'may be confidently excluded from the human race if they cannot understand the conception of food, and so any symbolism founded on food is universal in the sense of having an indefinitely extensive scope. That is, there are no limits to its intelligibility' (118). In *Words with Power*, in a formula for narrative somewhat less categorical than the generic *mythoi* which he proposes in *Anatomy*, Frye describes the material and imagery of all conceivable stories as deriving from four roughly distinguishable main areas: sexual life, food and whatever else sustains human life, freedom of movement, and property (the latter term to be taken, not in the strictly economic or legal sense, but as that which creates for the individual identity and significance).

Literature, in other words, tells the story of human beings as they struggle to stay alive, to gain their freedom, to unite with others, and to find meaning and happiness in life. In fiction and poetry, these images are not employed primarily as assertions about the world. 'As literature asserts nothing,' Frye observes, 'but simply holds up symbols and illustrations, it calls for a suspension of judgment, as well as varieties of reactions, that, left to itself, could be more corrosive of ideologies than any rational scepticism' (*WP*, 24). The danger of ideological forms of literary criticism is that they often try to enforce a uniformity of response to literary works, a uniformity which the works themselves do not support. 'The poem,' in contrast, as Frye understands it, 'like the rhetorical speech, is a focus of a community, but instead of demanding a uniformity of response it fosters variety' (*WP*, 67). The point Frye makes here is not very far from what Bakhtin means by the dialogic, even if the latter term is associated somewhat exclusively with novelistic genres; it is not just the novel, but literature in general, as a hypothetical and disinterested use of language, that is polyphonic, free, ultimately, 'from a unitary and singular language' (*Dialogic Imagination*, 314).

In his discussion of Shakespeare's comedies and romances in *A Natural Perspective*, Frye speaks of there being two possible responses in any audience. One is 'an attitude that comes to the theater with a mass of prejudices and clichés and stock responses, and demands that the play illustrate them' (52). As a popular writer, so Frye's argument goes, Shakespeare was happy enough to accommodate this desire for 'the apparent meaning, or moral, of the play' (52). There is an intelligent response as well, and this attitude 'is focused on its structure' and 'does not seek a hidden meaning in the play addressed only to it: it simply observes the dramatic tension' (53). The structure of a literary work – its tragic, ironic, or comic structure – is something that 'commands participation but not assent: it unites its audience as an audience, but allows for variety in response. The response to dramatic action, as to social action, ought to be a majority and not a totality. If no variety of response is permitted, as in extreme forms of melodrama and farce, something is wrong: something is inhibiting the proper function of drama' (50). A Nazi propaganda film inciting hatred of Jews aims at a very different response from that of *The Merchant of Venice*, a play which has particularly provoked a diversity of moods in its readers and audience. It is the fact that ideology seeks one response that often makes ideology or propaganda both so horrifying and so ludicrous.

In terms of cultural history, of course, ideology is 'the delta which all verbal structures finally reach' (*WP*, 19), since there are no enduring social mythologies. This is really what the New Historicists – with their almost exclusive focus on political content and their somewhat disingenuous inattention to the imaginative content of literary works – mean by culture: dead culture, that aspect of a literary work which does not outlive its time.[4] Frye points out that

every verbal structure, simply by being conditioned by its social and historical environment, reflects that conditioning. Metaphysical systems, down to Leibnitz at least, show a tendency to present themselves spatially, as it were, as structures devoted to unchanging truth, and so rising above time. However, they do not rise above time, and as time goes on this becomes increasingly obvious. The longer a thinker has been dead, the more likely his work is to be studied as an ideological document. (*WP*, 19)

But literature is not thought, and Frye's acute perception of the limitations in the approach of documentary critics, as he outlines it in *The Critical Path*, applies just as well to the New Historicists: they 'do not account for the literary form of what they are discussing'; they do not account for its poetic meaning; and they do not account for 'the fact that the genuine quality of a poet is often in a negative relation to the chosen context' (19–20).

In any work of art or literature, as Frye understands it, 'two centers of reference emerge, one contemporary with the [author] and the other with us. The principle involved is that there is a flexibility to the story that its ideological reference does not permit' (*WP*, 60). This ability of art and literature to survive their immediate historical context is related to the profound optimism implied in Frye's conception of imaginative culture. 'The artefacts of a vanished civilization,' he remarks of the artistic treasures retrieved by archaeology, 'were produced in the normal climate of human cruelty and folly, but they themselves are in an unchanging state of innocence. They are what we still want to see, and we can take pleasure in them while abstracting their social context from them' (*EAC*, 49). As he expresses the same thought in *Anatomy*: 'The imaginative element in works of art ... lifts them clear of the bondage of history ... the corruption out of which human art has been constructed will always remain in the art, but the imaginative quality of the art preserves it in its corruption, like the corpse of a saint' (348–9). Culture, for Frye, has a tendency to preserve at its core the most desirable impulses of human societies. It transmits an inalienable conception of human life that encourages us to imagine a better and more human world. Such a world, Frye claims, 'can be constructed only by the creative imagination, the one power that has been able to drive humanity beyond the needs of mere survival into a more abundant life' (*EAC*, 49).

We cannot avoid the fact that sedimented in all literary works is a passive aspect that belongs to ideology (*WP*, 18). A work such as *The Adventures of Huckleberry Finn*, to take an obvious example, reveals on the author's part a relatively conservative attitude to the dominant social attitudes of his day. This emerges, for example, in the racist caricatures of Jim and other black characters in the novel, and in the fact that Jim's and his family's quest for freedom, treated at times with humanity and sensitivity, is ultimately marred by the demeaning comic absurdities and manipulations of the plot. For some readers, this has made the novel obsolete except as a document of a history of social inequities and injustice experienced by African Americans in the United States. Such offensive elements constitute what we might call the 'wince factor' in literary works of the past, an inevitable result of the historicity of all texts, literary or otherwise, and not to exempt by any means those that are written today and that may often seem to us wisest in their advanced social attitudes. If the literature – and criticism – written now endures as art or as social document, it is the same fate that attends its survival: its ideological content, tested by time, will inevitably become embarrassingly conspicuous. It is the ideology of a text that dates a work the most, and it is now very difficult to teach a novel like *Huckleberry Finn* or *The Merchant of Venice* without being affected by serious misgivings about a good deal of its content.

That we grow aware of these aspects is all to the good. It is part of a process that makes us increasingly intolerant of areas of shameful abuse and injustice that we have denied and kept in the dark. Yet much of Twain's novel is itself a powerful expression of precisely this liberalizing impulse. It is informed by, and indeed has done a great deal to teach us, the very language of concern that has educated us to be sensitive to the ideological limitations of its own imperfect vision. The primary concern in *Huckleberry Finn* is, of course, the myth of freedom, and, to follow Frye's argument, it would be in the story's thematic structure and in its metaphoric imagery that this myth is most clearly articulated. The structure of a literary work, as Frye conceives it, does not by any means remove it from the most important social and human concerns. Rather, what gives literature its objectivity and authority is that inherent in its mythic and metaphoric structures is the implicit vision of a *social norm*.

The first essay in *Anatomy* opens by briefly introducing five modes: myth, romance, high mimetic, low mimetic, and irony. The formulation of this last mode, it seems to me, is particularly indicative of Frye's view of how the positive impulse and concern of literature are conveyed: 'If inferior in power or intelligence to ourselves, so that we have the sense of looking down on a scene of bondage, frustration, or absurdity, the hero belongs to the ironic mode. This still applies even when the reader feels that he is or might be in the same situation, as the situation is being judged by the norms of greater freedom' (34). The norms referred to here are never explicit, but they are nevertheless operative. The ironic mode and the norms that make it possible are, for example, clearly at work in many of the theoretic 'fictions' of contemporary criticism, in the stories unfolded by the likes of Foucault, Jameson, Greenblatt, and others, which so often portray a demonic world of power and subjugation, of human beings hopelessly entrapped in the clockwork of pervasive political and ideological structures. The implication of Frye's formulation is that even the most ironic literature – and we might add, then, the most ironic theory as well – involves the perspective of a higher order of reality, 'the paradisal pole that gives us a perspective on the hell-world, or ... provides the norm that makes irony ironic' (WP, 88). Without this perspective, the depiction of a nightmarish society or situation, such as the world of Kafka's The Trial or Beckett's Molloy, would hardly affect us as it does:

The real opposite of the dystopia is rather the sense of a social norm already mentioned, the sense that enables irony to be ironic. An audience watching a comedy recognizes the absurdity and grotesqueness of the characters who usually dominate the action, because it already possesses a vision of a more sensible society, and many comedies move toward some visualization of such a society in their final moments. (WP, 309)

The assumption of a social norm 'operates outside literature' as well: 'one can hardly imagine, say, doctors or social workers unmotivated by some vision of a healthier or freer society than the one they see around them' (WP, 309). But the exact nature of the world we desire, as Frye has observed, can be formulated only in the most platitudinous terms: that happiness and abundance are better than misery and want, freedom better than imprisonment, love and life better than hatred and death. It seems that more definite formulations are precisely what mark the shift from myth to ideology, from primary to secondary concerns. 'As soon as we make culture a definite image of a future and perhaps attainable society, we start selecting and purging a tradition, and all the artists who don't fit in (an increasing number as the process goes on) have to be thrown out' (AC, 346).

The most virulent opponents of current ideological approaches claim that today's politicized iconoclasts, with their questioning of the canon, are embarked on precisely such a 'selecting and purging.' But it could be argued that the champions of the canon are simply calling the kettle black. In both cases, it is the peremptoriness of points of view, the defensive refusal to entertain the significance of other perspectives, that has damaged the conditions favourable to genuine progress in knowledge, as opposed to contention and argument. A passage by Frye about philosophical argument in a notebook written around the completion of Fearful Symmetry comes to mind:

The problems of philosophy are not solved, but we do succeed in losing interest in them. We have not solved the medieval realist-nominalist dispute, the arguments for & against the validity of the ontological proof, or the Renaissance controversy over innate ideas; but we have acquired an overwhelming sense of their unreality which is better than a solution. If I hear undergraduates arguing over free will & necessity, I can only sit there in a smug stupor of inarticulate ignorance in which I am as convinced of my greater maturity & wisdom as though I were drunk. My brain beats out a drone bass indistinguishable in sentiment from the intellectual tortoises they're trying not to be: 'I don't know what you're talking about; but I have known, and you'll never catch me in *that* rat-trap again.' For if you can express your reasons for finding the question unreal you're still arguing about it, & still involved in its illusion of reality. (NB3, 64)

It is the danger of such 'illusion[s] of reality' that led Frye, from the beginning of his career, to identify himself unashamedly as a liberal, and in the latter part more defiantly as a bourgeois one. He obviously meant to be provocative, but he also meant what he said. The theme appears early. In a letter to Helen Kemp (4 September 1933), the twenty-one-year-old Frye mentions a test in a magazine that pegs him politically 'with perfect accuracy. On the fence between the Liberal and C.C.F. battalions, exactly where a follower of Spengler and Mantalini ought to be' (*Correspondence*, 1:155).[5] Frye's sympathy with the C.C.F. (Cooperative Commonwealth Federation) in Canada is mentioned in the notebook just quoted above, which dates from just after the war, but it is expressed in association with a tolerance that is more liberal than socialist, though – as he insists – it is

not merely liberalism or weakness of spirit: it is a product of a type of knowledge, even of vision, that I dare not & cannot decry. How does high Bhakti express itself? In charitable works. That to me means working for the C.C.F. In miracles of healing. I admire more the abortionist who risks a penitentiary sentence to help terrified women. In contempt of the world. My model there is an author who works for years on a book so 'dirty' it gets banned. These are all *new moral facts*; they are not expressions of rebelliousness or perversity. And because of them we must look for aspects of God which we have not looked for before. (NB3, 39)

In *The Critical Path* Frye opposes a myth of concern, a closed structure of belief which tends to express itself anxiously, to a myth of freedom, which is an expression of the pluralistic openness of certain aspects of modern culture. 'A plurality of ideologies,' he says in one of the *Words with Power* notebooks, 'is a good thing if it prevents one from becoming tyrannical. Perhaps the most effective element in democracy is its conception of the co-existence of ideologies' (NB27, 446). In another entry he writes: 'The language of ideology, being thesis-language, contains its own opposite. Ideology functions properly in a tolerance that tries to contain the opposite. Dogmas that exclude the opposite are pernicious. The worst are those that back up political dogma with a religious or quasi-religious one' (NB44, 7). What his 'bourgeois liberalism really amounts to,' he explains, 'is the sense of the ultimately demonic nature of all ideological constructs' (NB44, 702). In more positive terms, as he says at the end of *Anatomy*, with reference to Milton and Mill, 'liberty can begin only with an immediate and present guarantee of the autonomy of culture' (348–9).[6] Ultimately, Frye's bourgeois liberalism is really his profound belief in the 'liberty of the arts' as forming 'an essential part of the myth of freedom. To liberate the language of concern is to ensure that the whole imaginative range of concern is being expressed in society, instead of being confined to a selected type of imagination which is hitched to the tactics of one social group, as propaganda for it, or what we have called a rhetorical analogue to it' (CP, 166).

We live at a time when such rhetorical analogues, 'hitched to the tactics of one social group' or another, have great ascendency in literary studies. Frye, of course, grew up in a period when certain ideological constructs were also particularly dominant: 'In the 30s & 40s the Thomist one had Gilson & Maritain in the front line: they were gentlemen, of course, but a mean-minded fascism lurked in the background. I knew that the Thomist setup was an illusion, and that Marxism (which didn't have any gentlemen) would eventually be exposed as another illusion' (NB44, 702). It may be a healthy sign of the ongoing critical role of the liberal arts in society that the analogues flourishing today in the humanities represent, for the most part – in contrast with the nationalist and racist categories against which Benda's polemic was directed at the end of the 1920s – decentralized and minority views opposed to the social establishment. In this, they have much in common with the kind of counter-movement created by art and literature, with the 'imaginative wriggling out of a power struggle' that characterizes the strategy of culture at certain times – 'decentralizing where politics centralizes, differentiating where technology makes everything uniform, giving articulateness and human meaning to the small community where economy turns it into a mere distributing center, constantly moving in a direction opposite to that of the political and economic tendencies of history' (*EAC*, 166). The myths that 'are incarnated in works of literature,' Frye says in his interview with Cayley, 'create ... a cultural counter-environment to the ones that are ... twisted or skewed into ideological patterns of authority' (*NFC*, 90). At the same time, however, the pull of social anxieties means that intellectuals will always be tempted 'to help turn the wheel of history, to support social movements that are going in what they feel are the right directions, to show that in the power struggles of history ideas do after all count for something' (*EAC*, 162). With this can come the *trahison des clercs* that we began with, 'the betrayal, by the intellectuals, of their own standards in the interest of some form of mass movement' (162).

The problem with ideological thinking is that one must either take a position of relativism – the view, that is, that all ideologies are, ultimately, equal – or one must posit a significant degree of objectivity, of truth, of justice, against which to measure the distortion produced by ideological versions of reality. In the latter case, one is forced to admit that there is an element in human culture that escapes ideology, that is not imaginary, but *imaginative*, and that plays an indispensable role in society. It is not enough to say that 'ideology is inescapable,' for in order to engage in serious criticism of ideology, we must appeal to an element that is outside its sphere. At the same time, it is a banality to say that everything is ideological, if one means that no work of art or scientific discussion or legal argumentation is free of ideology. How can any human production be unaffected by systems of belief that, in any human society, disguise class interests and strategies of power? This does not mean, however, that the productions of time are expressions of nothing but ideology. Whether we are willing to admit it or not – that is, whether we are intellectually honest or not – we all assume a significant element of objectivity that is free of ideology and that enables us to criticize social conditions in the first place.

Frye gives the example of the authority of law in a society, 'an authority of its own that rises above its conditioning' (*EAC*, 162), meaning it to apply as well, of course, to scientific and scholarly knowledge and to the creative arts. 'It would be nonsense,' he admits, 'to think of any aspect of law as being in any way sacrosanct, autonomous, or detached from social influences or historical conditions. But to think of it as nothing but an instrument of social power would be equally wrong: it still contains an objective quality that lifts it clear of that' (161). Similarly, the perspective afforded by imaginative works of art and literature, as Frye sees it, is one in which the ideology of a group is ultimately superseded by the prior initiative of the imagination. At its most basic, this is simply the writer's impulse to compose a poem or a story, as opposed to the impulse to make a definite and unambiguous assertion about social reality. It is this imaginative structure of the literary work that constitutes an objective element that 'keep[s] something going in society that is not simply a conflict of pressure groups which are always and by nature anticultural' (161). Indeed, as we have noted, the intense conviction that lies behind so much contemporary criticism – the belief that it is our duty to root out the effects of power in discourse and to expose the complexity of ideology in all its intricate and cunning disguises – this conviction cannot stand on its own. Ultimately, it depends on something that, however self-evident, however much we may take it for granted, can have come to us only from a myth produced and fostered by the human imagination – an affirmative 'vision of fulfilled primary concerns, freedom, health, equality, happiness, love' (WP, 310), the vision of a world that, once and for all, makes human sense.

We must finally make a distinction, then, between the criticism that cannot get beyond protest or panegyric and the criticism that is genuinely imaginative. In the early notebook from which I have been quoting, Frye evokes the image of a moral and punishing God: 'Such a God at the beginning is a foreign body, a largely impotent critic of creativity, and as he gains more power he takes over more and more of the actor until he becomes the actor's essential self, a self no longer individual but universal' (NB3, 13). The impotent critic stage corresponds to ideological criticism when it is essentially moral and refers itself to a false polarity. The critic at this stage is, like Job's comforters – to harken back to the closing argument of Words with Power – an ideological censor, a kind of superego, telling us in his wrath what is bad and what is good. In a notebook entry written forty years later, during the writing of Words with Power, Frye writes: 'Marxism in theory transcends ideology, & some bourgeois masochists (Barthes) go along with this. But when we look at what Lenin says about religion it's clear that a counter-ideology is being set up: there's no transcendence of ideology. So my faith–ideology–secondary concern and charity–transcendence–primary concern still stands' (NB27, 206). Crucial here is the distinction that Frye makes between the faith that impels ideology and the charity that avoids false polarities, and thus fosters the imagination. It is perhaps this distinction above all that explains his unfashionable espousing of liberalism. In the same notebook written in the 1940s, he observes:

It's curious how insistently one tends to make cheap & flippant epigrams about things of which one is ignorant, & how much progress in wisdom is concerned with discovering the positive values of more & more things, or writers, & interpreting even their errors sympathetically. I still feel that in criticism everything positive stands, everything negative dates. As writing gets wiser it drops the tone of polemic. I think it's as literally true as so figurative a statement can be that without charity one is a sounding brass. (NB3, 43)

'And now abideth faith, hope, charity, these three; but the greatest of these is charity' (1 Cor. 13:13). Frye turned more than once to the episode, recounted in three of the Gospels, in which Jesus cures a paralytic, telling him to rise, take up his bed, and go home. 'Which is easier,' Jesus demands of the Pharisees, 'to say "Your sins are forgiven you," or to say "Rise and walk"?' (Luke 5:23). These words translate a miracle of healing into an imaginative fact. They represent a very specific statement: that the power to transcend the existing order of the world lies in the releasing of creative energy in the human soul. The function of criticism is not to be a moral censor or judge. It is to look for a transforming energy in everything we read and to help to set it free.

NOTES

1 Frye has noted, indeed, that the call for 'relevance' in education is a disturbing echo of the Nazi educational policy of 'target-knowledge' (NFC, 153).
2 There are numerous entries in the Words with Power notebooks in which we can see Frye turning over in his mind the crucial distinction between ideology and the authority of imaginative vision or poetic authority, the basic principle that 'poetic language ... not only is different from ideological language but puts up a constant fight against it to liberalize and individualize it' (NFC, 90). In Notebook 27, for example, he alludes to the fact that Wallace Stevens converted to Catholicism on his deathbed, and notes that '[m]any people, even though of Catholic background, felt betrayed by this. The point is the ideological horizontal bar: Stevens made a soft & sentimental move toward the pole of acceptance, instead of staying in the middle with his own poetic authority intact' (443). He describes the classical eighteenth-century 'phase of literature' as 'an extraordinary tour de force, a literature totally dominated by ideology and quite happy about it,' in which literature is unembarrassedly subordinated 'to canons derived from secondary concern' (450). He notes '[t]he function of literature as the (a) recreation and (b) recovery of mythical kernels in ideology. The conflict in the minds of poets; their authority; their conflicts

with ideologies. The theory of the arts as liberated prophecy. The classless society of culture as the everlasting gospel' (473). He comments: 'I must look up Origen & Clement: from what I remember, the Greeks kept a strong sense of mythology: it was the Romans who sold out totally to ideology' (490).

3 Eleanor Cook has depicted this shift in terms of the two genres that inform *Anatomy* as a piece of prose fiction: anatomy and confession, a generic duality which can be roughly correlated with the conceptual and the rhetorical. As she puts it: 'The genre of anatomy pulls us toward the discipline of philosophy, the discipline with which deconstruction has the greatest affinity. On the other hand, the genre of confession, which subsumes the social implications of art, pulls us toward social disciplines such as history and anthropology, disciplines with which, say, the New Historicists ... have the most affinity. I think it is fair to say that current critical energy is strongly bent toward the confessional genre' (17). Cook advocates some kind of dialectic of concern (confession) and detachment (anatomy), rather than the current polarization, which threatens to be a deadening one.

4 It is no accident perhaps that Stephen Greenblatt has confessed, in *Shakespearean Negotiations*, that part of the motivation behind his reconstructions of the past is, quite precisely, a desire to speak with the dead (1–20). The first chapter of the book begins: 'I began with the desire to speak with the dead' (1).

5 He continues: 'I think, with the C.C.F., that capitalism is crashing around our ears, and that any attempt to build it up again will bring it down with a bigger crash. I think with the Liberals that socialism, as it is bound to develop historically, is an impracticable remedy, not because it is impracticable – it is inevitable – but because it is not a remedy. I think with the C.C.F. that a cooperative state is necessary to preserve us from chaos. I think with Liberals that it is impossible to administer that state at present. I think with the C.C.F. that man is unable, in a laissez faire system, to avoid running after false gods and destroying himself. I think with Liberals that it is only by individual freedom and democratic development that any progress can be made. In short, any "way out" must of necessity be miraculous' (1:155–6).

6 See also Frye's discussion with Cayley, pp. 120–1. 'Actually, what I mean by bourgeois liberal ... is steering a middle course between the totalitarian mass man on the one hand and a kind of anarchism of the ego on the other' (121).

WORKS CITED

Althusser, Louis. *Lenin and Philosophy and Other Essays*. Translated by Ben Brewster. New York: Monthly Review Press, 1971.
Bakhtin, Mikhail. *The Dialogic Imagination: Four Essays*. Edited by Michael

Holquist. Translated by Caryl Emerson and Michael Holquist. Austin: University of Texas Press, 1981.

Benda, Julien. *The Treason of the Intellectuals (La Trahison des Clercs)*. 1928. Translated by Richard Aldington. New York: Norton, 1969.

Cook, Eleanor. 'Anatomies and Confessions: Northrop Frye and Contemporary Theory.' *Recherches Sémiotiques/Semiotic Inquiry* 13 (1993) 3: 13–22.

Eliot, T.S. *Selected Prose of T.S. Eliot*. London: Faber, 1975.

Frye, Northrop, and Helen Kemp. *The Correspondence of Northrop Frye and Helen Kemp, 1932–1939*. Edited by Robert D. Denham. 2 vols. Toronto: University of Toronto Press, 1996. 1: 155–6.

Greenblatt, Stephen. *Shakespearean Negotiations: The Circulation of Social Energy in Renaissance England*. Berkeley: University of California Press, 1988.

Huizinga, Jan. *Homo Ludens: A Study of the Play-Element in Culture*. Boston: Beacon Press, 1950

Lee, Alvin. 'Northrop Frye: Identity not Negation.' *Recherches Sémiotiques / Semiotic Inquiry* 13 (1993) 3: 33–46.

Lévy, Bernard-Henri. *Éloge des Intellectuels*. Paris: Bernard Grasset, 1987.

Salusinszky, Imre. 'Frye and Ideology.' In *The Legacy of Northrop Frye*, edited by Alvin A. Lee and Robert D. Denham. Toronto: University of Toronto Press, 1994. 76–83.

Winnicott, D.W. *Playing and Reality*. Harmondsworth, England: Penguin, 1971.

Northrop Frye as a Cultural Theorist

A.C. HAMILTON

I

In Frye's generation, those involved in the academic study of English literature were mainly historical scholars who engaged in source studies because they held that a literary work being the product of its author's life and times reflected its background of ideas, beliefs, reading, and events. In reaction, some of these later became critics – at that time a strongly pejorative label – who read a literary work 'as such' apart from all its literary and historical sources. Scholars may have enjoyed reading Milton's *Paradise Lost* as a poem rather than as a Puritan tract but in their professional endeavours its content – its relation to Milton and his age which they sought to document – alone mattered. As for its language, so far as they were concerned, it could have been translated from the Sanskrit. The New Critics turned from ideas to a poem's language as formally constructed into a unified work designed for pleasure as well as understanding, and by the 1930s and '40s, their formal study of a literary work began to supplant historical study. Those who flourished in the 1950s and '60s had been nurtured as formalist New Critics; and if they continued to write into the next two decades they found themselves in a new age of critical theory in which they were confronted not only by deconstruction but by that movement as it was soon absorbed by cultural criticism which expanded history into the broadly cultural. Instead of setting literary works apart from history in a direct and simple relationship as had been done by earlier positivist historical scholars – ironically, itself now a strongly pejorative label – cultural critics saw them, and themselves, entangled with all other kinds of discourse as part of a dynamic process.

As expressed by Louis Adrian Montrose: 'the newer historical criticism is *new* in its refusal of unproblematized distinctions between "literature" and "history," between "text" and "context"; new in resisting a prevalent tendency to posit and privilege a unified and autonomous individual – whether an Author or a Work – to be set against a social or literary background' ('Renaissance,' 6). With such a program, the New Historicism has succeeded in transforming the academic study of English literature; or, as Montrose declares, its theory together chiefly with feminist theory, 'has shaken the foundations of literary studies' ('Professing,' 25). It has done so, as I have argued elsewhere, in the simplest but most profound way possible: it changed the dominant master-metaphor of the Old Historicism. 'Earlier a literary work was held up as an artifact that *reflected* some particular historical context; now it is taken to be inextricably *embedded* in the culture of the age – no longer aesthetically transcendent, or even distinguishably literary, but culturally specific' ('The Renaissance of the Study,' 373).

In the new age of critical theory, which Frye largely spawned, it soon became evident that some are born cultural critics, some achieve greatness as cultural critics, and some have the role of cultural critic thrust upon them. Very roughly estimated, for there is much overlapping and any generalization tends to be parodic, those who were a product of the 1960s and flourished in the 1980s, most notably Stephen Greenblatt and Montrose, belong to the second category in which they have achieved considerable eminence. The revolution in English studies achieved by the New Historicists was a consequence of their dissatisfaction with earlier criticism. Greenblatt has traced his earlier allegiance to New Criticism under W.K. Wimsatt in the late 1960s until he took part in 'a shift away from a criticism centered on "verbal icons" toward a criticism centered on cultural artifacts' (*Learning*, 3). In describing the historical positioning of New Historicism, and particularly its concern with writing as a mode of action indicated by its tendency to hypostatize 'Power,' Montrose notes that academic critics today are impelled 'by a nagging sense of professional, institutional, and political impotence' ('Renaissance,' 11–12). Jean E. Howard has recorded how she grew weary 'of teaching texts as ethereal entities floating above the urgencies and contradictions of history and of seeking in such texts the disinterested expression of a unified truth rather than some articulation of the discontinuities underlying any construction of reality,' and how later she found that 'an analysis of Renaissance culture can be made to speak to the concerns of late twentieth-century culture' ('New Historicism,' 15).

Many critics born before 1940 who continued to write into the 1980s and 1990s found themselves thrust – 'interpellated' is a more apt term – into the third category if they wanted to communicate with the younger generation. A critic who would seem to belong to this category – admittedly borderline because he was born in 1945 – is Gary Waller. Since he was not born a cultural critic, occasionally he looks back wistfully to a simpler age of critical innocence; and yet cultural criticism was not thrust upon him for he readily embraced it, proclaiming as his masters 'Gramsci and Althusser, Benjamin and Brecht, Foucault, Derrida, Hayden White, Harold Bloom, Hans Georg Gadamer, Hans Robert Jauss, Raymond Williams' (418). Yet those who properly belong to this category – to continue to generalize broadly – still find their masters in the traditional critics of English literature. For them, the identity of a literary work remains unproblematic in spite of the claim of cultural critics that literary and non-literary 'texts' are indistinguishably mingled. For them, that claim is the ultimate *trahison des clercs*. Even while speaking the new critical language, their bottom line is that a literary work is *sui generis* being fiction and not fact, a product essentially of the poet's creative imagination rather than of ideology. As a self-contained aesthetic object and therefore in some real measure autonomous, it is distinguished in kind from its sources, background, and the author's life as a thing in itself apart from the Other.

An interesting example of a critic in this category is Harry Berger, Jr. He belongs to the earlier generation – his first book appeared in 1957 – and remains, as he has acknowledged, an 'old New Critic' ('Bodies,' 147). Since he continued to write, he found his generation admonished by the next because 'we did not inscribe our own presuppositions, our ideological missions, our political positions, into our discourse.' He has done his best to adapt but confesses that 'when I use terms like *inscribe* and *discourse* I find myself caught between a feeling of adolescent pride and an impulse to giggle' ('Kidnapped Romance,' 208–9).

The clash of critical generations is illustrated in Montrose's Introduction to the 1988 reprinting of Berger's 1960s Spenser essays in *Revisionary Play*, and I pause over it because it serves to place Frye as a cultural critic. Writing in 1968, Berger allows the sociopolitical study of Spenser by earlier historical critics to be 'solid and important' even though conservative; in rebuttal, Montrose dismisses their scholarship because it 'merely impoverished the text' (8). Yet Montrose is almost as harsh towards Berger, complaining that his writings 'have tended to avoid direct confrontations of sociopolitical issues' though he blames 'the absence of a historically specific sociopolitical dimension' on the time they were written, a time when 'the sociopolitical study of Spenser was epitomized by the pursuit of topical identifications or the cataloguing of commonplaces' (7). He refers, of course, to the earlier historical scholarship that set up a correspondence between characters and their actions in a literary work and people and events in history. In contrast, the New Historicism of which he is the most eloquent theorist sees a work embedded not in history but, as the word used three times in two sentences indicates, in a *sociopolitical* context, both determined by it and actively determining it. In effect, the two are not to be distinguished: texts are inescapably historical; history survives only as texts, a symbiotic relationship which he has formulated chiastically as 'the historicity of texts' and 'the textuality of history' ('Elizabethan Subject,' 305).

Montrose levels two additional charges against Berger: first, that he fails to acknowledge that Spenser is 'a gendered and classed subject acting and acted upon in a particular society'; and second, he does not sufficiently recognize that his interpretation of Spenser is itself 'a historically determinate social act' (7). For Montrose, since 'the human subject is always already inscribed in ideology' (12), possessing only a 'socially constructed subjectivity' – evidently all human beings and all equally, everywhere and at all times – poet and critic alike are 'an effect rather than a source of culture' (7, 11). In line with these charges, Montrose generously praises the 'resolutely secular humanist orientation' of Berger's essays as is evident when he contrasts 'the dominant vertical axis of Dante's narrative with the radical horizonality of Spenser's' (9). He praises Berger's 'humanist emphasis upon the individual and collective capacity of *homo faber* for fashioning both the world and the self' but blames him for his lack of 'a clearly countervailing perspective on the limitations and illusions that make problematic any claim for human agency' (10, 11). While Berger foregrounds 'the unique human subject ... as the locus of meaning and value,' he fails to show that the experiences of that subject 'are always already subject to the pervasive shaping and constraining power of sociocultural codes and categories, institutions and practices' (11). From Montrose's perspective, then, Berger remains more of an unregenerate literary critic than a reborn cultural critic.

As the godfather of critical theory, Frye was notorious for his refusal to acknowledge his offspring. Nor did he make any effort to accommodate his criticism to later critical fashions, declaring in 1975 that his *Anatomy of Criticism* was not revisable, being 'a book of its own period, the mid-fifties, and to try to dress so middle-aged a production in the unisex jeans of the seventies would be an indignity and not a renewal of youth' (SM, 100). Occasionally he was sufficiently provoked to complain about 'the wasteland of critical theory' and 'the present plague of darkness' in 'a confused and claustrophobic battle of methodologies' (MM, 93, 236, 19). Or against critics who place a literary work 'in a vast chaos of *écriture* where there are no boundary lines between literature and anything else in words' (MM, 235–6), saying defiantly in 1984 that 'Keats and Shelley are poets and not philosophers, and Kant and Hegel philosophers and not poets' (MM, 109). It is not until *Words with Power* appeared in 1990 that he took issue with New Historicism although he maintains that he has 'followed [his] own course in this book without reference to other critical schools' (xix). The simplest but far too simple explanation is that having been born in 1912, he was too far removed from the current critical scene to change. I shall argue rather that he did not need to adapt because he is the unique example of our first category: he was born a cultural critic. Cultural criticism was not something thrust upon him or to which he turned because he was dissatisfied with other kinds of criticism but was bred in the bone. It shaped his career as a cultural critic, making him receptive, for example, to the interpenetration of his views on culture with those of Spengler, Blake, and Arnold.[1]

The immediate problem in arguing that Frye was born a cultural critic is with the label itself. Among contemporary cultural theorists, Raymond Williams may be usefully labelled a socialist, Fredric Jameson a Marxist, Alan Sinfield a cultural materialist, and Louis Montrose a New Historicist, but Frye is too encyclopaedic in the range and comprehensiveness of his criticism to be called anything but a literary critic although here 'literary' means the broadly cultural. When Frye claims that 'as long as I have been a literary critic, I have been interested in the relations between a culture and the social conditions under which it is produced' (DG, 15) or when he claims that the critical path he followed all his life directed him to 'the social function of words' (WGS, 170), he seems to have considered himself a cultural critic. Yet for Montrose, whom one may conveniently label a cultural critic, culture *is* the 'historically specific sociopolitical dimension' of both poet and critic, and quite rightly he would be suspicious that Frye's separation of 'culture' from 'social conditions' suggests that for him literature exists apart from the sociopolitical and that 'social' means other than relationships of power. When Frye defines a major literary work as 'a place in which the whole cultural history of the nation that produced it comes into focus' (EI, 123), the term, 'the whole cultural history of the nation,' means something entirely different from the 'historically specific sociopolitical dimension' of the poet and therefore of his work. No New Historicist would allow that there is a 'whole' cultural history, or that culture has its own 'history,' or that there is a whole cultural history of a 'nation.' Nor would such a critic define literary criticism as 'the conscious organizing of a cultural tradition' (GC, xviii).

In his own way, Frye was already a New Historicist in the *Anatomy of Criticism* (1957) by rejecting the one-to-one relationship between a literary work and history posited by the Old Historicists of his time. For him, a literary work does not passively reflect its immediate historical context but actively shapes an extended cultural context with which it is intrinsically, inextricably linked. In place of the New Historicist's dominant metaphor of embeddedness, he commonly speaks of a literary work being *rooted* in its social context – a metaphor that suggests that the work may grow or develop rather than being set in bedrock or enclosed in concrete. Or he speaks of *interpenetration*, 'the interrelating of different subjects in a way that preserves their own autonomy' (SM, x). There is also a difference of focus between him and Montrose, one expanding and the other narrowing. Frye speaks of culture, of culture as a whole, and that whole as part of a larger verbal universe that includes the Word of God; Montrose speaks of history, of history as the sociopolitical, and the sociopolitical as a power struggle. One seeks the larger cultural overview; the other the historically specific. In Montrose's terms as cited above, Frye is equally at fault with Berger in failing to acknowledge that like the poet he is 'a gendered and classed subject acting and acted upon in a particular society' and in seeing himself, as he sees Spenser, 'transcending his own gendered and historically specific subject position' ('Introductory Essay,' 13). In Frye's terms, Montrose is at fault with Berger in contrasting 'the dominant vertical axis of Dante's narrative with the radical horizontality of Spenser's' (9) not because it is untrue of Spenser but because both poets are involved in both dimensions of human existence. Hence to visualize the poet's relation to society, Frye posits a plus sign with the poet as its centre:

The horizontal bar forms the social and ideological conditioning that made him intelligible to his contemporaries, and in fact to himself. The vertical bar is the mythological line of descent from previous poets back to Homer (the usual symbolic starting point) which carries on into our own time. (WP, 47; cf. MM, 85)[2]

The horizontal bar represents the 'historical dimension of ideology' and therefore the poet's 'historicity ... which many critics think makes up the entire area of criticism' (*WP*, 48). Clearly Frye alludes here to the New Historicists and is suggesting that poetry's relation to culture may be understood only by considering its relation both to the poetic tradition and to its social and ideological conditioning.

That diagram lies also at the centre of Frye's critical theory, and it leads to the question that must be asked of him, as of any cultural critic, What is culture? even while granting the force of Raymond Williams's statement that 'culture is one of the two or three most complicated words in the English language' ('Keywords,' 76). There are two supplementary questions inescapable in an age of multiculturalism: Whose culture? Who speaks for it?

II

A brief history of the major influences that fashioned Frye's sense of culture during his formative years may begin when he entered Victoria College in 1929 at the age of seventeen. His imaginative reception to the story of the fall in his Methodist upbringing – a matter to be considered later – led him inexorably to the first book outside the Bible that profoundly affected him: Oswald Spengler's *Der Untergang des Abendlandes*, translated in 1926, 1928 as *The Decline of the West*.[3] It gave him, as he testified, 'a vision of coherence' (*NFC*, 48), 'the sense of the whole of human thought and culture spread out in front of me' (*RW*, 321). In place of the usual chronology of historical accidents in a particular age or country, Spengler's book offered a world-history, *Weltgeschichte*, or rather *Welt als Geschichte*, the World as History, by analysing a number of morphologically similar but 'windowless' cultures, each undergoing an organic cycle of birth, growth, decline, and death. In Spengler's Introduction, Frye may have first encountered a significant use of the word 'culture':

I see, in place of that empty figment of *one* linear history ... the drama of *a number* of mighty Cultures, each springing with primitive strength from the soil of a mother-region to which it remains firmly bound throughout its whole life-cycle ... Each Culture has its own new possibilities of self-expression which arise, ripen, decay, and never return ... I see world-history as a picture of endless formations and transformations, of the marvellous waxing and waning of organic forms. (21–2)

As rephrased by Frye, Spengler 'showed how all the cultural products of a given age ... form a unity that can be felt or intuited, though not demonstrated, a sense of unity that approximates the feeling that a human culture is a single larger body, a giant immersed in time' (*SM*, 111). As Frye has acknowledged, once he perceived that Spengler was a literary or cultural critic, 'my conception of the real area covered by the word "criticism" vastly expanded' (*SM*, 111). As a result, he became a cultural critic in the sense that a literary work was seen to embody the larger culture to which it belongs rather than its particular historical context.

Frye was chiefly interested in Spengler's book because its concept of an organic culture provided a 'grand narrative' or myth of a fall that made sense of an overwhelming number of otherwise unconnected facts. His Methodist upbringing had shown him that the Bible occupied the centre of authority in society because it contains the most significant stories out of which all verbal discourses, but especially all literary works, descend. These stories, which he calls myths, had consolidated into an encyclopaedic, canonical body that expresses the essential concerns of Western culture. He calls them myths because they 'strike their roots into a specific culture' (*CP*, 35) and together form a vast mythological universe within which we live. Armed with this vision, he realized that cultural criticism, unlike historical criticism, need not belittle a literary work: 'to make a great writer gain rather than lose by a historical treatment takes a sense of the interlocking relevance of all the literature of his age, conceived as a unit of culture complete in itself' (*NFCL*, 152).

Frye may have been influenced by Spengler in *Fearful Symmetry* (1947), for he avoided the usual scholarly effort to explain Blake's works in terms of biography or historical context or to interpret them by close reading in order to place him 'in his historical *and cultural* context' (5, my italics). Yet Blake supplanted Spengler, for Frye was taught by him to see culture not in the Spenglerian terms of 'soul' and 'destiny,' but as 'the totality of imaginative power, of which the matrix is art' (*FS*, 89), and to read major literary works in the terms Blake uses to describe the New Jerusalem as 'the total form of all human culture and civilization' (91). Such identification of culture with the creative imagination revealed in the arts made Frye a proponent of nineteenth-century Romanticism, which countered the medieval-Renaissance Christian mythological universe by regarding the forms of human civilization 'as man-made rather than as God-made' (*FI*, 3). In *Fables of Identity*, he claims that 'the imaginative or creative force in the mind is what has produced everything that we call culture and civilization. It is the power of transforming a sub-human physical world into a world with a human shape and meaning, a world not of rocks and trees but of cities and gardens, not an environment but a home' (152).[4]

Three modern writers who are important in the cultural history to which Frye belongs are Matthew Arnold, F.R. Leavis, and Raymond Williams. All three are connected by their concern with the traditional 'social contract' according to which, as Frye explains, 'society precedes the individual, who is born involuntarily into it, and is forced to accept the heritage of a mental and bodily conditioning which he can alter only within strictly prescribed limits' (RW, 209). Individuals are willing to surrender certain freedoms and rights for the general social good, with the consequence that society rather than the individuals who compose it becomes the source of authority. In his interpretation of this contract, Frye may be called a conservative because he believed that 'the individual grows out of the group, not the other way round' (DG, 186) and that only by adjusting to society is genuine individuality possible: 'he is not a real individual until his energy flows freely into his social relations' (SM, 39). Yet he was also a radical because, following Rousseau and Marx, he believed that the individual should become fully aware of his social conditioning and do something about it. His double commitment led him to support a new social contract, which he associated with culture as defined by Arnold.

In *Culture and Anarchy*, Arnold defines culture as 'the best that has been thought and known in the world' (79). One may suspect, of course, that by 'the best' he means the best that was thought and known by the educated Victorian middle-class to which he belonged and for which he spoke. However the term may be defined and whatever his political agenda, Arnold upholds culture as a cohesive force that binds all individuals into a society through their shared concerns and values, as the context for his statement indicates:

[Culture] seeks to do away with classes; to make the best that has been thought and known in the world current everywhere; to make all men live in an atmosphere of sweetness and light, where they may use ideas, as it uses them itself, freely, – nourished, and not bound by them.

Since culture is not primarily intellectual but involves 'all sides of our humanity,' he distinguishes between our ordinary selves which 'do not carry us beyond the ideas and wishes of the class to which we happen to belong,' leaving us 'separate, personal, at war,' from our best selves by which 'we are united, impersonal, at harmony' (99). While much in this concept of culture appealed to Frye, his comment in *Fearful Symmetry* that 'Arnold's view of both culture and society is conservative, traditional and evolutionary; Blake's is radical, apocalyptic and revolutionary' (90) reveals where his critical allegiances lie.

Leavis inherited Arnold's concept of culture but was more gloomy about its future. In an early pamphlet, significantly entitled *Mass Civilization and Minority Culture*, he begins by citing Arnold on culture but goes on to lament that 'the prospects of culture ... are very dark. There is the less room for hope in that a standardized civilization is rapidly enveloping the whole world' (169). For Leavis, the only hope was to identify culture with the values of an intellectual élite: 'in their keeping ... is the language, the changing idiom, upon which fine living depends, and without which distinction of spirit is thwarted and incoherent. By "culture" I mean the use of such a language' (145). As a consequence, his criticism alternates between nostalgia for a lost organic society, which never existed, and denunciation of the present 'technologico-Benthamite' age. In their day, Leavis and Frye were polarized as critics on the importance of value judgments and critical theory but Leavis was Frye's ally in his vigorous defence of English studies, and within it literary criticism as a discipline, of the university as the creative centre of civilization, and especially of the place of the literary tradition within culture.[5]

Raymond Williams is a central figure in any attempt to understand Frye's concept of culture though not because of any influence. As far as I know, Frye never refers to him or to his major book, *Culture and Society*, which appeared one year after the *Anatomy*. Yet Williams said that Frye was 'one of the four or five people, in contemporary cultural studies, who need to be faced because of the solidity and influence of their work.'[6] The link between them would seem to be Arnold. In response to T.S. Eliot's definition of culture as the development of a whole society that includes 'all the characteristic activities and interests of a people,' such as Derby Day, a cup final, the dog races, and the music of Elgar (*Notes*, 31), Williams expanded his definition to include 'the whole way of living of a people' (*Culture*, 83): the forms of production along with consumption, such as coal mining and the London Transport. As a Marxist, he espoused a 'cultural materialism' according to which culture includes 'all forms of signification, including quite centrally writing, within the actual means and conditions of their production' (*Culture*, 210). For Williams and Frye, Arnold would seem to be hopelessly élitist, middle-class, and reactionary; yet Williams concludes, and Frye would agree, that 'we shall, if we are wise, continue to listen to him, and, when the time comes to reply, we can hardly speak better than in his own best spirit' (128).

This brief history is summed up in Frye's 'Levels of Cultural Identity' (1989). His first, elementary level, 'the sense of custom or life-style: the distinctive way that people eat, dress, talk, marry, play games, produce goods, and the like' (*EAC*, 168), is identified by Williams as culture itself in his description of 'the whole way of living of a people.' Greenblatt expands that description in defining culture as social practices that are historically specific to the age of late capitalism: 'a culture is a particular network of negotiations for the exchange of material goods, ideas, and – through institutions like enslavement, adoption, or marriage – people' ('Culture,' 229. Characteristically, he writes of 'a culture' rather than culture.) To this level Frye adds a middle level that relates to society rather than to the individual: '[it] is the product of tradition and history, and consists of the distinctive political, economic, religious, and other institutions that shape a nation's life and give direction to the main currents of its ideology' (*EAC*, 168). This level of culture as a shared heritage shows the influence of Arnold's educational contract which binds individuals into a society. It leads Frye to call culture 'the social manifestation of the educational system' (*CDC*, 11), and speak of a classless society as 'the final embodiment of culture' (*DG*, 93).

For Frye there is a third level of culture, which, characteristic for him, he calls 'an upper level': here culture is defined as 'the product of a nation's specialized creative powers' (*EAC*, 169). Greenblatt adds to his definition of culture cited above that 'Anthropologists are centrally concerned with a culture's kinship system – its conception of family relationships, its prohibitions of certain couplings, its marriage rules,' and adds to this sentence that they are also concerned with a culture's narratives: 'its myth, folktales, and sacred stories.' Just such narratives in their descent from myth provide the basis for Frye's third level, one that leads him to define culture as 'the indestructible core of a human society, so far as it is a human society and not a mere aggregate of atoms in a human mass' (*CDC*, 10). As suggested above, this level of creativity may be traced to Coleridge, for whom culture is cultivation in the sense that the arts create a level of nature higher than the merely physical. It provided Frye with one of his most dominant themes: that we do not live directly in nature but 'inside the construct of culture or civilization' (*EAC*, 146).

Cultural critics recognize that a society shares a dominant ideology which preserves its deepest concerns, ideas, assumptions, feelings, hopes, anxieties, beliefs, and values, the authority of which it seeks to legitimate through its social institutions and for the sake of its preservation is prepared to uphold by whatever means necessary. The dominant Elizabethan ideology, for example, was called the Elizabethan World Picture by E.M.W. Tillyard; and in terms which he would endorse, Montrose says it 'inscribed the English commonwealth within a divinely created and providentially directed cosmos' that was 'metaphysically legitimated' ('Elizabethan Subject,' 308). Frye also recognizes the central importance of society's ideology though he prefers to call it a social mythology because it existed as a canon of stories or myths or a mythology until society projected it as an ideology by translating its metaphors into ideas and beliefs in order to rationalize support for its authority.

As I have traced elsewhere,[7] but include here because it distinguishes him as a cultural critic, Frye calls society's mythology 'the myth of concern' which 'crystallizes in the centre of a culture,' and which, with 'its roots in religion,' serves to bind the community to common acts and assumptions (CP, 35, 36). In his later writings, he distinguishes between a primary mythology which he identifies with literature and a secondary mythology which he identifies with ideology.[8] The first addresses the individual's primary concerns: 'that life is better than death, freedom better than slavery, happiness better than misery' (MM, 119); the second, society's concerns: the anxiety to maintain its authority and prestige by preserving its hierarchy and class structure, its religious and legal institutions, and its defence against all rival ideologies (see MM, 88). A literary work is 'an ideological product, an expression of the culture of the age' but the critic's task is 'to reveal in such works the primary myth underlying the ideological surface' (MM, 268).

For the New Historicist, such as Montrose, the human subject being a construct and not an essence is, as noted earlier, 'always already inscribed in ideology' – a powerful metaphor which implies the permanent branding of a slave. The inference that we are embedded in a particular, historically specific culture has its parallel in Frye's no less radical claim: 'nobody can create, think or even act outside the mythology of his time' (DG, 185), though he allows exceptions: Rousseau, Marx, Darwin, Freud, and Einstein 'who have changed our mythology' (RW, 189, 323) and, of course, his spiritual preceptor, Blake. Frye allows that poets 'normally reflect the ideologies of their own times, and certainly they are always conditioned by their historical and cultural surroundings,' but he adds that 'there has always been a sense of something else that eludes this kind of communication' (*MM*, 21). In part, he is referring to the vertical bar noted above, the mythological line of descent to which all poems belong. Within mythology, poetry creates a counter-mythology which allows it to escape the paralysing, alienating, and dehumanizing tyranny of the present. While for Greenblatt, a poem may subvert ideology by exposing its contradictions, it does so only in a way that may be contained; for Frye, its content may be a product of ideology but not its mythological structure, with the consequence that it transcends ideology.

III

The Old Historicists simply assumed that any work may be studied as a product of the author's life and times. It would not surprise them that E.R. Curtius, for example, should acknowledge that *European Literature and the Latin Middle Ages*, published in 1948, 'is not the product of purely scholarly interests. It grew out of vital urges and under the pressure of a concrete historical situation' (x). Yet they assumed that as scholars they attempted to present facts about history impersonally, impartially, and objectively, and they condemned any scholar whose work revealed personal bias or prejudice. In opposition, the New Historicists claim that all scholarship is inescapably subjective because we are all equally products of our own age. Howard writes: 'first of all, it seems necessary to abandon the myth of objectivity and to acknowledge that all historical knowledge is produced from a partial and a positioned vantage point' (22-3). Even the critical method of the New Historicists was seen to be a product of its age, the political turbulence among students in Reagan's California of the 1960s and 1970s, as Montrose has spelled out: 'the reorientation in the field [of literary studies] under way since at least the beginning of the 1980s is largely the work of scholars who were students during the turbulent '60s, and who have responded to the radically altered sociopolitical climate of the current decade ... with intellectual work that is explicitly sociopolitical in its manifest historical content' ('Professing,' 25).

New Historicists have made us aware of our own historicity by adapting to their purposes the *ad hominem* argument that anything we say about the ideology of an earlier work is largely a product of our own ideology. As expressed by Montrose: 'our professional practice, like our subject matter, is a production of ideology: By this I mean not merely that it bears the traces of the professor's values, beliefs, and experiences – his or her socially constructed subjectivity – but also that it actively instantiates those values, beliefs and experiences' ('Professing,' 16). Hence critics in the 1980s found discontinuities, discord, disruption, and division in earlier cultures because they held that just these qualities characterized their own culture at the time of the Cold War with its threat of nuclear annihilation. Greenblatt has acknowledged that 'it is all too easy for us to perceive the possibility of ironic dissent ... the difficult task is to perceive the celebration of order' (*Learning*, 110). That task has proven far too difficult for many modern critics whose writings mirror only themselves, as Frye complains in the course of defending a liberal, that is, a liberating education: 'there is nothing liberating in merely seeing our own prejudices and stereotypes in a mirror, or in kidnapping the culture of the past to make it conform to them' (*DG*, 93).

Frye called *Fearful Symmetry* 'a very anxious, troubled book' because 'it's written with the horror of Nazism just directly in front of it all the time,' and said that 'the most fruitful part' of *Anatomy of Criticism* was written 'in that period of hope between 1945 and 1950' ('Interview,' 41). Salusinszky has shown that *The Critical Path* is 'inseparable from its own social context: that is, a profound crisis in the universities, reflecting the broader social crisis over the war in Vietnam, the crisis that had been threatening to tear apart the cohesive ideology of the Western liberal societies' (76). Yet Frye's writing relates more directly to his life than to his times, as he acknowledged: 'everything I write I consider autobiography, although nobody else would' (*OE*, 211). In a 1981 interview, he said that 'I'm really building everything around a highly personal vision, a vision that I think I've had since I was a child,' adding that 'consciousness of it came in various stages. I suppose it began to take its present form in my undergraduate years at university' (*WGS*, 219). In an interview four years later he explains that vision in terms of the general human condition:

I suppose I'm really saying what is true of almost all members of the human race, that they get what I call their archetypes in their childhood and then spend the rest of their lives elaborating them in various ways. I was brought up in a middle-class, non-conformist environment. I have been more or less writing footnotes to the assumptions I acquired at the age of three or so ever since. (*WGS*, 269)

He felt strongly that 'you keep revolving around your childhood all your life' (*WGS*, 263) but as a child of 'three or so' just what did he know? What could he have known even implicitly about those assumptions?

Possibly Frye's claim may have been influenced in retrospect by the Platonic theory of anamnesis: that we do not acquire knowledge in later life but recollect what we already know but have forgotten. A more likely explanation is a concept that he preferred to anamnesis, Søren Kierkegaard's 'repetition,' which is 'not the simple repeating of an experience, but the recreating of it which redeems or awakens it to life' (*AC*, 345). Certainly there is no better explanation of the many books that followed the *Anatomy* not by repeating his earlier insights into the place of literature within culture but by their creative repetition in a new context. The importance of repetition in this sense is suggested by his definition of knowledge as 'a constant recreation of old knowledge' (*DG*, 183); by the central place of convention in his criticism; by his remark that recreation is 'the constructing of human culture and civilization' (*CR*, 54). Like other artists, the poet does not imitate fallen physical nature but recreates the nature that God had first created, thereby renewing it. In *Creation and Recreation*, Frye suggests that Kierkegaard's concept derives from biblical typology: the fulfilment of the type in the future antitype 'is at once a contrast and a complement to the Platonic view of knowledge as recollection of the past' (61). One may infer, then, that he regarded each of his books as a creative repetition of the assumptions he acquired at the age of three or so. But what were those assumptions?

Frye was very much aware that by virtue of birth he was a product of a specific society: a male born into an Anglo-Saxon, lower middle-class, liberal, Methodist, rural Eastern Canadian family.[9] It was a nonconformist upbringing because Methodism is a Protestant denomination characterized by its insistence on private religious experience based on the Bible rather than, as in Anglicanism, the public expression of common doctrinal belief based on the Thirty-Nine Articles. As he explains in *The Double Vision*: 'in Methodism, even of the episcopal variety to which my family belonged, there was an emphasis on religious experience as distinct from doctrine and on very early exposure to the story element in the Bible' (3). Since he believed that people derive their assumptions from stories ('Interview,' 31), presumably his assumptions as a child would have been derived from the encompassing biblical story of creation, fall, redemption, and restoration, and in particular from the story of Adam and Eve who lived in a higher state of nature until, losing paradise through disobedience to God, they were forced into the lower world of fallen nature. Yet since he calls these assumptions archetypes shared by almost all members of the human race and not just by Methodists, they are not culturally specific but multicultural and therefore related to the basic concerns of the primary mythology as noted above: 'that life is better than death, freedom better than slavery, happiness better than misery.'

A further clue to the nature of these assumptions may be found in Frye's reference to a 'highly personal vision' which he says he thinks he has had since a child. We may only guess its nature; and my guess, which I infer from the visionary element that informs his criticism, is that it was a typically Wesleyan moment of illumination: the sense of a sudden awakening or rebirth gained through a glimpse of a higher, real world of a redeemed nature to which we rightfully belong rather than the unreal world of fallen nature to which we have been exiled. Such a vision would explain a number of qualities characteristic of his criticism: its evangelical zeal and strongly apocalyptic urgency; his critical posture of always 'standing back' from a literary work in its culture; as a loner, his detachment from the social ideology that encompasses our lives; his fascination with the creative imagination especially of poets who reveal that higher nature; and his commitment to the concerns of the primary mythology. It would explain also why throughout his many books and articles he always upholds individual dignity, liberty, equality, and fraternity.

The assumptions implicit in such a vision are those of the primary mythology: that there is a life of freedom and happiness above and beyond our present life that leads only to death. They would not be consciously known to a child of three or so but they were there and needed only to be recollected by being recreated in his books. He wrote footnotes to these assumptions because he hoped that any member of his world-wide audiences would share them, for they express the concerns of a mythology shared by all human beings who by being members of the human race share the same identity. Frye is *the* cultural critic of our generation because he is the voice of that primary mythology expressed in poetry. What is special about him is his ability to awaken in us the mythology we already know. As he explains in *The Great Code*, his strategy as a teacher is 'to get the student to recognize what he already potentially knows, which includes breaking up the powers of repression in his mind that keep him from knowing what he knows' (xv). That helps to explain why in his time he was the most popular literary critic in the world – popular in the sense in which he applies that term to literature: one who requires the minimum of special education from a reader. It may also explain why he used the *lingua franca* appropriate to a 'public address' format (*WP*, xix) in order to address his audiences about matters that concern their common humanity.

Frye's hope that he may play a role in holding traditional culture together and passing it on to the next age (*WGS*, 268) may well be fulfilled because the multiculturalism characteristic of his criticism will have its place in an increasingly globalized world.

NOTES

1 On this subject, see White, 'Frye's place.'
2 Here I draw upon Hamilton, 'Northrop Frye and the New,' 77.
3 Here I draw upon my account of Spengler's influence on Frye's cultural history in *Northrop Frye*, 55–9.
4 Frye's frequent pairing of 'culture and civilization' suggests the influence of Coleridge, whom Frye later singles out as one who gave him a sense of 'what literature is doing in the world' (*WGS*, 285). For Coleridge, culture is the harmonious development of those qualities and faculties that characterize our humanity in contrast to civilization or what is often called the standard of living. See especially Williams, *Keywords*, 81. Once culture is set up as distinct from the lived experience of ordinary people, it becomes a critique of civilization, and heightens the tension between the social élite and the masses.
5 In *Northrop Frye*, I consider some connections between Frye's criticism and Leavis's but the matter deserves extended study.
6 As I note in *Northrop Frye*, 246 n. 20.
7 See 'Legacy,' 9–10.
8 This matter is treated by Salusinszky. See also White, 'Ideology.'
9 For a fuller treatment, see my 'Northrop Frye as a Canadian.'

WORKS CITED

Arnold, Matthew. *Culture and Anarchy.* Edited by Stefan Collini. Cambridge: Cambridge University Press, 1993.
Berger, Harry, Jr. 'Bodies and Texts.' *Representations* 17 (1987): 144–56.
– '"Kidnapped Romance": Discourse in *The Faerie Queene.*' In *Unfolded Tales: Essays on Renaissance Romance*, edited by George M. Logan and Gordon Teskey. Ithaca: Cornell University Press, 1989. 208–56.

- *Revisionary Play: Studies in the Spenserian Dynamics.* Berkeley: University of California Press, 1988.

Curtius, E.R. *European Literature and the Latin Middle Ages.* Translated by Willard R. Trask. New York: Pantheon, 1953.

Eliot, T.S. *Notes towards the Definition of Culture.* London: Faber & Faber, 1948.

Frye, Northrop. Interview with Imre Salusinszky. In *Criticism in Society.* London: Routledge, 1987. 26–42.

Greenblatt, Stephen. 'Culture.' In *Critical Terms for Literary Study,* edited by Frank Lentricchia and Thomas McLaughlin. Chicago: University of Chicago Press, 1990. 225–32.

- *Learning to Curse: Essays in Early Modern Culture.* New York: Routledge, 1990.

Hamilton, A.C. 'The Legacy of Frye's Criticism in Culture, Religion, and Society.' In *The Legacy of Northrop Frye,* edited by Alvin A. Lee and Robert D. Denham. Toronto: University of Toronto Press, 1994. 3–14.

- *Northrop Frye: Anatomy of His Criticism.* Toronto: University of Toronto Press, 1990.

- 'Northrop Frye and the New Historicism.' *Recherches sémiotiques / Semiotic Inquiry* 13 (1993): 73–83.

- 'Northrop Frye as a Canadian Critic.' *University of Toronto Quarterly* 62 (1993): 309–22.

- 'The Renaissance of the Study of the English Literary Renaissance.' *English Literary Renaissance* 25 (1995): 372–87.

Howard, Jean E. 'The New Historicism in Renaissance Studies.' *English Literary Renaissance* 16 (1986): 13–43.

Leavis, F.R. 'Mass Civilization and Minority Culture.' In *Education and the University.* Cambridge: Cambridge University Press, 1979. (First pub. 1943.) 141–71.

Montrose, Louis Adrian. 'The Elizabethan Subject and the Spenserian Text.' In *Literary Theory / Renaissance Texts,* edited by Patricia Parker and David Quint. Baltimore: Johns Hopkins University Press, 1986. 303–40.

- 'Introductory Essay.' In *Revisionary Play: Studies in the Spenserian Dynamics,* by Harry Berger, Jr. Berkeley: University of California Press, 1988. 1–16.

- 'Professing the Renaissance: The Poetics and Politics of Culture.' In *The New Historicism,* edited by H. Aram Veeser. New York: Routledge, 1989. 15–36.

- 'Renaissance Literary Studies and the Subject of History.' *English Literary Renaissance* 16 (1986): 5–12.

Salusinszky, Imre. 'Frye and Ideology.' In *The Legacy of Northrop Frye,* edited by Alvin A. Lee and Robert D. Denham. Toronto: University of Toronto Press, 1994. 76–83.

Spengler, Oswald. *The Decline of the West*. Translated by Charles Francis Atkinson. New York: Knopf, 1939.

Waller, Gary F. 'Author, Text, Reading, Ideology: Towards a Revisionist Literary History of the Renaissance.' *Dalhousie Review* 61 (1981): 405–25.

White, Hayden. 'Frye's Place in Contemporary Cultural Studies.' In *The Legacy of Northrop Frye*, edited by Alvin A. Lee and Robert D. Denham. Toronto: University of Toronto Press, 1994. 28–39.

– 'Ideology and Counterideology in the *Anatomy*.' In *Visionary Poetics: Essays on Northrop Frye's Criticism*, edited by Robert D. Denham and Thomas Willard. New York: Peter Lang, 1991. 101–11.

Williams, Raymond. *Culture and Society: 1780–1950*. London: Chatto & Windus, 1960.

– *Keywords: A Vocabulary of Culture and Society*. London: Fontana, 1976.

– *Writing in Society*. London: Verso Editions, 1983.

Reading Frye in Hungary: The Frustrations and Hopes of a Frye Translator

PÉTER PÁSZTOR

I

Reading Frye in Hungary seems almost to be a story of non-reading. So far, no serious study has appeared that addresses both the theoretical and practical implications of Frye's critical system with regard to Hungarian literature and criticism. However, the story of Frye in Hungary may still prove to be interesting and important from a cultural-historical point of view.

The way in which I have come to this story is that exactly ten years ago I proposed the publication in Hungarian of *The Great Code*. The publisher accepted the idea and contracted me to do the translation. But just before I got down to serious work, the contract was annulled. In 1992 I managed to persuade the very same publisher – Hungary's most important publisher of literature in translation – to renew the contract. This time I jumped headlong into the laborious task, hoping that this would ward off the further frustration of another cancelled contract. I submitted the completed manuscript early in 1993, and to my utter surprise managed to talk the publisher into doing *Words with Power* too. But while I was working on *Words with Power*, there was complete silence about *The Great Code*: instead of the printed book, all I got were promises, and I completed *Words with Power* with little hope of ever seeing either book in print. The same fate seemed to be in store for me as for József Szili, an eminent literary theoretician and translator of René Wellek and others, who had completed the Hungarian version of the *Anatomy* in 1991, but whose hopes of ever getting his manuscript published had waned. Then, in August 1995, the publisher told me he would bring out *The Great Code* in December, but not *Words with Power*; I could do what I liked with the manuscript. In January 1996, I got another final promise on *The Great Code*, for June. I was sceptical, but now, as of 1 July 1996, we at last have a Hungarian Frye (see Pásztor).

Why have the Frye translations suffered such a plight? The immediate answer, one always invoked by publishers, is the economic situation. Because of weak consumer buying-power, publishers cannot price such books to cover the cost of publishing them, so they are put off until the losses can be made up from the profits generated by Stephen Kings, or donations from benefactors. Yet, despite all this, Eliade is brought out in Hungarian, Roger Scruton is brought out, Derrida is brought out – while Frye, one of the most quoted authors in the humanities, has to wait ten years. I am conscious that speculations as to what went wrong on the part of the baffled translator – who expended so much labour on rendering Frye's thoughts, so deeply and consciously rooted in English, into a language utterly different – might sound somewhat paranoiac. But they are characteristically Eastern European.

While the delay probably had nothing to do with the quality of the translation, there were many difficult and problematic passages. The title *The Great Code*, for instance, would, if translated word for word, sound awful, and mean something more like *The Great Supermarket Bar-Code*; so it was rendered as *Double Mirror*. This may be disputed, as Frye originally uses the metaphor for the typological relationship between the Old and New Testaments. The publisher and the editor, however, liked it very much because they saw it as rather eye-catching, and therefore more suited to their purposes. And I myself am inclined to think that in Hungarian it is a solution that at least tries to resonate as heavily as the original. On the one hand Frye clearly extends the typological relationship between the two parts of the Bible beyond the Bible, and thus on to the relationship between the Bible and literature, so it is not altogether misleading. On the other hand it alludes to one of Frye's central theses: that literature does not reflect 'life,' but a society's mythology, and that literature, like the Bible, is therefore primarily self-referential. Here I experienced a feeling common among translators, that what we lose on the swings we make up on the roundabouts: I may have had to give up philological exactitude, but I gained a new element in meaning.

Another vexing translation issue concerned the very last paragraph of the book, where we are told that the Bible or other great cultural achievements grow hair after having been locked in a mill to grind our prejudices and aggressions.[1] This is meant to work as a kind of Zen-

Buddhist paradox to heighten the consciousness of the reader, and it probably does achieve such an effect after one or two readings; but after several readings with the aim of rephrasing it in another language, it increasingly smacked of mixed metaphor.

In fact, I have asked several native English speakers whether this hair-growing was a mixed metaphor or not, and even though some of them tried to assure me that, if the context was established, there was no reason why the Bible could not do so, I still find it awkward: in Hungarian expository prose a book growing hair is simply inconceivable. I found a further oddity in a cultural achievement's being locked in a mill to *grind* our aggressions and prejudices, though 'grind' here is probably meant to convey something like 'repeat' or 'rotate,' as with a prayer wheel.[2] What strengthens my feeling of awkwardness even more is that Frye is seldom like this. His chapters often end in a similarly heightened tone – a metaphor, or a paradox, designed to exemplify, and lead the reader through, his different levels of meaning, from the literal to the anagogic – but nowhere else in his work have I come across anything open to such doubt. Frye's metaphors are generally as congruous and clear as you would expect of a writer of expository prose with a highly refined literary sensibility.

Another characteristic of Frye's style in *The Great Code* (and, I think, only in *The Great Code*) that I found rather difficult to cope with during translation was the way in which he puts down his ideas in loosely connected, sometimes even disconnected paragraphs, leaving the reader (and even more the translator) desperately searching for links. This was probably an outcome of the pressures of writing on a subject that Frye had been working on all his critical life; he had an enormous amount of material to handle, both theoretical and practical, of which, presumably, he wished to lose little; so he compressed, and compressed so thoroughly that he ended up with a relatively slim volume for an opus of such scope.[3] This, however, is most certainly not a fatal flaw, if it is one at all: the unexpected popularity, and even the critical reviews, of the book attest to that. But while working on the text, trying to grasp how one passage evolved from the other, I could often sympathize with Frye's own feeling while writing that he had been like Milton's Satan journeying through chaos (*GC*, xxiii).

All of this would be of little significance, just a trade secret of translation, if the translator had not been compelled to wonder why his Frye had been waiting so long to appear. These are normally issues that it is the task of the translator to resolve one way or another (or not resolve at all), and keep quiet about. From the particulars of his work he can seldom draw conclusions of import. But when his work remains unpublished for so long, his self-probings and self-justifications may have a larger cultural bearing.

Obviously, any book that is to be published in another language undergoes a process of assimilation to the prevailing cultural discourses in the intended language. Such a process is bound to be more delicate in the case of a prose treatise like Frye's than in the case of a postmodern metafiction. Now, Hungarian is a culture divided by warring discourses. How is the translator to place Frye among these divisions? With which cultural discourse is he to align him? Among the many divisions in Hungarian culture that had to be directly faced in the course of translation were the denominational differences in theological language. Basic terms have different Catholic and Protestant variants; even the primary term 'Christian,' together with several, mostly Old Testament, names, are spelled and pronounced differently. It is staggering for anyone to learn that a name like Isaiah, resonant with so much religious and cultural significance, has in Hungarian a Catholic and a Protestant version (Izajás and Esaiás), both, however differently, assimilating the Hebrew name to the Hungarian sound system. This state of terminological affairs is a result of the unusually long-lasting Protestant–Catholic animosity in Hungary, which was never really resolved by the conflicting parties, merely subsumed by violent secularization under the Communists. Now that recent Hungarian history has blunted the cutting edge of this conflict, people in secular quarters, feeling that the discordant terminology is anachronistic and confusing, have been calling for a unified terminology. This would be impossible except by fiat, because on the one hand structures and allusions from five hundred years of religious and cultural history cannot simply be discarded, and on the other hand certain groups would justly feel discriminated against. A characteristic Frygian solution would be to let things fossilize, as he says concerning the male metonymy in English (*WP*, 190). But then what course should a translator of Frye take? Frye clearly strives for catholicity – he is far beyond denominational divergences – but at the same time he springs from, and continues, a Protestant tradition. It was clear from the very outset that the Protestant Bible (translated by Gáspár Károli in 1590) had to be used, because it has had a role in Hungarian culture similar to that of the Authorized Version in English culture. I could then easily have resorted to saying that the use of the Károli Bible demands an accompanying Protestant terminology; but would this not push

Frye's catholicity in a partisan direction? What is more, because the Protestant–Catholic animosity is by and large anachronistic, the secular reader, to whom the book is primarily addressed, might find this option rather provincial. So after all I used a rather eclectic theological terminology, mingling Protestant and Catholic variants. But while trying to make up my mind about an adequate solution, and when my self-examination inclined me towards a partisan Protestant option, I had thought that it could be justified by one of the great morals of the Frye Code: that though it matters where one comes from, what really matters is where one goes. Nothing would exemplify this better than a partisanly Protestant discourse arriving at an all-encompassing catholicity. Right or wrong, however, the translator has had to make concessions, to pay heed to a politics of culture.

II

Thus, not finding sufficient grounds for the delay of the Hungarian Frye in the economic (ir)rationale of the post-Communist transition, or, hopefully, in the quality of the translation, we might begin to search for reasons in the climate of Hungarian literary discourse and culture in general. The first question that presses itself is why, in fact, plans for publishing Frye in Hungary were proposed only as late as the mid-1980s. The ideological commissars definitely did not forbid the reading of Frye in Hungarian. The publishing policy of the authorities since the mid-1960s was that practically any non-Marxist book could be brought out, as long as it was not openly anti-Marxist and by a Hungarian (or Eastern European) author. This, of course, did not in the least mean that the great masterpieces of Western thought could find their way easily into print in Hungarian. Editors had to engage in horrifying and often unending ideological tugs-of-war, devising elaborate (and schizophrenic) mechanisms, like the so-called 'red tail': the afterword explaining to the reader how he or she should read the 'notable bourgeois idealist' work with proper Marxist-Leninist eyes. Granted sufficient and enduring pressure by intellectuals, from the late-1960s on many important works were published; editors could even allow themselves a certain degree of complacency in regard to the number and scope of significant Western books available. However, Northrop Frye was not among them, even though in Romania and Yugoslavia translations of the *Anatomy* had appeared in 1972 and 1979 respectively.

Frye does not seem to have been wanted in Hungary in the 1970s and early 1980s – it would hardly make sense to expect any influence by him earlier than that – but it would be too easy to claim that his visionary poetics couldn't have found a place where Marxism dominated literary scholarship. As in the case of publishing policies, in scholarship the situation was complicated.[4] There is no denying that Marxism gained ascendancy over literary scholarship by sheer force. However, as a result of both the post-1956 leniency on the part of the authorities and the high-aesthetics of Georg von Lukács, Marxist scholarship could maintain a scholarly standard by the 1970s. (This was not exactly the case in some of the other Communist countries, where criticism hardly meant more than politburo propaganda somewhat disguised in literary terms.) Hungarian Marxist critics could boast a more or less coherent literary terminology expounded in a scholarly-theoretical language. By the 1970s Hungarian literary scholarship had produced a large body of work, in all major fields, the intellectual force of which was at times brilliant. The trouble was that much of the brilliance served to foster the Marxian literary stance, which thus became a full-fledged critical universe. And equipped with all the necessary props, including critical canons and a literary canon moulded to its requirements, this critical universe took on an immense ability to assimilate. The system was vicious: the critic with scholarly aims had to face it, and facing it meant absorbing the idiom, the language, and the basic assumptions, which in their turn determined conclusions.

In such intellectual circumstances, critics who wanted to be worthy of the name could only point out directions, ways of escape, or else find minor enclaves where they could become a saving remnant of the traditions of European scholarship in the face of Marxist canons of mimesis, realism, sociopolitical content, and authorial intent. What were some of these escape routes and enclaves?

The most common route was positivism. But establishing the positive facts of the discipline still left it prey to ideology: more often than not what you got were scores of facts, mostly historical and biographical, that left the real questions to be asked and answered by the established order. In one respect, however, positivism could pretend to an opposition of sorts: Communist bowdlerization had corrupted even the classics, and new corrected critical editions were prepared from the 1970s on.[5]

But facts could be used by others too. The first and only serious scholarly attempt to rival Lukácsian aesthetics came about as a result of the activities of a literary historian and educator, Béla G. Németh, who, together with his students, began to give close readings to Hungarian and European classics using methods borrowed from New Criticism, Structuralism, Russian Formalism, and German poetics. However, the labours of these 'textual critics' could not achieve a breakthrough at the time: the literary authorities simply trampled their work underfoot.

In addition to being resisted by the authorities and by the exponents of positivism, the work of these critics was resisted by literary elements that also strove to express their independence. Hungarian literature has a highly national quality, precisely because in the lack of independence through the ages national aspirations were expressed, not by communal bodies and politicians, but by the poets. Certain literary canons were quite naturally formed by such aspirations, and upholding them under Communism could mean an independent outlook from the ruling 'internationalist' idiom. Now, critics of this inclination feared that the textual critics intended just another attack on these traditional canons.

Equally vehement resistance to the textual critical enterprise came from the so-called literary essayists. Though looked upon somewhat derisively by scholarly critics, these essayists, often leading writers and poets, have had an immensely important role in Hungarian letters and literary scholarship because they, more than anyone else, with their highly poetic and metaphorical language, could maintain their independence from the ruling idiom. Now these writers feared that the autonomy of literature was under siege again by extra-literary forces.

In the late 1970s and early 1980s these groups were all trying to assert themselves – which was in no way a normal or easy task, given that the formation of intellectual circles and schools, with their representative magazines, was strictly forbidden by the authorities. This desperate need for self-assertion wanted supportive ideas, of which Northrop Frye could offer very few. His basic principles either ran contrary to each of their positions, or sought to find places for them within a larger scheme (yet again unacceptable for groups labouring to throw off the yoke of another 'larger scheme'). So it is not surprising that we find no significant recognition or account of Frye's work in Hungarian at the time. We do, however, find sporadic references to his 'valuable insights' – which may sound a little déjà vu for students of Frye – along with various kinds of misreadings that may themselves be culturally significant.

One among a number of possible examples is a paper entitled 'Myth Criticism, or the Myth of Deep Structure,' by Zsolt Virágos, which is a highly polemical overview of American myth-criticism that refers to Leslie Fiedler and others, but mostly to Frye, citing several of his works. The argument is that seeing myths in works of art is justified, but seeing myths as the source of works of art, as myth critics invariably do, lacks all foundation. Their 'hunting for myths' is motivated by a 'seeing-what-ever-I-want-to-see' approach and is 'a forced attribution of functionally invalid contexts and the turning of peripheral connections into central criteria.' Little as we learn about it, Frye's Hegelian, absolute, closed, and prescriptive '*taxonomia universalis*' is given a final blast from the canon of 'the reflection of social conditioning' – the reflection of *the* reality as determined from the divine perspective of the Marxists (135–6).

The interested reader would receive no better guidance if she or he turned to the *Világirodalmi lexikon* (Encyclopaedia of World Literature), a massive monument to the universal claims of Marxist criticism and their absurdity, as well as to the genuine literary scholarship done in spite of, or in areas left unpatrolled by, the ideological guardians. The Frye article, however, was not left unguarded, as it was written by the editor-in-chief of the encyclopaedia, István Szerdahelyi, one of the leading literary commissars at the time (and otherwise an authority on versification). After assigning him the usual label of an archetypal and myth critic, he says that Frye stressed the 'importance of historicity' and 'attempted a – highly debated – typology of genres, of artistic creation and reader response' in the *Anatomy* (Király et al., 3:371). Whether the slightly derogatory tone reflected the official position vis-a-vis Frye or not I am not sure, but stating that according to Frye the work of art is 'none other than the transformation of archetypal images, myths and rituals' (3:371) certainly points to the fact that he was not carefully read.[6]

Frye was clearly not wanted, and not read seriously. While, as I have mentioned, this should not be any surprise from certain points of view, it is odd if we bear in mind that this period, the 1970s, marked the height of Frye's influence. It was, however, not only Frye who was not wanted. We Hungarians have our own great mythographer, Karl Kerényi, most of whose works in the archetypal field still remain to be published in Hungarian.[7] The narrative understanding (to borrow a term from Ricoeur) characteristic of both men, the differences notwithstanding, was so distant from, so much without points of contact with, the derived theoretical reason of both the established critical order and the attempts to escape from it, that at the time they could hardly be responded to systematically. For many, thinking in such uncritical, pre-rational terms as myth and archetype meant submission to collectivity, ultimately Nazism, of which Hungary had ample reminiscences. But more of this later.

In the meantime along came the very slow years of the early 1980s when it clearly dawned on so many that the Marxian universe, even at its best, was wholly closed, especially with regard to reform, whether in criticism or elsewhere. This realization brought about an overwhelming abjection in many, but the abjection had some surprising results. Out of it, as no larger aim could be envisaged, people – especially men of letters, writers, and critics – slowly began simply not to care less about paying lip-service to the authorities. They began to do whatever they deemed their discipline demanded of them. Some were given the sack, others silenced. But the process went on – out of abjection.

During the first period of the changes (roughly, 1983–7), with respect to literary criticism this meant an increased, and increasingly public, interest in various critical theories. The textual critics and others were busy translating books like Gadamer's *Truth and Method* (1984) and Auerbach's *Mimesis* (1985). New introductions to literary theory were written, and one of the important ones, by a Transylvanian critic, Éva Cs. Gyimesi, was the first to give a fuller and more favourable account of Frye's work (67–8).[8] This was also when hermeneutics, post-structuralism, post-modernism, and deconstruction found their Hungarian advocates.

It was in the very searching atmosphere of this period that a few young critics, including myself, discovered Frye and became, in one way or another, devoted to his work. By far the most important one among us was a university lecturer and Shakespeare scholar, Tibor Fabiny, whose critical, teaching, and even publishing enterprises have all been profoundly influenced by Frye, and have influenced many others in their turn. In 1982 Fabiny started a workshop with colleagues and students to study Shakespeare's imagery, with special attention to emblems. Numerous publications associated with the workshop have drawn heavily on Frye, while others have included translations of some of Frye's essays in the fields of iconology, Renaissance symbolism, hermeneutics, and biblical typology. Apart from publishing about, and publishing, Frye, Fabiny has written a book in English, *The Lion and the Lamb*, which, though utterly individual in its interpretations and conclusions, continues the typological program set out in *The Great Code*.

Equally importantly, there are now signs that some of Fabiny's students are beginning the work of applying Frye's ideas to Hungarian literature. One of them, László Szilasi, has published an excellent essay on how Frye's concept of romance clarifies our understanding of our most popular nineteenth-century novelist, Mór Jókai. On the one hand, Szilasi argues, the Jókai cultists take his work literally as scripture, while on the other his critics have compiled long lists of the 'flaws' in his novels when they are compared to other great novels of the period. In fact these 'flaws' conform exactly to Frye's description of romance. Thus Jókai should be studied as a writer of nineteenth-century romance, not judged against the canons of nineteenth-century realism.

So by the mid-1990s we have a strong and determined 'procurator' of Frye in Hungary; we have his students; we have a number of essays by Frye in Hungarian and a few on him; and we have seminars and lectures discussing his work. Gradually Frye seems to be finding his way into Hungarian letters. But in order for this movement to be complete, as I see it, a thorough theoretical reckoning of Frye's work by a student of Hungarian literature is required. Such a reckoning probably hinges upon the publication of at least one of Frye's books in Hungarian and, as we have seen, this has been delayed, despite the great transformations in politics, culture, and criticism. To see the possible reasons why, we have to continue with the story of the changes.[9]

III

As the genuine possibility of fundamental political changes began to appear on the horizon from about 1988, critical interest, naturally, also shifted in that direction. There were the important immediate tasks of writing on formerly suppressed authors, works, and subjects, the most pressing being the literary history of the past forty years. At last critics were not tongue-tied in expressing their political concerns. None the less, serious troubles arose. The formation of a multi-party system, desirable as it was, also meant that the only seeds of such a system could be two basically literary circles, as there were no other social formations apart from the Communists.

Now these two literary brotherhoods were divided upon a conflict that had taken place in the 1930s, which was, yet again, never resolved by the parties involved, but subsumed by the Nazification of the country during the war, and then afterwards by the Communists, who not only silenced but manipulated it, playing the parties off against each other. In the 1930s the issue had been the modernization of the country: whether to follow Western models or find more indigenous solutions to genuinely pressing social problems. Though the debate had been marred by different kinds of group hatred, including anti-Semitism, it had had cultural and social import. The renewed battle in the late 1980s and early 1990s seemed to carry little of the social meaning it had once had.

The two groups are aligned more along habits of thought and culture than formulated ideologies or programs. It is difficult to find suitable English terms for them, but 'Urbanites' and 'Populists' might do. Urbanites are mostly city intellectuals, modern and secular, today usually liberal in politics. Populists are usually first-generation intellectuals with a humble, peasant background, a strong sense of social responsibility, and a commitment to maintaining traditional Hungarian culture. Today they are mostly conservative. Each group sees in the other the personification of evil. Urbanites are regarded by Populists as a bunch of rationalists, rootless egotists hell-bent on destroying whatever was left of traditional Hungarian culture and communal values, and prepared to employ any means towards this end, even clandestine co-operation with the Communists. The Populists are seen by the Urbanites as a bunch of outsider pseudo-intellectuals, who, lacking individual talent, cling to myths and subordinate the individual to collectivity: they are therefore potential Nazis, only waiting for an opportunity to get rid of free-thinking Jews, and are capable of anything, even clandestine co-operation with the Communists.

The effects of all of this were of course devastating. This was especially true in the field of culture, where the primary function of debate, whether political or literary, became the manifestation of camp-allegiances: reading became an act of hunting for certain terms and phrases that betrayed the author's fealties, irrespective of the genuine learning and criticism that might have been involved.

Clearly the catholicity of Frye could not be put to use on either side. So, although plans to publish the *Anatomy* and *The Great Code* had been accepted, and translators contracted just before the onset of this culture war, when anything that might help to demolish the old order was being taken advantage of, the former was put off forever, it seems, and the latter postponed several times when the flames of this conflict flared up again. One could never adduce direct evidence for this, but these are cultural conditions and reflexes that cannot be disregarded. And it may well be that the *The Great Code* was finally brought out recently only because the conflict has abated somewhat in the past two years.

Whether or not the delay in its publication was caused by the culture war, Frye's *The Great Code* seemed to me to be germane to it in many respects. Earlier I spoke of the difficulties in assimilating a work undergoing translation to the prevalent discourses in the intended language, and at first I had expected to have to accomplish acrobatic feats of tact in finding a linguistic space for Frye's pertinent cultural-ideological observations between these warring discourses. To my utter surprise, I did not have to, for in Frye's text I saw both sides' positions implied, both sides impugned, and also a possible means of bridging the gap between them.

The Populist–Urbanite animosity has often been thought of as a conflict between East and West, of Eastern rural traditionalism and authoritarianism versus Western modernization and democratization. This idea has a long history in Hungarian thought, much longer than the history of Populists and Urbanites. One of its most important formulators was Endre Ady, a notable modernist poet working in the first two decades of the century, and regarded by both groups as a kind of forerunner, who wrote in a passionate essay in 1905 that Hungary was 'a ferry-nation, which even in its most formidable dreams only runs between two shores: from East to West, but preferably backwards' (2:215). It is no wonder, then, that the East–West metaphor is often used to explain the Populist–Urbanite rancour. But it has also been resisted, on the grounds that Populism has itself been calling for social and political democracy all along (not to mention the fact that similar agrarian-populist movements in the West could hardly be associated with anything Eastern).

We would be far less off the mark, I suggest, if we were to see the Populist and Urbanite positions as particular variants of Frye's concept of the the myths of concern and freedom, which he dwelt on in *The Critical Path*, where he states that a condition of whatever we can live with in the world around us is the tension between freedom and concern, and that should either gain the upper hand the result would be a 'squalid tyranny' or a 'lazy and selfish parasite on a power-structure' (*CP*, 55). This would be a wonderful moral for us in Hungary, just as it was for the West in times of student unrest, except that it is not *The Critical Path* that is being read, or is about to to be read, in Hungary – besides which, the symmetry, the schematism of the concept, would make it too easy to dismiss.

It is *The Great Code* that is being read, where the freedom–concern dialectic does not appear, but where the issue behind it looms large, and in a far less symmetrical manner. In Frye's dicussion, all levels of biblical imagery and narrative attest to the mutual interdependence of the myths of freedom and concern. And it was this very aspect of *The Great Code* that I found particularly poignant in relation to this culture war of ours. For if, from the perspective offered by Frye, we were able to see the Populist position, with its idealization of rural existence, as an inheritor of the Paradisal-pastoral imagery of the Bible; and likewise were able to see the Urbanite position, with its idealization of the free and urbane life of the cities, as an inheritor of the New Jerusalem imagery of the Bible; and were able to acknowledge that these images in their undisplaced biblical context are metaphorically the same – then we would be provided with a frame of reference that could eliminate the debilitating exclusivity of the two positions.

Naturally, I do not suppose that by reading Frye the Populists and Urbanites are going to set aside all their differences and fall upon one another's bosoms; far too many wounds have been inflicted on both sides for that sort of thing. But I do believe that these moments in Frye constitute weighty calls for a greater degree of tolerance on their parts. More important, however, there are fortuitously an increasing number of intellectuals who wish to resist the regimental drive and seek ways out of the cultural-political impasse created by the debate. Frye's frame of reference could assist their efforts, in a way that would neither do away with the issues involved nor regard them entirely as meaningless remnants of the past. Many of these intellectuals wish to do just that, but, however one might sympathize with such a position, it would leave one more question of our cultural history unresolved, and we have had to experience this kind of irresolution and its inevitable repercussions far too often.

One of the difficulties involved in such an application of Frye's concepts concerns the understanding of myth. A notable Urbanite novelist maintained in a television interview, in the early 1990s when the battle was raging, that what differentiated his group from the Populists was that they thought critically and individually and in rational terms, while Populists thought in myths, and as a result subordinated the individual to collectivity. Whatever one may think of this formulation, it certainly points to the misgivings of many Eastern European intellectuals. These misgivings are corroborated by historical evidence, for example in the way that one of this century's leading students of myth, Mircea Eliade, was tempted in the 1930s by the Romanian Nazi movement (see Eliade). Frye is of course all too aware of the problem, which is why he dwells so much on the problems of ideology and myth. His distinctions between myth and the ideological applications of myth, between primary and secondary concerns, are powerful arguments that should be sufficient to quell liberal anxieties regarding myth.

Among the arguments that seek to show that myth is not by definition authoritarian, one seems to me particularly pertinent to the present

Hungarian cultural-political quarrel over national identity, a quarrel that is of course at the heart of the Populist–Urbanite dispute, but that involves far wider groupings, which I will call liberals and nationalists.[10] The argument occurs in Frye's discussion of the royal metaphor, the unifying image of society as one body, especially its reversal 'from a metaphor of integration into a wholly decentralized one, in which the total body is complete within each individual' (GC, 100). If this decentralization of the royal metaphor could be the symbolic counterpart of the political ideal of democracy, as Frye suggests (GC, 101), it could also be of great service in a democratic construct of national identity.

Hungarian liberals have maintained, as in the case of myth, that any construct of national identity that points beyond citizenship and political rights subjugates individual freedom. Although this fear has historical justification, there are certain problems with it, both for those many Hungarians (one-third of the total) who live outside Hungary's borders and need a construct of national identity that is not bound to mere citizenship, and for those within Hungary, whose experience of social life is marked by political corruption, vast indifference towards social affairs and social responsibility, lack of solidarity, and an increase in crime. The situation, in short, is like the one described in *Words with Power*: 'There are people but there is no community; there is solitude but no individual space' (WP, 230). Nationalists have maintained that this is partly the result of the lack of any sense of social cohesion, and have called for a renewed stress on national identity, while liberals have rejected these attempts. Though little heard amidst the battle cries, historians and cultural critics have advocated an understanding of national identity that avoids its authoritarian pitfalls by separating it from citizenship and rooting it solely in cultural tradition. Frye's decentralization of the royal metaphor, which calls attention to the cultural-linguistic nature of social identity and stesses that it is a metaphor affording several possible interpretations, together with the fact that the general context of his discussion is the biblical aspect of the European cultural tradition, should provide useful arguments for these attempts. Coupled with his fundamentally liberal outlook, it may even help in spanning the gulf between liberals and nationalists. The issue is pressing: extreme nationalists, who have no inclination to pay heed to the many qualifications of the royal metaphor but only wish to idolize it, like the ancient Egyptians described by Frye (GC, 88), may, in a disrupted society under threat of massive pauperization, construct for us a truly dangerous form of national identity.

A good number of Frye's critics have acknowledged the learning and mastery of his critical system, while maintaining that it is far too idiosyncratic to be readily applicable as a scholarly-critical procedure. I myself have some doubts whether as a *system* Frye could have a direct and extensive influence on Hungarian critical scholarship, though certain of his observations and critical concepts (on typology, archetypes, genre, etc.) will be, and have been, made use of. But I presume that the real influence of his system in Hungary will take the form of a challenge. Most important, one hopes that it will challenge Hungarian critics to rediscover the role of the Bible in the interpretation of our literature. This will take a long time. However, one of the central axioms of his system, his notion that critical concepts should be derived from literature and not elsewhere, or in other words the narrative understanding that keeps his system within the literary universe but still retains its theoretical nature, could have a much more immediate impact on Hungarian letters. This is especially so now that, in the past year or so, literary criticism has returned to the theoretical interests of the mid-1980s: there are great public debates between followers of hermeneutics and deconstruction, and the old controversy between essayists and scholars has flared up again, bringing up precisely the issue of the scientific nature of literary theory as opposed to the imaginative nature of the literary art it deals with.

However, the doubt concerning Frye's system's directly influencing the academy remains. Perhaps his own recognition of this is one of the reasons that he chose a 'public address format' (*WP*, xix) for his books. Another reason is his desire to address the 'cultural needs' of a 'lay public' (*WP*, xix). The arduous cultural–ideological impasse created by the Populist–Urbanite and nationalist–liberal conflicts reflects some of the immediate cultural needs of the Hungarian lay public that the *The Great Code* seems to me to have an immediate bearing upon. Whether for this or other reasons, the lay public has certainly been quick to respond to the publication of the book: the first printing sold out inside two months. Scholarship, on the other hand, has been slower to respond.

Pressing cultural-ideological needs and the positive reaction of the lay public may still lead to a serious *critical* reckoning with Frye. Of course, the tempering potential that I attribute to Frye with respect to our conflicts may only be desperation at the sight of overwhelmingly inexorable historical forces that are far beyond the translator – whose natural task, however, is mediation. In any case, the reading of Frye in Hungary has at last begun.[11]

NOTES

1 To quote exactly: 'The normal human reaction to a great cultural achievement like the Bible is to do with it what the Philistines did to Samson: reduce it to impotence, then lock it in a mill to grind our aggressions and prejudices. But perhaps its hair, like Samson's, could grow again even there' (GC, 233). My own Hungarian translation, rendered back into English (an admittedly awkward procedure), would be something like: 'People generally react to a great cultural achievement like the Bible by doing what the Philistines did to Samson: divest it of its power, then lock it in a mill to grind, and in the mill of our aggressions and prejudices to be ground. But Samson's hair could grow again even there.' (In Hungarian the use of personal pronouns is gruesomely limited; and so, in addition, a more literal translation of the last sentence would have had to go: 'But perhaps the Bible's hair, like Samson's ...') For the sake of interest here is the French version by Catherine Malamoud, which, as far as I can tell, seems to be aware of the oddity but does not resolve it: 'Devant une grande réalisation culturelle telle que la Bible, la réaction normale des hommes est d'en faire ce que les Philistins ont fait a Samson: la réduire à l'impuissance, puis l'attacher à une muele, pour moudre nos agressions et nos préjugés. Mais peut-être que sa chevelure, comme celle de Samson, pourrait repousser même en cet endroit' (310).

2 Interestingly, in Hungarian grinding and mills have a rich array of connotations and metaphorical usages. To be ground up means to lose one's moral integrity under pressure of external forces. Or emotion can be refined by grinding, so that we have lovers in folk-songs taking their sorrows to mills to have them ground. In a poem, the painter-poet Béla Kondor thinks of himself as a miller, continually grinding and being ground – in fact, this was what prompted my solution.

3 *Words with Power* caused no such problems for me, possibly because when translating it I already had my Frye terminology and syntax ready at hand. Still, I found *Words with Power* to be much easier to work on, and I think Frye himself felt the need to cover 'much the same set of phenomena' (*WP*, xii) as in the *The Great Code* partly because of these difficulties. At least this is what I make of the remarks about the 'deficiencies' of the *The Great Code* in the introduction to *Words with Power*.

4 In the following summary overview I have been especially influenced by Szegedy-Maszák and Kulcsár Szabó.

5 Though bowdlerization continued even into the early 1980s: in the Hungarian version of Thomas Pynchon's story 'Entropy,' an 'ex-Hungarian freedom

fighter' is referred to simply as an 'ex-Hungarian' in order to avoid the troublesome allusion to 1956.

6 There is another interesting error in the bibliographical section of the article, where *A Natural Perspective* is referred to as *A National Perspective,* and is further translated into Hungarian in that sense. Could this be a Freudian slip, reflecting a common prejudice that a positive view of myths implies nationalism?

7 Kerényi emigrated to Switzerland in 1943 as an act of opposition to the Nazification of the country. He wanted to return to Hungary in 1947 but, luckily for him, was not given permission by the Communists. Kerényi died in 1973, and in the 1970s was much revered for his stance against Nazism. However, the inference was not drawn from this that one can treat myths without necessarily succumbing to nationalism or Nazism. Of late this attitude with respect to Kerényi is changing.

8 Transylvania used to be part of Hungary, but was annexed by Romania in 1920. Professor Gyimesi, a prominent dissident in the 1980s, teaches at the Hungarian department of the Kolozsvar (Cluj) university in Romania. She used the Romanian edition of the *Anatomy,* which seems to me to prove that available translations are indispensable for the assimilation of foreign thinkers.

9 For a thorough and scholarly discussion in English of the changes see Tőkés's monumental study.

10 The latter term has rather bad connotations, and in other contexts I would prefer to use 'patriots,' but if I used it here it would imply that liberals are not patriots, which I do not believe. For clarity's sake by 'nationalists' I do not mean right-wing extremists.

11 Péter Pásztor's translation of *Words with Power* and a translation of *Anatomy of Criticism* by József Szili have both been published in Hungary since this paper was written.

WORKS CITED

Ady, Endre. *Ady Endre Publicisztikai Írásai* (The Journalism of Endre Ady). 3 vols. Edited by Erzsébet Vezér. Budapest: Szepirodalmi, 1977.
Cs. Gyimesi, Éva. *Teremtett világ: rendhagyó bevezetés az irodalomba* (Created World: An Irregular Introduction to Literature). Bucharest: Kriterion, 1983.
Eliade, Mircea. *Autobiography.* San Francisco: Harper & Row, 1981.
Fabiny, Tibor. *The Lion and the Lamb: Figuralism and Fulfilment in the Bible, Art and Literature.* London: Macmillan, 1992.

Király, István, and István Szerdahelyi et al., eds. *Világirodalmi lexikon* (Encyclopaedia of World Literature). 18 vols. Budapest: Akadémia, 1970–95.

Kulcsár Szabó, Ernő. *Az új kritika dilemmái: az irodalomértés helyzete az ezredvégen* (The Dilemmas of a New Criticism: The Situation of Literary Understanding at the end of the Millenium). Budapest: Balassi, 1994.

Malamoud, Catherine, trans. *Le Grand Code: La Bible et la littérature* (*The Great Code*, by Northrop Frye). Paris: Éditions du Seuil, 1984.

Pásztor, Péter, trans. *Az Ige hatalma* (*Words with Power*, by Northrop Frye). Budapest: Európa, 1997).

– *Kettős tükör: A Biblia és az irodalom* (*The Great Code*, by Northrop Frye). Budapest: Európa, 1996.

Szegedy-Maszák, Mihály. 'Merre tart az irodalom (todomány)' (Where is Literature/the Study of Literature Heading?). *Alföld* 2 (1996): 3–23.

Szilasi, László. '"Oda alant lakik, aki azt mozgatja": Jókai Mór *Szegény gazdagok* című regényének románcos olvasata' ('There below liveth the one that moveth': A reading of Jokai's *The Poor Rich* as Romance). *Alföld* 9 (1994): 44–57.

Szili, József, trans. *A kritika anatómiája* (*Anatomy of Criticism*, by Northrop Frye). Budapest: Helikon, 1998.

Tőkés, Rudolf. *Hungary's Negotiated Revolution*. Cambridge: Cambridge University Press, 1996.

Virágos, Zsolt. 'A Mítoszkritika, vagy a mélystrúktura mítosza.' In *Acta Germanica et Acta Romanica* (Proceedings of the First National Germanistic Symposium, September, 1980). Szeged: no pub., 1981. 131–41.

Interpenetration as a Key Concept in Frye's Critical Vision

ROBERT D. DENHAM

The 'subject' swallows everything objective to it: hence the pan-historical critics of today, the Hegelian pan-philosophical absolute knowledge, the pan-literary universe which only three people understand: Blake, Mallarmé, and myself. The *final* answer, naturally, is interpenetration.

Northrop Frye, Notebook 44, 717

One does not read very far in Frye before realizing that he is a dialectical thinker, his mind repeatedly moving back and forth between opposing poles of reference: knowledge and experience, space and time, stasis and movement, the individual and society, tradition and innovation, Platonic synthesis and Aristotelian analysis, engagement and detachment, freedom and concern, *mythos* and *dianoia*, the world and the grain of sand, immanence and transcendence, and scores of other oppositions. A second self-evident feature of Frye's expansive body of work is its drive toward unity. He always resists the Kierkegaardian 'either/or' solution. But for Frye unity is never achieved at the expense of variety, and in his notebooks he never tires of insisting that opposites are never resolved by reconciliation, harmony, or agreement. Such terms relate to propositional language and are forms of what he calls 'imperialistic compulsion' (NB53, 214). In one of his notebooks from the mid-1960s Frye says: 'I have always distrusted what I call Reuben the Reconciler in thought: the syncretism that "reconciles" Plato & Aristotle or St. Thomas & Marx. I think every great structure of thought or imagination is a universe in itself, identical with and interpenetrating every other, but not similar or harmonizable with any other' (NB19, 172). And in one of his late notebooks Frye reiterates the point:

If it was Vico who began the philosophy of history, it was Hegel who saw that a philosophy of history had to include a history of philosophy. Philosophy begins in an assertion of territoriality; it grows and diversifies through criticism, dispute, 'refutation,' and so on; but its real being is in a tradition of consensus. Every poem is 'unique,' in the soft-headed phrase, and 'archetype spotting' is a facile and futile procedure; but the traditions and conventions of poetry make a shape and a meaning. They move toward a future (emergence of primary concerns), and they expand into a wider present.

   Criticism also has a tradition that gives a consensus to all the disagreement, including, not impossibly, all the blather and stock response. Because, as I've said from the beginning, even the bullshit documents a history of taste.

   The bullshitters, of course, are always chasing donkeys' carrots (or bulls' tails), looking for a final reconciliation of all disagreements in the bosom of Marx, S. Thomas, the Great Mother, or what not. The correct form of this is the 'God exists in us and we in him' formula of Blake, Juliana of Norwich, and many others. (NB53, 149–51)

Later in the same notebook he says:

Conversion is imperialism, reconciliation at the price of subjection. If a Jew tells me he can't accept Jesus as the Messiah, there isn't, in these days, any question of conversion on either side, merely a realization that we both see the same things from different points of view: in short, interpenetration.

   Two levels of history: aggressive and cultural. The aggressive is imperialist and seeks the reconciliation of the pax Romana: agreement on the linguistically aggressive dogma. Cultural history interpenetrates: variety and unity, but no uniformity. (NB53, 191, 196)

The key concept in these notebook entries is interpenetration. If opposites are not to be reconciled or harmonized in some way, what does it mean to say that they interpenetrate? It would be foolish to suggest that there is an authoritative answer to the question, but if we consider some of the ways Frye used the word, we may gain an insight into the remarkable religious quest recorded in the notebooks that Frye kept for more than fifty years. Before exploring the idea of interpenetration itself, I want to consider briefly the origin of the idea. Here, as throughout, I will generally let Frye's notebook entries speak for themselves, providing only a bit of connective tissue.

The Birth of an Idea

Interpenetration, Frye says in an interview with David Cayley, is a 'key idea that has always been on my mind' (*NFC*, 61). 'Always' is certainly a hyperbole, but Frye did come to the intuition early. What helped crystallize the idea, first of all, was his reading of Spengler as a teenager. In 1930 Frye happened upon *The Decline of the West* in the library at Hart House, the student centre at the University of Toronto, and he reread the book during the summer of 1931. What attracted Frye to Spengler was his view of the organic growth of cultures and his meditation on the destiny of art forms. But Frye was always somewhat puzzled by his fascination with Spengler, and it was only years later, he reports in one of his notebooks, that he realized his attraction was also 'the result of divining in him the principle of historical interpenetration: everything that happens is a symbol of everything else that's contemporary with it. Such a perspective helps one to escape from the abstracting of culture, including the arts and sciences, from what I've called the dissolving phantasmagoria of political events' (NB53, 22). He puts it almost the same way in another notebook: 'the great intuition I got from Spengler, and later from Vico, was the sense of every historical phenomenon being symbolic of every other phenomenon contemporary with it' (NB44, 554).

If Spengler helped to crystallize the idea for Frye, Whitehead's *Science and the Modern World* helped to articulate it. 'I can still remember the exhilaration I felt,' Frye recalls, 'when I came to the passage' in Whitehead's book (*DV*, 40–1).[1] The word *interpenetration* does not actually appear in *Science and the Modern World*, which was the first book of philosophy that Frye 'read purely on [his] own and purely for pleasure' (*DV*, 40). But the passage that struck Frye with such force came from Whitehead's chapter entitled 'The Romantic Reaction': 'In a certain sense everything is everywhere at all times. For every location involves an aspect of itself in every other location. Thus every spatio-temporal standpoint mirrors the world' (*Science and the Modern World*, 93).[2] At several places in the papers he wrote as a student at Victoria and Emmanuel Colleges Frye uses the word *interpenetration* in the sense of religious syncretism or assimilation, but in a paper on Calvin he presented at the Theological Society of Emmanuel College in 1935 he remarks, in what seems to be a clear reference to the passage in Whitehead, that 'the centre of the universe is wherever one happens to be' (*Student Essays*, 414). And he concludes that paper by contending that when our understanding of the Spenglerian rise and fall of civilizations and the Incarnation 'interpenetrate and focus into one, we shall have a theology which can accommodate itself to twentieth-century requirements' (416). Interpenetration, then, was an idea which, in its Whiteheadean sense, Frye began to exploit at an early age: he was twenty-two when he wrote the paper on Calvin.

A third defining source for interpenetration was the Buddhist tradition, especially the Avatamsaka and Lankavatara sutras. In a notebook from the 1980s Frye recalls that learning about interpenetration from Whitehead 'was followed by [Peter] Fisher's introducing to me the Lankavatara Sutra, where it [interpenetration] was said to be in the Avatamsaka Sutra' (NB11h, 12). Fisher was one of Frye's students, who, after graduating from college, had approached Frye about doing an M.A. thesis on Blake. As Frye reports this episode in his preface to Fisher's book on Blake, Fisher 'nearly walked out again when he discovered that I had not read the *Bhagavadgita* in Sanskrit, which he took for granted that any serious student of Blake would have done as a matter of course.' Frye adds that he had earlier been misled in his reading of Oriental philosophy by bad translations, but that thereafter his and Fisher's 'conversations took the form of a kind of symbolic shorthand in which terms from Blake and from Mahayana Buddhism were apt to be used interchangeably' (Fisher, v).[3] These conversations were frequent: in the late 1940s and early 1950s Frye and Fisher met every Monday to drink beer and talk about literature and philosophy and religion.

A few years later Frye seems less certain about the sequence of his early encounter with Whitehead and the Mahayana Buddhist texts. In a notebook devoted to his Emmanuel College lectures, 'The Double Vision,' he writes:

The theme I want for the third lecture takes me into fields I'm ill prepared to enter, and unless I can connect it with something already central in me I don't know how I can complete it in time. The general idea is that harmony, reconciliation (whether of God and man or of two arguments) and agreement are all terms relating to propositional language. The poetic counterpart is what I've been calling interpenetration, the concrete order in which everything is everywhere at once. Whitehead's SMW [*Science and the Modern World*] says this in so many words: I must have got it from there originally, though I thought I got it from Suzuki's remarks about the Avatamsaka Sutra. (NB53, 17)

In trying to remember when he first encountered 'Suzuki's remarks,' Frye is doubtless referring to D.T. Suzuki's comment in *The Lankavatara Sutra* that interpenetration in the *Avatamsaka Sutra* 'constitutes the central thought of the sutra' (xxxvi). Suzuki's book appeared about the time Frye came across the passage in Whitehead – the early 1930s: his detailed exposition of the *Avatamsaka Sutra* did not appear for another two decades.[4]

In any case, there are three primary contexts for Frye's early encounter with the idea of interpenetration – the historical by way of Spengler, the philosophical by way of Whitehead, and the religious by way of the Mahayana sutras. In Frye's later work interpenetration usually appears in a religious context (it is found in key passages in *The Great Code* and *The Double Vision*), and in the notebooks, where the word *interpenetrate* or some form of it appears more than 150 times, the context is most often religious as well. There are also decidedly literary and political or cultural uses of the term. Before looking at the fundamentally religious meaning of interpenetration, we should consider the ways the term *interpenetration* is used in these other contexts. But whatever the context, interpenetration is one of the many verbal formulas Frye uses to force language to express the ineffable. 'I don't believe affirmations,' Frye says in a notebook from the years he was writing *Words with Power*, 'either my own or other people's. The motto I've chosen for the book (*quique amavit cres amet*) represents a hope but not a faith: I can't pin down my faith so precisely. What I believe are the verbal formulas I work out that seem to make sense on their own' (NB44, 200).[5] Or again, in a notebook from the early 1970s Frye writes, 'It is possible that I ought to write two short books ... The first book, which could conceivably be the Birks Lectures, would be on the three awarenesses of religion, that of the light–dark dialectic of the Father, of the journey of the Logos through the seven creative stages, and of the decentralized interpenetration of the Spirit. Caution: don't say "solving the problem of," which is projection: say "finding the verbal formulas for"' (NB24, 44).[6] Frye's notebooks are an extended quest in search of verbal formulas, one of which is interpenetration. He uses the word to help define a certain kind of experience, understanding, process, concept, and vision. But around the word *interpenetration* cluster a host of additional verbal formulas that help to define it.

The Contexts of Interpenetration

Historical Interpenetration

As indicated, one of the principles that Frye learned from Spengler was the interpenetration of symbolism: 'everything that happens in the world symbolizes everything else that happens' (NB54.3, 10). 'Nobody,' Frye says, 'had really established this before, though there are hints of it in Ruskin; today it's a staple of pop-kulch McLuhan-Carpenter stuff, but they (at least McLuhan) got it through Wyndham Lewis, whose *Time and Western Man* is a completely Spenglerian book' (NB54.3, 10). What Lewis attacks in this book is what he calls 'time-philosophy,' and although he is thoroughly anti-Spenglerian, Lewis does show 'how twentieth-century philosophy, literature, politics, popular entertainment, music and ballet, and half a dozen other social phenomena all form an interwoven texture of "time-philosophy," and are all interchangeable symbols of it' (*SM*, 189).[7] What Frye is getting at is the unity of culture viewed organically, rather than in a linear or cyclical way. The various units of cultural history are of a piece, and within a given 'culture,' as Spengler uses the term, its philosophies and myths and metaphors mirror each other or, as Frye says in the notebook just quoted, they 'are intertwined in a historical progression' (NB54.3, 10).[8] In short, they interpenetrate, thus providing Frye a way to move beyond the endless repetitions in the cyclical view of history. 'In the cyclical vision *everything*,' he says in a notebook from the late 1970s, 'becomes historical, and there is no Other except the social mass. The impulse to plunge into that is strong but premature. Something here eludes me. The answers are in interpenetration and Thou Art That' (NB11e, 44).[9] Or again:

With the Fall man lost good & got the knowledge of good & evil, a cyclical & interpenetrating knowledge in which evil is primary & good a secondary derivation from it. So much I've always got clear. Man also lost life, life which is the *opposite* of death, life where death is an alien & non-existent possibility like unicorns, and got the interpenetrating cycle of life & death, where death is not only natural & inevitable, but implied in the very conception of life itself.

I'm intellectually a prisoner of my own profession: for me, to know anything is to find a verbal formula for it. Hence the above represents something I've always known but never really knew. I suppose the good–evil & life–death cycles are only aspects of a total pattern of double-gyre or antithesis which can 'exist' only in that form, as CP [*The Critical Path*] says. Youth & age, male & female, master & slave, & so on. So the cycle is the demonic analogy of interpenetration. (NB24, 185–6)

The apocalyptic analogy of interpenetration, as we will see, is the Incarnation, because the Incarnation liberates one from the myth of eternal recurrence.

Philosophical Interpenetration

Philosophically, Frye sees interpenetration as synonymous with the identity of the one and the many, of particularity and totality. He announces in a 1971 notebook that this identity is, in fact, the motto of the so-called third book, the elaborate, encyclopaedic work that he planned to write after finishing *Anatomy of Criticism* (NB24, 213). 'The rush of ideas I get from Hegel's *Phenomenology* is so tremendous,' Frye says, 'I can hardly keep up with it. I note that there's a summary in my edition that quotes Plotinus as saying that what is beyond is also here. So Plotinus has interpenetration' (NB53, 97).[10] Sometimes Frye speaks as if interpenetration takes the form of a Hegelian synthesis, or at least the dialectic described by Hegel as an *Aufhebung* (a lifting up, a preserving, and a cancelling): once a philosophical position (thesis) has found its antithesis, the new synthesis that results lifts up the old position to a new level while at the same time preserving it as part of the new synthesis. In one of his *Great Code* notebooks, where he is trying to work out the structure of the second part of the book, Frye says, 'Unity is a (relatively static) thesis; its negation is not so much the decentralized Bible as the recreation in which it becomes a historical process, and interpenetration, the real decentralized Bible, is the Aufhebung which follows' (NB54.5, 125). At other times, however, Frye draws back from Hegelian synthesis because of its emphasis on propositional agreement: 'Hegel showed how the thesis involved its own antithesis, although I think the "synthesis" has been foisted on him by his followers. Anyway, the expansion to absolute knowledge is too close to what Blake calls the smile of a fool. My goal would be something like absolute experience rather than absolute knowledge: in experience the units are unique, and things don't agree with each other; they mirror each other' (NB53, 17).[11] In the same notebook Frye observes that 'Whitehead surrounds his principle of interpenetration by talking about the prehension of an event and its relation to other events: particularity and totality make nonsense without each other' (NB53, 32). 'Every location,' to repeat Whitehead's formulation, 'involves an aspect of itself in every other location. Thus every spatio-temporal standpoint mirrors the world' (*Science and the Modern World*, 93). In his notes for a lecture on Blake's illustrations for the Book of Job, Frye observes that the checkered pavement with intersecting circles in plate 20 is a 'symbol of an interpenetrating world where everything is everywhere at once' (NB57, 135). Another example is in Borges's story 'The Aleph,' 'which illustrates the principle of interpenetration, everything everywhere at once' (NB52, 135).[12]

There were other philosophical formulas. Following the claim in one notebook that the whole–part antithesis is resolved by interpenetration, Frye inserts the parenthetical remark 'Coleridge through Barfield' (NB44, 353). The reference is to Owen Barfield's *What Coleridge Thought*, a book that provides a detailed exposition of Coleridge's understanding of interpenetration, a dynamic and generative process that does not reconcile polarities but recreates a new entity from them.[13] Coleridge, in fact, uses the word *interpenetration*, maintaining that only through the imagination can one see the power 'of interpenetration, of total intussusception, of the existence of all in each as the condition of Nature's unity and substantiality, and of the latency under the predominance of some one power, wherein subsists her life and its endless variety' (*Theory of Life*; qtd. in Barfield, 52–3). Polarity, the two forces of one power, is, Coleridge says in the *Statesman's Manual*, 'a living and generative interpenetration' (qtd. in Barfield, 36). Barfield points to analogues of Coleridge's theory of polarity in Ramon Lull and Giordano Bruno, two thinkers who also held an attraction for Frye.[14] Here is one of Frye's versions of polarity: 'The revealed community would have to be based on some such conception as Christ, who is conceived metaphorically, as an interpenetrating force we're a part of and yet is also a part of us' (NB58, 12).

Frye was also drawn to physicist David Bohm's notion of the 'implicate order,' in which 'the totality of existence is enfolded within each region of space (and time)' (Bohm, 172).[15] Or, in Frye's words, 'Where religion and science can still get together is on the conception of the objective world as an "unfolding" of an "enfolded" or unborn order, which is beyond time and space as we experience them' (NB44, 19). At the conclusion of *The Double Vision* Frye refers to Bohm's implicate order as the 'interpenetrating energies' of the spiritual world (84). Barfield was familiar with Bohm's work, and Frye may well have first encountered Bohm in *What Coleridge Thought*. In any case, Coleridge's polarity,

Bohm's implicate order, and Barfield's thesis about identity (one becomes two while remaining one), are, like Whitehead's spatio-temporal standpoints mirroring the world, different philosophical translations of the principle of interpenetration.

Frye would maintain, I believe, that the idea that two things are the same thing (as in metaphor) is better captured by the word *interpenetration* than by the word *identity*; for *interpenetration*, whether of unity and variety, wholes and parts, totality and particularity, self and other, human and divine, suggests more strongly than does *identity* that each half of the dialectic retains its own distinctiveness. Unity, as Frye is fond of insisting, does not mean uniformity. Moreover, interpenetration is a more dynamic concept than identity, the former implying a free flow back and forth between the 'two forces of one power.'

Social Interpenetration

Interpenetration appears frequently in the notebooks in a social context. 'I think that in proportion as we move away from secondary concern with its hierarchies to primary concern our cosmology will decentralize, become increasingly classless in its assumptions, and come to focus on the central idea of interpenetration' (NB52, 74). The centralizing tendency in human affairs is aggressive and authoritarian, and like his preceptor Blake, Frye always resists all forms of imperialism. 'The crusade,' he says, 'is expanding empire, in Blake's terms, not decentralizing (interpenetrating) art. (Note that decentralizing is one stop on the way to interpenetration)' (NB46, 42). The movement toward interpenetration, then, is a movement away from power, ideology, and secondary concern, while the focus of the genuine community is dialogue. Dialogue, like decentralization, is not the same thing as interpenetration,[16] but the two ideas are related in many of the notebook entries.[17] At one point Frye says that authentic dialogue is interpenetrative, adding that 'Plato, the inventor of dialogue, goes in an anti-dialogue direction. He begins what Aristotle, especially in his conception of *telos*, greatly develops: the *tendentious* argument, the writing cat-walk leading to an end, the end being really the justification of existing authority' (NB11f, 92). Ideology is monologic and exclusive, but in dialogue the opposites of different ideologies interpenetrate (NB44, 102). The ultimate revelation, Frye says in a 1969 notebook, is 'through mysticism to dialogue – interpenetration of Word.' And 'the final sense of interpenetration,' he adds, is 'the key to dialogue as well as identity' (NB11f, 89, 92).

In the one essay where interpenetration is headlined – 'Culture as Interpenetration' – Frye speaks less abstractly, using the concept to describe the synthesis of the indigenous and immigrant cultures in Canada. We see this synthesis realized, he observes in his notes for this essay, in Leonard Cohen's *Beautiful Losers*, a novel about 'a Montreal Jew writing with genuine compassion about a seventeenth-century Algonquin woman turned Catholic saint, with twentieth-century themes mixed in' (NB54.6, 12). 'I speak of interpenetration,' Frye adds, 'because it seems to me that one decisive feature of high culture is cross-fertilization, something that's beyond the external influence of a mother country and the internal response to it' (NB54.6, 29). Socially and culturally, then, interpenetration derives in part from Frye's own liberal politics – his utopian vision of a classless society in which differences are abolished not so much by acceptance or reconciliation as by identification. Community, communion, and commonwealth are ideas that cluster in the margins of Frye's comments on interpenetration, ideas not unrelated to his own personal identification with the principles of the Co-operative Commonwealth Federation.[18] 'Centralizing and homogenizing versus interpenetration,' Frye says in thinking about one of the themes of *The Double Vision*: 'probably it's the germ of Utopia: nowhere becoming everywhere' (NB46, 37).

While individuals can themselves interpenetrate with each other and with texts, individual egos cannot:

I gather that Bakhtin's 'dialogism' is gradually replacing 'deconstruction' as a buzzword. Of course there's dialogue between writer & reader, but much more goes on than that: it's more like an interpenetrating of identities. Montaigne's 'consubstantial' remark shows that the writer's ego and the reader's ego *can't* interpenetrate: they're like the old-style atoms, or, more accurately, like the Leibnitzian monads. In this century we have to forget that 'atom' means the unsplittable (or did mean it) or that the individual is the 'individable.' Two egos identifying would be like two billiard balls copulating.[19]

Or, as Frye puts it in another entry: 'love is interpenetration, but it has to extend beyond the sexual interpenetrating of intercourse. Every act of hostility is penetration with a threat, with a desire to dominate or acquire for oneself. Love means entering into and identifying with other people and things without threats or domination, in fact without retaining an ego-self' (NB44, 501).

In the process of identity, individuality, which Frye says is 'the ethical and political side of the principle of interpenetration' (NB11e, 37), does not disappear. There is one power, as Coleridge says, but still two forces. Or, as the idea gets expressed in another verbal formula, 'Man is awake at night & sees that the moon & stars are orderly as well as the sun. He also sees the sun vanish into the dark world & reappear. The Logos & Thanatos visions, then, may begin as bordering haloes of one world; but each is the world, & they interpenetrate. The morning has come, and also the night' (NB12, 401).

Metaphor as Interpenetration

'I know,' Frye says, 'that the theory of metaphor is very complex, or has been made so by exuberant philosopher-critics, but I want to explain its basic principle very simply. A statement of identity like A is B introduces us to a universe in which unity and multiplicity are alternating aspects of the same phenomena. Paul's Christ in me and I in Christ is the obvious introduction for this [Emmanuel College] audience' (NB53, 32). Frye's view of metaphor, unique among literary critics and philosophers of language, is based on the principle of identity. If Frye is able to state 'very simply' the principle that the metaphorical and the literal meaning are the same, his explanation of the principle is complex and extends over his entire career. It begins in *Fearful Symmetry*, is developed in *Anatomy of Criticism*, and becomes an insistent theme in subsequent books.[20]

From the point of view of natural language, Frye observes, literal meaning has always been regarded as the descriptive, denotative meaning: the literally true is the same as the descriptively accurate. But in Frye's view of language, outlined in the first chapters of both *The Great Code* and *Words with Power*, metaphorical meaning is identified with literal meaning. Frye begins with the assumption that 'the centripetal aspect a of verbal structure is its primary aspect' (GC, 60). Because what words primarily do with precision and accuracy in poetry is to hang together as a verbal structure, the literal and metaphorical meanings are therefore the same. Speaking of biblical metaphor, Frye writes:

The Bible means literally just what it says, but it can mean it only without primary reference to a correspondence of what it says to something outside what it says. When Jesus says (John 10:9), 'I am the door,' the statement means literally just what it says, but there are no doors outside the verse in John to be pointed to ... Metaphorical meaning as I use the term, like myth, has for me a primary and a derived sense, the primary one being so broad that it is really a tautology. All verbal structures have a centripetal and a centrifugal aspect, and we can call the centripetal aspect their literary aspect ... The primary and literal meaning of the Bible, then, is its centripetal or poetic meaning. It is only when we are reading as we do when we read poetry that we can take the word 'literal' seriously, accepting every word given us without question. This primary meaning, which arises simply from the interconnection of words, is the metaphorical meaning. (GC, 60–1)

Metaphor (identity with), as opposed to simile (identity as), asserts counter-logically that two things *are* the same thing. Frye refers to this paradox in *The Double Vision* as 'metaphorical literalism.' 'In the myth-metaphor world all truth is paradox: a Hegelian thesis where thesis contains and implies antithesis, but lives with it and doesn't transcend it. A is/isn't B. This did/didn't happen' (NB44, 706). In *Words with Power* he distinguishes three aspects or levels of metaphorical experience: the imaginative, the erotic, and the existential or ecstatic. As we move up the ladder of metaphorical experience, the gap between identity and difference continues to lessen until we reach the highest state (the ecstatic), where, Frye says, we have 'a sense of presence, a sense of uniting ourselves with something else' (85). In one of his *Words with Power* notebooks Frye writes, 'the second stage of response is a still photograph or picture of the plot, when it's mythos-language; when it's logos-language there's a large element of diagram, which is also pictorial. That's been there since Plato's divided line. This opens up an expansion of mythos or narrative to any kind of verbal sequence, & of metaphor or juxtaposition to any kind of pattern. Then, moving back through erotic & enthusiastic metaphor, we see that what we get into is identity as and with – and that, of course, to the part–whole antithesis resolved by interpenetration' (NB44, 353).

In his published work Frye uses the word *interpenetration* only twice in the context of metaphor. 'Imaginative literalism,' he says in *The Double Vision*, 'seeks what might be called interpenetration, the free flowing of spiritual life into and out of one another that communicates but never violates' (18). In *The Great Code* he uses the word to describe the kind of vision contained in metaphors of particularity, such as Blake's 'To see the world in a grain of sand,' as opposed to metaphors of unity and integration.[21] But in the notebooks Frye repeatedly writes about interpenetration, most often in connection with the goal of what I have called his religious quest. The topics explored in the notebooks are wide-ranging, but if we step back from them and attempt to see them as a whole, the conclusion seems inescapable that Frye is, in fact, on such a quest. What emerges from the infinite variety of the notebooks is an anabatic journey: Frye's central mission is to ascend the imaginative ladder to the ultimate level of spiritual vision. The journey is similar to Hegel's quest in *The Phenomenology of Spirit* for the absolute ideal, except that the verbal formulas used to describe it are altogether different. And one of the key verbal formulas is *interpenetration*.

Interpenetration as Spiritual Vision

In a notebook from the late 1960s, when Frye was thinking through the intricate schema for the third of the eight major books he planned to write, he says, 'I still have to work out the right verbal formulas for the similarity–identity business. All religions are one, not alike; "that they may be one," not that they should all think alike: community means people thinking along similar lines & motivated by similar drives; communion means that all men are the same man. The Hegelian–Marxist "synthesis" is this identity projected as the end of a process, but that's illusory. These are of course only hunches, but the right formulas are there if I can find them. And identity is important because it's the key to the interpenetration climax' (NB12, 559). As suggested above, Whitehead was important in Frye's understanding of this climax. The passage from *Science and the Modern World* was, Frye said in 1990, 'my initiation into what Christianity meant by spiritual vision' (*DV*, 41). Fifty-five years earlier, as we have seen, Frye used interpenetration in a theological context in his Emmanuel College paper on Calvin. But over the years Frye lost interest in theology, having discovered that visionary texts, like Blake's, provided a more adequate account of the stages and the end of the quest. Thus, the attraction that the *Avatamsaka Sutra* held for him.

The *Avatamsaka Sutra* is a massive, dense, extravagant, and repetitive text that forms the basis of the Chinese Hua-yen school of Buddhism, founded by Tu-shun (or Fashun) in the sixth century. Its ideas were chiefly disseminated during the next century through the lectures of Fa-Tsang (643–712). In India the *Avatamsaka* (Sanskrit for 'flower ornament') was a central text of the Yogacharins, and in Japan the *Avatamsaka* sect was known as Kegon. There is no evidence that Frye read the *Avatamsaka Sutra* outside the selections in the third series of D.T. Suzuki's *Essays in Zen Buddhism*. In fact, in one of his notebooks Frye says, 'I can't make any sense out of these infernal Sutras: they seem designed for people who really can't read' (NB53, 17).[22] But what Frye did fasten on from the *Avatamsaka Sutra* was the idea of the identity of everything and the interpenetration of all elements in the world. Suzuki calls this the 'fundamental insight' of the sutra (*Essays*, 84). 'It is,' he adds, 'philosophically speaking, a thought somewhat similar to Hegel's conception of concrete universals. Each individual reality, besides being itself, reflects in it something of the universal, and at the same time it is itself because of other individuals. A system of perfect relationship exists among individual existences and also between individuals and universals, between particular objects and general ideas. This perfect network of mutual relations has received at the hand of the Mahayana philosopher the technical name of interpenetration' (*Essays*, 84–5).

This is the idea that captivated Frye. The sutra represents the idea in experiential and intuitive rather than philosophical terms, though Suzuki's commentary on the sutra, which is based chiefly on book 39 ('The Entry into the Realm of Reality'), is in the main *expressed* philosophically (he calls interpenetration a 'doctrine'). Suzuki again: 'In the world of the *Gandavyuha* [book 39] known as the Dharmadhatu [realm of reality], individual realities are folded into one great Reality, and this great Reality is found participated in by each individual one. Not only this, but each individual existence contains in itself all other individual existences as such. Thus there is universal interpenetration, so called in the Dharmadhatu ... This is not philosophical penetration of existence reached by cold logical reasoning, nor is it a symbolical representation of the imagination. It is a world of real spiritual experience' (*Essays*, 96).[23] Such passages are doubtless what Frye remembered when he was preparing his Emmanuel College lectures, some forty years after he had encountered Suzuki's *Essays in Zen Buddhism*. Like Suzuki, Frye often speaks of interpenetration as an experience.[24]

As an experience, interpenetration implies process and is thus a temporal term, related to *mythos* rather than to *dianoia*: 'the conception of interpenetration has to apply to movements of time' (NB11f, 97). But Frye often speaks of interpenetration as a concept, and therefore as a thematic or spatial idea, as in this notebook entry: 'Any thematic stasis of the Christian *commedia* is likely to sound a trifle Buddhist, as the Eliot quartets do. So does the *Paradiso*, for that matter. The fictional emphasis is on escape from prison; the thematic on smashing the walls of a mental prison, the iron bar in Zen. Romance, which presents this as contained, leads fictionally to Jerusalem & Eden; thematically to the Avatamsaka conceptions of universal identity and interpenetration' (NB19, 130). On still other occasions Frye, aware of the limitations of spatial and temporal categories, seeks to push language beyond Spenglerian time and Whiteheadean space. 'The third chapter,' he says in one of his *Words with Power* notebooks, 'goes beyond space into the conception of interpenetration, the fourth one beyond time into the conception of "mystical dance," or time as interiorly possessed contrapuntal movement' (NB52, 697). The interpenetrating vision, which is the climax of the anabatic quest, comes when space is annihilated (NB27, 164, 168).[25]

Philosophical systems can themselves interpenetrate: 'I suspect,' Frye says, '... that the key to philosophy is the exact opposite of what philosophers do now. It's the study of the great historical systems, each of them a palace and a museum, that's genuine philosophy. At a certain point they interpenetrate into a house of many mansions, a new Jerusalem of verbal possibilities, but that's a tremendous state of enlightenment' (NB44, 110). Religions interpenetrate as well.

In 1935 Frye wrote, with particularly acute prescience, to Helen Kemp: 'I propose spending the rest of my life, apart from living with you, on various problems connected with religion and art. Now religion and art are the two most important phenomena in the world; or rather the most important phenomenon, for they are basically the same thing. They constitute, in fact, the only reality of existence' (*Correspondence*, 1:425–6). As it turned out Frye, who was twenty-two at the time, did devote his whole career to seeking the unified vision of religion and art. To discover verbal formulas for expressing that vision was, again, at the centre of his mission. When in 'The Aleph' Borges's narrator arrives at the 'ineffable core' of his story, he reflects that 'all language is a set of symbols whose use among speakers assumes a shared past. How, then, can I translate into words the limitless Aleph, which my floundering mind can scarcely encompass? Mystics, faced with the same problem, fall back on symbols' (*The Aleph*, 12–13). The authors of the *Avatamsaka Sutra* also fall back on symbols – mirrors, many-faceted jewels, the pores of Buddha, the net of Indra. Frye, less given both to symbolism and to falling back, reaches forward to interpenetration as one of his central verbal formulas. There are, as suggested, numerous contexts for his use of the word, but the most frequent context in the notebooks is a religious one. 'The Holy Spirit, who, being everywhere at once, is the pure principle of interpenetration' (NB52, 715). Frye also associates interpenetration with anagogy, kerygma, apocalypse, spiritual intercourse, the vision of plenitude, the everlasting gospel, the union of Word and Spirit, the new Jerusalem, and atonement. These are all religious concepts, any one of which would be worth exploring in an effort to get at the core of the paradox of interpenetration. This paradox involved for Frye a continuous restating of the claim that X is Y, that X identifies itself with Y, that X interpenetrates Y, that X incarnates itself in Y. Incarnation, or Blake's human form divine, is perhaps the ultimate radical metaphor for Frye. 'That God may be all in one,' he says: 'that's the text for interpenetration' (NB11e, 99). Or, in a notebook from the late 1960s, the Incarnation (along with identity, mutual awareness, and natural inclusion) is synonymous with interpenetration: 'The conception of interpenetration is that of natural inclusion. We are in God; God is in us. Therefore there are two worlds, as at the end of Paradiso, one the other turned inside out. My consciousness of things put those things inside me, but whatever is conscious has me inside them. I fell over this years ago in dealing with art & nature: in art nature is turned inside out. But I didn't see it as interpenetration, or an aspect of it. Perhaps this mutuality of awareness is identity' (NB12, 503).[26]

I conclude with two notebook entries that centre on the Incarnation, the first from 1946, when Frye was reading the *Lankavatara Sutra*, and the second from 1989, when he was preparing his lectures on the 'double vision.'

I can take no religion seriously, for reasons I don't need to go into here, that doesn't radiate from a God-Man, & so Christ & Buddha seem to me the only possible starting points for a religious experience I don't feel I can see over the top of. Hinduism has the complete theory of this in Krishna, and perhaps Judaism in the Messiah, but I'm not satisfied that even Hinduism is really possessed by the God-Man they understand the nature of so clearly. Now in Christianity & Buddhism I reject everything involved with the legal analogy, the established church, & so cling to Protestantism in the former & Zen in the latter. I'm just beginning to wonder if Protestantism & Zen – not as churches but as approaches to God-Man – aren't the same thing, possessed by the same Saviour. (NB3, 110)

I want to proceed from the gospel to the Everlasting Gospel, and yet without going in the theosophic direction of reconciliation or smile-of-a-fool harmony. The synoptics make Jesus distinguish himself from the Father, as not yet more than a prophet: it's in the 'spiritual' gospel of John that he proclaims his own divinity. (That's approximately true, though one has to fuss and fuddle in writing it out.) Yet John is more specifically and pointedly 'Christian' than the synoptics: the direction is from one spokesman of the perennial philosophy and a

unique incarnation starting a unique event. Buddhism and the like interpenetrate with the Everlasting Gospel: they are not to be reconciled with it. (NB53, 30)

Juxtaposing these two passages, separated by more than four
decades, may help us to see the interpenetration, as it were, of East and
West in Frye's thought. In his published work one gets little sense that
Eastern art and religion are at all formative. To be sure, there is the note
on Blake's mysticism at the end of *Fearful Symmetry*, where Frye likens
Blake's view of art to the spiritual discipline of yoga and where he says
that Blake's vision is 'startlingly close' to Zen Buddhism 'with its para-
doxical humor and its intimate relationship to the arts' (431). And in the
Anatomy one runs across references to the Brihadaranyaka Upanishad,
Chinese romances, the No drama, the *Mahabharata* and the *Ramayana*,
Chinese and Japanese lyric poetry, and Lady Murasaki's *Tale of Genji*.[27]
But in most cases Frye is using these texts for purposes of illustration
only, and if they were removed nothing much would be lost. Sometimes
Eastern literature has a more functional role to play in Frye's argument,
as in his use of *The Dream of the Red Chamber* and Kalidasa's *Sakuntala* in
The Secular Scripture (103–9, 147–8). But no one comes away from the
published work thinking that Eastern literature is at all fundamental to
Frye's criticism. Similarly, with Eastern religion and philosophy. There
are scores of references to Hinduism, Buddhism, and Taoism scattered
through Frye, from *Fearful Symmetry* to the two Bible books. But here
Frye's interest is primarily in the occasional analogue: Eastern religion
and philosophy lie on the periphery of his major concerns. In the notebooks, however, Frye's interest in the East is much less marginal. Notebook 3, for example, contains extensive entries on the path of Patanjali's
eight-fold yoga, which Frye turns to in order 'to codify a program of
spiritual life' for himself (NB3, 78).[28] He also writes about other forms of
yoga: *bhakti* yoga, the path to the devout love of god, and *jnana* yoga, the
path of abstract knowledge.[29] He has entries on Bardo, the 'in-between'
state in Tibetan Buddhism that connects the death of individuals with
the rebirth that follows.[30] And the notebook includes several extended
reflections on the *Lankavatara Sutra*. When we read in Eastern religious
texts, Frye says 'that all things exist only insofar as they are seen of Mind
itself, that suggests pantheism to a Western mind. Such pantheism corresponds to the hazy impression the Westerner has of all "Eastern" philosophy: that it is an attempt to forget that one is an ego & try to
hypnotize oneself into feeling that one is a part of the great All. But it is
clear, first, that the Lankavatara is based on a conception of a divine

man; second, that it does not teach a doctrine but inculcates a mental attitude' (NB3, 111).

The divine man – to return to the passages juxtaposed above – is perhaps the epitome of interpenetration for Frye. What Frye doubtless has in mind is the Mahayana idea of *trikaya*, which includes the Buddha as both a transcendental reality and an earthly form.[31] In Christianity, the interpenetration of the human and the divine is the descending movement of the Incarnation and the ascending one of the Resurrection. 'In the Incarnation the Word comes down and the Spirit, having finished his job, goes up. Here the Spirit is the Father of the Word. In Acts 1–2 the Word goes up and the Spirit comes down. Here the Spirit is the successor or Son of the Word' (NB44, 522). The 'Logos as incarnation,' Frye says in Notebook 12, gives place to the interpenetrating epiphany (59). In one of his late notebooks Frye recalls that a 'student asked me about the difference between analogy and metaphor. I said that such a statement as "God is love" could mean that love, a mere finite word, was being used as an analogy to something infinite, or that the two were being metaphorically identified. It then occurred to me that the metaphorical meaning was only possible in an incarnational context. Useful people, students' (NB52, 258).[32]

'All religions are one,' Frye writes, 'not alike: a metaphorical unity of different things, not a bundle of similarities. In that sense there is no "perennial philosophy": that's a collection, at best, of denatured techniques of concentration. As doctrine, it's platitude: moral maxims that have no application. What there is, luckily, is a perennial struggle.'[33]

The effort to restate in sequential, continuous prose the role played by interpenetration in Frye's own perennial struggle is perhaps ultimately doomed to fail because the notebook entries come to us in the form of aphorisms. Frye always said that the chief problem he faced in writing was fusing the notebook aphorisms into a sequential argument. Although there are connections among the entries in the notebooks, their form remains essentially discontinuous. But there is a spatial as well as a linear form (to borrow Joseph Frank's categories), and Frye's aphorisms seem to invite our arranging them in patterns independent of any sequence. The final stage of Frye's ogdoad project, the series of 'eight masterpieces in one genre' that he first formulated at age nine, was to be a book of aphorisms. He refers to the eighth book as *Twilight*, as his valedictory, as 'my *Tempest*, the work of my old age.' Late in his life he speaks of the '"twilight" of my ogdoad fantasy ... as something perhaps not reached' (NB44, 326). While it is true that

Frye did not produce a separate book of aphorisms, the word *perhaps* suggests that he intended the notebooks to be his *Twilight*. They are, in any case, the Daedalean workshop from which *Twilight* could be constructed, and one chapter of that book would surely be devoted to interpenetration.

NOTES

1 See also *NFC*, 61, where Frye further reports that he 'later found' the idea in Whitehead.

2 The only place in Frye's work where he quotes the passage is in *DV*, 41. Wallace Stevens quotes the same passage in 'A Collect of Philosophy' (*Opus Posthumous*, 273), and Frye, citing the reference in Stevens, does refer to Whitehead's 'great passage' in 'Wallace Stevens and the Variation Form' (*SM*, 292). Cf. the gloss on the passage from Whitehead in the notebook Frye devoted to his 'double vision' lectures: 'in an interpenetrating world everywhere is the one particular spot' (NB52, 55).

3 Frye was familiar with *The Lankavatara Sutra* through the edition that Fisher introduced him to – the 1932 translation by the renowned Buddhist scholar D.T. Suzuki. In NB3 Frye reports that Fisher had in fact given him a copy of the *Lankavatara* (109). Frye was perhaps familiar as well with Suzuki's commentary on the sutra, *Studies in the Lankavatara Sutra*, where Suzuki says that the *Avatamsaka Sutra*, 'the consummation of Buddhist thought,' represents 'abstract truths so concretely, so symbolically ... that one will finally come to the realisation of the truth that even in a particle of dust the whole universe is seen reflected – not this visible universe only, but the vast system of universes, by the highest minds only' (95–6). Here we have an echo of Blake's 'world in a grain of sand.'

4 D.T. Suzuki devotes about half of his *Essays in Zen Buddhism*, 3rd series, to the *Avatamsaka Sutra*. This is the book by Suzuki that Frye quotes from in *GC*, (168), referring to the Buddhist view of interpenetration as a gloss on Blake's seeing the world in a grain of sand. Frye's knowledge of the *Avatamsaka Sutra* seems to have come entirely from Suzuki's work. The English translation of the complete sutra, *The Flower Ornament Scripture*, did not appear until 1993. The interpenetration of the whole and its parts is also central to the *Lotus Sutra*, which forms the basis of the T'ien-t'ai school of Mahayana Buddhism, but I have found no references in Frye's published or unpublished works to this sutra.

5 The motto that Frye has in mind for *WP* – 'And those who have loved now

love the more' – is the last half of a couplet from the *Vigil of Venus*, 'Cras amet qui numquam amavit, quique amavit cras amet.'

6 Frye presented the Birks Lectures on 'Revelation and Response' at McGill University, 4–7 October 1971.

7 It is not possible to date NB54.3 with certainty; it appears to be from the mid-1970s. Frye's remarks on Lewis in *SM*, which elaborate the somewhat cryptic references in the notebook, were written at about the same time, the essay having first appeared in *Daedalus* in 1974.

8 Cf. this entry from NB44, 709: 'Malraux says Spengler's book started out as a meditation on the destiny of art-forms, then expanded. What it expanded into, I think, was a vision of history as interpenetration, every historical phenomenon being a symbol of the totality of historical phenomena contemporary with it. That's what fascinated me, though of course I didn't know it for many years.' Frye makes a very similar remark on p. 61 of the interview with David Cayley referred to above. Malraux's comment on Spengler is from *The Voices of Silence*, 619.

9 This notebook is difficult to date with certainty, but, since Frye says that he bought the notebook when he was in New Zealand (19), it was written after his 1978 lecture tour there. 'Thou Art That' or 'That Thou Art' (*Tat Tvam Asi*), one of the principal precepts of Vedanta contained in the Hindu Upanishads, means that the Absolute is essentially one with oneself.

10 Frye is referring to the A.V. Miller translation of Hegel's *Phenomenology of Spirit*. The quotation from Plotinus ('Everything that is yonder is also here') is from J.N. Findlay's analysis on p. 517. Frye's marginal annotation beside the interpenetration passage in his own edition of Whitehead's *Science and the Modern World*: 'this doctrine of the universal mirror is a point for me, I think. The passage is almost identical with Plotinus, V, 8' (Cambridge: Cambridge University Press, 1938), 114.

11 Blake's reference to 'the smile of a fool' is in his attack on Sir Joshua Reynolds's ideas of harmony: 'Such Harmony of Colouring is destructive of Art One species of General Hue over all is the Cursed Thing calld Harmony it is like the Smile of a Fool' ('Annotations to the Works of Sir Joshua Reynolds,' *The Complete Poetry and Prose*, 662).

12 See *The Aleph and Other Stories*, 3–17. In this story, Carlos Argentino Daneri explains to the narrator that the Aleph in his cellar 'is one of the points in space that contains all other points ... the microcosm of the alchemists and Kabbalists, our true proverbial friend, the *multum in parvo!*' (10, 12).

13 See especially, chap. 3, 'Two Forces of One Power.' Barfield's interest in interpenetration is recorded in another notebook as well (NB52, 74).

14 For Frye's extensive commentary on Lull's contemplative mysticism see 'The

Life and Thought of Ramon Lull,' an essay written during Frye's final year at Emmanuel College, in *Northrop Frye's Student Essays*, 217–34. Bruno appears throughout his published and unpublished work. Among the Romantic poets, Keats relies on the concept of interpenetration, his version contained in the word *interassimilate*. Compare Shelley's idea that the elevating delight of poetry 'is as it were the interpenetration of a diviner nature through our own' (*Defence*, 31).

15 Bohm opposes the implicate or enfolded order to the explicate (mechanistic) or unfolded order; see, especially, chaps. 6–7. The enfolded order includes both matter and consciousness. On Bohm, see also NB44, 24, and NB27, 145.

16 In a notebook entry about the conclusion to his first Emmanuel College lecture on 'the double vision' Frye says: 'spiritual language is interpenetrative, going much farther than any damn "dialogue." Discursive language, being militant, aims at agreement and reconciliation' (NB53, 250).

17 Here, for example, are two entries from the 'double vision' notebook: 'The movement I'm talking about is away from classbound ideologies toward a primary concern to which the keys are interpenetration and decentralization' (NB52, 85). 'Interpenetration and decentralized myth [are] the goal I'm heading for' (NB52, 95).

18 The CCF was a democratic socialist party, organized by farm and labour groups in Calgary in 1932, which sought 'a commonwealth in which the basic principle regulating production, distribution, and exchange [would] be the supplying of human needs instead of the making of profits.' It was the forerunner of the New Democratic Party. Frye always maintained that his own identity was rooted in his association with Victoria University, the United Church of Canada, and the CCF.

19 NB44, 428. 'Dialogism' is the term used by Mikhail Bakhtin to designate the ways that different 'voices' in a literary text disrupt the authority of a single voice (monologism). See his *Problems of Dostoevsky's Poetics* and *The Dialogic Imagination*. 'Montaigne's "consubstantial" remark' refers to a passage in 'Of Giving the Lie': 'I have no more made my book than my book has made me; a book consubstantial with its author, concerned only with me, a vital part of my life; not having an outside and alien concern like all other books' (*Essays*, bk. 2, trans. Charles Cotton).

20 See, e.g., *FS*, 114; *AC*, 73–82; *GC*, 59–61; *WP*, 69–96; *MM*, 97, 232–3.

21 *GC*, 166–7. In *WP*, 126, Frye actually makes a third reference to interpenetration in connection with metaphor, but it is only to cite his earlier use of the word in *GC*. Compare Blake's aphorism with that of the masters of the T'ien-tai school of Mahayana Buddhism: 'The whole world is contained in a mustard seed.'

22 In another notebook, Frye remarks, 'I find these sutras a lot of blithering crap, but I suppose they made sense as vade mecums of practical meditation' (NB11h, 12).

23 Dharmadhatu ('realm of dharma') refers, in Mahayana Buddhism, to the unchanging totality in which all phenomena are born, live, and die. Li Tongxuan, the eighth-century Chinese Buddhist layman, begins his commentary on the *Gandavyuha* by saying, 'The inherent baselessness of physical and mental objects is called reality. The interpenetration of one and many, the disappearance of the boundaries of the real and artificial, of affirmation and negation, is called the realm' (Appendix 3, *The Flower Ornament Scripture*, 1565). Thomas Cleary translates Li Tongxuan's guide to bk. 39 in its entirety (pp. 1565–1627).

24 Interpenetration is described as an experience in NB52, 509, 821; NB11e, 37; NB53, 17; and NB54.4, 122.

25 If interpenetration is finally beyond space and time, Frye none the less makes repeated efforts to represent the idea diagrammatically. What he calls the 'interpenetration of the cyclical & dialectical' (NB11f, 296) appears, of course, as a tacit diagram at several places in *AC*, most visibly, so to speak, in his account of the phases of the *mythoi*. In the notebooks Frye makes dozens of actual sketches of what he calls the Great Doodle, a schematic way of representing a temporal pattern imposed upon a spatial one, or vice versa.

26 In *WP*, Frye remarks that Paul's phrase 'all in all,' forming a vision in which human beings are the centre and God the circumference of an expanding sphere, 'suggests both interpenetration, where circumference is interchangeable with center, and a unity which is no longer thought of either as an absorbing of identity into a larger uniformity or as a mosaic of metaphors' (186).

27 See *AC*, 56, 143, 156, 283, 288, 297, 317, and 324. In *SR*, Frye calls attention to the connection between Shelley's use of 'interpenetration' in *A Defence of Poetry* and the apocalyptic visions of the Eastern poets (160).

28 Frye actually doesn't get beyond the fourth stage – *pranayama* – but he outlines in some detail what he proposes to do in the first three stages – *yama*, *niyama*, and *asana*, or the ethical and moral practices and the bodily positions.

29 On the verso of the flyleaf of NB3 Frye wrote 'Paravritti of July 26/46' (Sanskrit for 'the highest wave of thought').

30 References to Bardo are scattered throughout Frye's unpublished writings – from his diaries in the late 1940s and early 1950s to his final notebook. In recounting one of his Monday sessions with Peter Fisher Frye wrote in his 1949 diary that 'we went on to discuss the life–Bardo cycle. Normally we are dragged backwards through life & pushed forwards through Bardo, &

attempt to find some anastasis at the crucial points, or else go through a
vortex or Paravritti which leads us, not to escape, but to implement charity
by going forwards through life, as Jesus did, & withdraw in retreat from
Bardo' (an unpublished entry, dated 7 February 1949). Frye had a desire all
his life to write what he called a Bardo novel; his most extensive outline of
the project is in NB2.

31 See Suzuki, *Studies in the Lankavatara Sutra*, 308–14.

32 For the use of interpenetration in the eighth-century debate about the two
natures of Christ, see John of Damascus, *On the Orthodox Faith*, bk. 3, chaps.
3–4. The interpenetration of God and man is also found in Sufism. See, for
example, Ibn al-Arabi's *The Wisdom of the Prophets*.

33 NB44, 48. The allusions here are to William Blake's *All Religions Are One*
(1788) and Aldous Huxley's *The Perennial Philosophy* (1945).

WORKS CITED

Bakhtin, Mikhail. *The Dialogic Imagination*. Translated by Caryl Emerson and
Michael Holquist. Austin: University of Texas Press, 1981.
– *Problems of Dostoevsky's Poetics*. Translated by Caryl Emerson. Minneapolis:
University of Minnesota Press, 1984.
Barfield, Owen. *What Coleridge Thought*. Middletown: Wesleyan University
Press, 1971.
Blake, William. *The Complete Poetry and Prose of William Blake*. Edited by David
Erdman. Rev. ed. Berkeley: University of California Press, 1982.
Bohm, David. *Wholeness and the Implicate Order*. London: Ark, 1980.
Borges, Jorge Luis. *The Aleph and Other Stories*. Translated by Norman Thomas di
Giovanni. New York: Bantam, 1971.
Cayley, David. *Northrop Frye in Conversation*. Concord, Ont.: Anansi, 1992.
Fisher, Peter. *The Valley of Vision: Blake as Prophet and Revolutionary*. Edited by
Northrop Frye. Toronto: University of Toronto Press, 1961.
The Flower Ornament Scripture. Translated by Thomas Cleary. Boston:
Shambhala, 1993.
Frye, Northrop. *Northrop Frye's Student Essays, 1932–1938*. Edited by Robert D.
Denham. Toronto: University of Toronto Press, 1997.
Frye, Northrop, and Helen Kemp. *The Correspondence of Northrop Frye and Helen
Kemp, 1932–1939*. Edited by Robert D. Denham. 2 vols. Toronto: University of
Toronto Press, 1996.
Hegel, G.W.F. *Phenomenology of Spirit*. Translated by A.V. Miller. Oxford: Oxford
University Press, 1977.

Ibn al-Arabi. *The Wisdom of the Prophets*. Aldsworth: Beshara, 1975.

Malraux, André. *The Voices of Silence*. Translated by Stuart Gilbert. Princeton: Princeton University Press, 1978.

Shelley, Percy Bysshe. *A Defence of Poetry. Shelley's Critical Prose*. Edited by Bruce R. McElderry, Jr. Lincoln: University of Nebraska Press, 1967.

Suzuki, D.T. *Essays in Zen Buddhism*. 3rd series. London: Rider, 1953.

– *The Lankavatara Sutra: A Mahayana Text*. London: Routledge & Kegan Paul, 1932.

– *Studies in the Lankavatara Sutra*. London: Routledge & Kegan Paul, 1930.

Whitehead, Alfred North. *Science and the Modern World*. New York: New American Library, 1948.